# MAKING MUSIC MEANINGFUL

## A Source Book for Beginning Teachers

Franklin E. Churchley
Noel T. Gantly
Betty A. Hanley
Gerald N. King
Carolyn Ritchey Kunzman
R. Dale McIntosh

with

Bonnie Butchart Smith

  Wm. C. Brown Publishers

**Book Team**

Editor *Meredith M. Morgan*
Production Coordinator *Audrey Maiers-Reiter*

**WCB** **Wm. C. Brown Publishers**

President *G. Franklin Lewis*
Vice President, Publisher *Thomas E. Doran*
Vice President, Operations and Production *Beverly Kolz*
National Sales Manager *Virginia S. Moffat*
Group Sales Manager *John Finn*
Directory of Marketing *Kathy Law Laube*
Marketing Manager *Kathleen Nietzke*
Managing Editor, Production *Colleen A. Yonda*
Production Editorial Manager *Julie A. Kennedy*
Production Editorial Manager *Ann Fuerste*
Publishing Services Manager *Karen J. Slaght*

**WCB Group**

President and Chief Executive Officer *Mark C. Falb*
Chairman of the Board *Wm. C. Brown*

Typography and design by Dale McIntosh, Betty Hanley, Greg Launder, Todd Phillips, Chris Vater, and Sam Nelles.

Music notation created on Professional Composer ™ by Mark of the Unicorn, and Notewriter ™ by Passport Designs and assembled in Aldus Pagemaker ™. PictWriter ™ by Sun Valley Software was used to import many of the musical examples. Text was created in Microsoft Word ™.

Printed in Times Roman, Goudy, and Helvetica.

Musical examples printed in Sonata ™ and Petrucci ™.

Copyright © 1992 by Wm. C. Brown Publishers. All rights reserved

Library of Congress Catalog Card Number: 91-75357

ISBN: 0-697-15368-1

No part of this publication may be reproduced, stored in a retrieval system, or transmitted, in any form or by any means, electronic, mechanical, photocopying, recording or otherwise, without the prior written permission of the publisher.

Printed in the United States of America by Wm. C. Brown Publishers,
2460 Kerper Boulevard, Dubuque, IA 52001

10 9 8 7 6 5 4 3 2 1

# CONTENTS

Preface .................................................................................... vii

Acknowledgements ............................................................... ix

**Planning for Teaching Music** ............................................. 1

    Why Teach Music in the Schools ....................................... 3

    Lesson Planning ................................................................ 11

    Evaluation ......................................................................... 37

    Methods ............................................................................. 45

        Orff Schulwerk .......................................................... 45
        Kodály ........................................................................ 47
        Dalcroze ..................................................................... 48
        ETM ............................................................................ 49
        MMCP ........................................................................ 50

**Making Music** ...................................................................... 51

    Songs and Strategies ........................................................ 53

    Primary Songs ................................................................... 55

        Ah, Poor Bird ............................................................ 57
        Barnacle Bill .............................................................. 58
        Barnyard Song .......................................................... 59
        Bee, Bee, Bumble Bee ............................................. 60
        Billy Bad .................................................................... 61
        Bingo .......................................................................... 62
        Blue Bells ................................................................... 63
        Bluebird ..................................................................... 64
        Bounce High ............................................................. 65
        Bow Wow .................................................................. 66
        Categories ................................................................. 67
        Charlie Over the Ocean ........................................... 68
        Clap Your Hands ...................................................... 69
        Eency Weency Spider ............................................. 70
        Elevator ..................................................................... 72
        Engine, Engine Number Nine ................................ 73

Hey, Hey Look at Me ...................................................................74
Hot Cross Buns ...............................................................................75
I'm a Little Candle ..........................................................................76
Ich-a-back-a ....................................................................................77
If You're Happy ..............................................................................78
Long-Legged Life ...........................................................................79
Old Brass Wagon .............................................................................80
Poor Bird .........................................................................................82
Prendés i garde ................................................................................83
Pussywillow .....................................................................................84
Rain, Rain Go Away .......................................................................85
Row Your Boat ................................................................................87
Snail, Snail ......................................................................................88
Starlight, Star Bright .......................................................................89
Telephone Song ...............................................................................90
Weavily Wheat ................................................................................91
What Kind of Cake ..........................................................................92
What the Turkey Said .....................................................................93
Who's that Yonder ..........................................................................94

## Intermediate Songs ...................................................................95

Are You Sleeping (Frère Jacques) ...................................................97
Bonavist' Harbour ...........................................................................98
Brave Wolfe ....................................................................................99
Canoe Song ...................................................................................102
Come to the Land ..........................................................................103
Der Hans ........................................................................................104
Donkey Riding ..............................................................................106
Eggs and Marrowbones .................................................................108
Ezekiel Saw the Wheel ..................................................................111
Fish and Chips ...............................................................................113
Five Hundred Miles .......................................................................115
The Ghost of John .........................................................................116
God Rest You Merry, Gentlemen ..................................................118
The Grand Old Duke .....................................................................120
Great Big House ............................................................................121
Hallowe'en Night ...........................................................................123
Hebrew Round ...............................................................................124
Hoosen Johnny ..............................................................................126
Hungarian Dance ...........................................................................127
Hurling Down the Pine ..................................................................128
The Huron Carol ............................................................................129
I'll Give my Love an Apple ..........................................................131
J'entends le moulin ........................................................................133
Jack was Ev'ry Inch a Sailor .........................................................135

| | |
|---|---|
| Joshua fit the Battle of Jericho | 137 |
| Kookaburra | 138 |
| Land of the Silver Birch | 139 |
| Loo-Lah | 140 |
| Merrily We Roll Along | 141 |
| O Canada | 142 |
| Old Smokey | 144 |
| Old Texas | 145 |
| Orthodontist Blues | 146 |
| Praetorius Round | 149 |
| The Riddle Song | 150 |
| Rocky Mountain | 152 |
| Sakura | 154 |
| The Sloop John B. | 157 |
| Song for the Mira | 159 |
| There's a Hole in my Bucket | 162 |
| Toembaï | 163 |
| Tom Dooley | 165 |
| Turn on the Sun | 166 |
| Tzena | 168 |
| When the Saints | 169 |
| Where the Coho Flash Silver | 170 |
| Who Built the Ark | 173 |

**Listening** ... 175

| | |
|---|---|
| Air Gai | 177 |
| Epitaph for Moonlight | 179 |
| Morris Dance | 181 |
| Parade | 183 |
| The Swan | 184 |
| Walking in the Air | 185 |
| Walking Notes | 186 |

**Composing Music** ... 187

**Singing** ... 195

**Playing Instruments** ... 211

| | |
|---|---|
| Recorder | 213 |
| Guitar | 246 |
| Ukulele | 262 |
| Piano | 282 |

**Understanding Music**..............................................................317

    **Materials of Music**..................................................319

Appendix A — Literacy Concepts Cross Referenced ......359
                   Melodic and Rhythmic Patterns..............................360

Appendix B — 1-, 2- and 3-Chord and Pentatonic Songs ...............361

Appendix C — Piano Keyboard .......................................363
                   Autoharp Chord Chart ...............................364
                   Curwen Hand Signs ...................................365
                   Guitar Chord Chart ....................................366
                   Ukulele Chord Chart ..................................368

Appendix D — Music Signs and Symbols ........................369

Appendix E — Glossary ..................................................373

General References ..............................................................380

Classified Index ....................................................................381

Alphabetical Index of Songs ...............................................383

# Preface

This book is written for pre-service and in-service elementary classroom teachers of music. It provides a rich resource of songs and musical activities with some of the concepts that may be drawn from them and sample strategies that can make learning music meaningful.

Sections on approaches to music education, lesson planning, student evaluation, methods, composition, singing, and listening are designed to help the reader become aware of some of the important issues and trends in music education. The section on music materials provides the beginner with essential vocabulary and a coherent, concise explanation of concepts which elementary school children are expected to form. The "Playing Music" section for recorder, guitar, ukulele, and piano offers an opportunity for the development of performance and reading skills and a way of reinforcing and practising musical understanding.

The songs appear alphabetically by title in two sections — Primary and Intermediate. Cross referencing to concepts and a classified index make this material easily accessible. While a scope and sequence chart has been provided to help the classroom teacher organize music experience beyond a single lesson, the flexible organization of the book avoids locking instructors into any pre-conceived pattern of teaching, allowing them to follow their own methods and plans.

The book focuses on the music itself. Specific suggestions are provided for using songs as starting points leading to musical learnings. The suggestions are meant to open doors for the exploration of new ideas rather than be narrowly prescriptive. Some songs have extensive strategy statements, since beginning teachers need detailed sequences. Other songs have brief suggestions for teachers to build upon. Some of the material is more appropriate for primary students while some of the songs and activities are more suitable for intermediate grades.

The contents of *Making Music Meaningful* should provide teachers with some of the music they need as well as suggestions for teaching it. The text is not intended to be comprehensive; it is an initiation. We hope that the eventual outcomes result in more meaningful music experiences and learning for you and for children in schools.

*University of Victoria*
*June, 1991*

# Acknowledgements

The authors are indebted to students and instructors from the University of Victoria, Memorial University, Malaspina College, East Kootenay Community College, and Okanagan College who participated in testing the trial stages of this book and provided valuable feedback.

Gratitude is also due to the following authors, publishers and copyright holders for permission to use their material:

"Song for the Mira" words and music by Allister MacGillivray, © 1975 by Cabot Trail Music, used by permission from publisher; "What the Turkey Said" by Moiselle Renstrom from *Sing a Song* from THE WORLD OF MUSIC (series) © 1936 by Ginn and Co., used by permission of Silver Burdett & Ginn Inc.; "Bold Wolfe" reprinted by permission of the publishers from *Ballads and Sea Songs of Newfoundland* by Elizabeth Bristol Greenleaf and Grace Yarrow Mansfield, Cambridge, Mass., Harvard University Press, © 1933 by President and Fellows of Harvard College, © 1961 by Elizabeth Bristol Greenleaf and Grace Yarrow Mansfield; "I've Got the Million Dollar Orthodontist Stainless Steel and Rubber Band Blues" ("Orthodontist Blues") by Douglas Skilling from *Canada is... Music 7/8*, © 1984 by Gordon V. Thompson Music, a division of Warner/Chappell Music Canada Ltd., Toronto, Canada. Used with permission. "I'll Give My Love an Apple" from *Traditional Songs of Nova Scotia* by Helen Creighton, used by permission of McGraw–Hill Ryerson Limited, Toronto; "The Riddle Song," reprinted from *Multicultural Perspectives in Music Education.*, edited by William M. Anderson and Patricia Shehan Campbell, published by Music Educators National Conference (MENC), Reston, Virginia, 1989. Reprinted with permission from the MENC. "The Huron Carol," English text by J.E. Middleton, used by permission of the Frederick Harris Music Company Limited, Oakville, Ontario, Canada, All Rights Reserved; "Being a Friend," used by permission of Claire Hatcher, Laurel Patton, Leah Stuart, and Betty Schofield; "Summer Song" and "New York Strum" used by permission of Chalmers Doane, Doane Musical Enterprises Ltd.; Lloyd Arntzen for "Where the Coho Flash Silver;" Waterloo Music Company for "Ah, Poor Bird," "Edi Beo Thu," and "Prendés i garde." "Lots of Fish in Bonavist Harbour" and "Hurling Down the Pine," collected by Kenneth Peacock and published in *Songs of the Newfoundland Outports*, National Museum of Canada, 1965. Used by permission of Canadian Museum of Civilization. "Epitaph for Moonlight" by Murray Schafer, used by permission of the publishers, Berandol Music, Markham, Ontario.

Every effort has been made to locate copyright owners to secure permission to use their material. Any omissions discovered will be rectified in subsequent printings.

The authors are indebted to Bonnie Butchart Smith for the Ukulele section and to Gerard O'Leary for instructional suggestions in the guitar and ukulele sections.

# PLANNING

# for Teaching Music

# Why Teach Music in the Schools

Music can and should have enriched your lives at home and school. Even if your own experiences with music as a youngster weren't positive or memorable, without any reading or careful thinking, you could probably make up a quick case for including music in the curriculum. However, how consistent would your rationale be? That is, would your reasons be of an educational nature, making music a vital part of the child's total experience, or would they be superficial, leaving music (and the other arts) to hold a tenuous, peripheral position in the curriculum, a subject to be encouraged in times of economic growth, but the first to be eliminated in times of restraint? Will any justification do, or are some reasons more vital than others? Indeed, how convinced are you that music plays a truly important role in the education of our children?

The following discussion will challenge you to think more carefully about the reasons for teaching music in the schools and the educational consequences of sets of beliefs. From an understanding of the why, come the what and how of instruction. It is therefore necessary for you as a future educator to be aware of the variety of often conflicting reasons which are most frequently used to justify music programs so that you can think about them and form a reasoned judgment about their merits and educational implications. Remember that what you believe influences what you do.

One way of bringing order to a "shopping list" of ideas is to group thoughts into useful categories. An examination of the non-musical and musical benefits of music education will provide a framework for probing the most prevalent, and in some cases ancient, arguments in its defense. While it is probable that over simplification will occur, each framework will be briefly discussed.

## Non-musical Values

In this category are to be found arguments which don't focus on the music itself but instead on its effects in such areas as academic growth, social development and psychological well-being. The subsequent questions in the boxes will invite you to imagine what kind of music class would be a consequence of the teacher's belief in a variety of scenarios and to think more deeply about what certain beliefs mean in practice. Keep in mind which kind of class will best promote **educational** reasons for including music in the school curriculum. Throughout the year you might want to return to some of these questions as you learn more about what a music program can offer students. Consider each non-musical value in turn.

1. **Music for Academic Purposes** – If music is to be included in the school curriculum and given a higher status than a "frill," proponents of this argument propose it must have an academic justification: it must demonstrate that the use of music helps promote cognitive development which is, in practice, the main function of schooling. This umbrella houses two conflicting views: advocates of the first view use music to assist learning in other subjects; those of the second, consider music to be an academic discipline in its own right with an important body of knowledge to be mastered.

Examine the first position. In it, music is a valuable tool because singing songs helps children learn to read and play with language, songs can be used to drill otherwise dull math tables and, in general, develop memory. (Note the abundance of "educational" songs many of which could result in musical malnutrition for young children.) Music makes social studies more interesting through the use of relevant songs - the folk songs of a period bring history to life. Music acts as a good background to art and creative writing lessons, sometimes acting as a source for stimulation, sometimes, a soothing background. In this view music is considered to be "integrated" in the school day so there is no music period as such.

> **What music background will a music teacher who holds this view likely have?**
>
> **What kind of musical learning would occur in classrooms of teachers who think of music as a means of enhancing learning in other subjects?**

Advocates of the second viewpoint who think of music as a serious academic endeavour for itself argue that music is like any other academic study: the teaching of music theory and analysis develops mental acuity just as does the teaching of mathematics and science courses; the mental discipline and critical judgment needed to perform or create music are necessary capacities for success in the world. Furthermore, there is a vast cultural heritage with which students should be acquainted and appreciate if they are to be truly educated. Such music classes have the added benefit of helping to identify the talented students.

> **What music background would a teacher who holds this view have?**
>
> **What will be the focus of the music class?**
>
> **Will this type of music class meet the needs of all students or only those of superior ability?**

**2. Music as a socializing force** – The power of music to inculcate social norms has long been acknowledged. Historically, the study of music has often been encouraged in the public schools because music could be used to reinforce the social and religious values of the community. The slogan "The boy who blows a bugle will never blow a safe," popular in the thirties exemplifies the attitude. It is evident that being a member of a choir, orchestra or band helps develop in participants social skills such as the ability to cooperate with others and work towards a common goal, and the need for commitment to the group. Performance groups do provide opportunities for the reinforcement of social values.

At the local level, music performances serve an important public relations function for the school, drawing large numbers of parents who have an opportunity to witness a positive, exciting event. More importantly, these programs preserve a sense of community which is increasingly absent in a volatile society. As a bonus, students who learn to sing or play an instrument will have life-long skills which they can use in their leisure hours.

> **What repercussions would such beliefs have in the selection of music and in the types of activities experienced in the classroom?**

The power of music to unite and motivate people has made its control an issue for some groups. It is unnecessary to look far back in history (although examples abound there as well) to identify institutions, governments and religious groups who, holding to the belief that the wrong kind of music would counteract their envisioned utopia, have attempted to control what music will be created or performed.

> **Can you think of any examples of such attempts to control music and music education?**

**3. Music to influence mood** - Music has the power to affect people. There are examples in history: it is written that David calmed Saul with his beautiful music and, in Italy, people were said to dance the tarantella to avoid the deadly effects of the poisonous bite of the tarantula spider. You have probably selected music because it suited your mood, might cheer you up, or make you feel romantic. The playing of "O Canada" while the red maple leaf rises behind the victorious athlete sends shivers along the spine. Music can also bring back memories of past events: "They're playing our song."

> **Should music be used in the schools primarily because it is a mood modifier (drug)?**

That music appears to affect our moods, is pleasurable for most people, and is often used for entertainment leads to the belief that music is purely an emotional phenomenon to be enjoyed however one is able. Knowledge and understanding are likely to interfere with enjoyment. One consequence of such beliefs is the widespread concern that students should like what they do in music class.

> **Is the purpose of music in the classroom fun, entertainment, or a change of pace?**
>
> **What educational justification is there for including music in the curriculum solely because it is a source of pleasure?**
>
> **What would you expect to see happening in a classroom in which the teacher believes music should be mainly fun?**
>
> **Does understanding enhance or destroy enjoyment?**

How music affects the human brain and human behaviour is an exciting area of research. Music therapists have been applying findings about the effects of music to help people. Others are also applying these findings but with different ends in mind: advertisers to sell products, building designers to enhance the environment, dentists to allay fears, car manufacturers to increase production, to name a few. Music can be used to manipulate us to work faster, buy more, and even feel certain ways as the producers of *Muzak* will attest. *Fahrenheit 451* is not so distant. To counteract this assault on our ears some thinkers, such as Canadian composer R. Murray Schafer who commented on the fact that we have no "ear lids," advocate a greater awareness of the soundscape and the effects of noise pollution.

> **What role should music education play in this "battle" for minds?**
>
> **What kind of music program would a teacher whose only concern was the manipulative power of music provide for students?**

Another essentially non-musical way of considering music is to examine what functions it fulfills in society. You will note some unavoidable overlap with previous topics.

**4. The uses of music** - Musical works have been created for a variety of purposes ranging from ceremonial, to work-related, to entertainment and to background music. Sometimes the music has evolved from the people (folk music), sometimes it has been commissioned for a particular occasion (Handel's *Water Music*), or to be performed by a particular group. Marches, lullabies, campfire songs, fanfares, political rally songs, sambas, blues and film music are examples of the ways people use music to enhance an event, make it more tender, express deeper feelings, and create dramatic tension. The list is seemingly endless. Only since the nineteenth century when composers, deciding they were more than servants, left the safety of the patronage system was music written "on speculation". The idea of functional music stood in disrepute with artists of the time, and to some extent artists of the twentieth century, because composers were considered to be inspired geniuses privy to an understanding of the true meaning of life, shaking a metaphorical fist at the Philistines about them. In fact, larger works still had to be sponsored by some wealthy person or group if they were to be performed, and the artist at least to some extent had to acknowledge public taste. The situation stands pretty much the same today with the Canada Council and wealthy foundations acting as contemporary patrons.

> **What kind of music class would result if the functional values of music were stressed?**

The non-musical values discussed so far may strike you as very important reasons for valuing music and including it in the school curriculum. All of the benefits, and in some cases warnings cited may be real and important, but do they alone or collectively constitute a compelling argument for music education? A look at the musical values will provide you with a different perspective.

## Musical Values

Proponents of this view argue that as valuable as some of the non-musical benefits of music education might be, many of them can better be attained using other means. Besides, they do not present music's essential, unique contribution, a contribution shared by all the arts, that of providing insight into human feelings and thus into the human condition.[1] Music is valuable for itself because it is analogous to the "feeling life" unique to humans: the way music sounds is a metaphor for the way people feel.[2] Instinctively we are attracted by this argument (we have all experienced the capacity of music to evoke feelings), but it sounds "pie in the sky" and impractical. What does this argument offer the music teacher?

A brief digression is necessary before we look closely at application. A person does not experience or know the world through either feelings or cognition: both intertwine and contribute to our understanding of self, of the world and our interaction with it. A denial of either is a denial of human nature. In recent developments in cognitive psychology researchers have been expanding our understanding of what it means "to know." That intellectual capacity is the prime and often only reliable source of knowledge of the world and man (the scientific paradigm) has been challenged. It appears that there are other equally valid modes of experiencing the world. The ability to think musically has been posited as a specific form of intelligence.[3] The final word has not been written, but a broader conception of cognition is being formed, one which gives greater importance to the subject, the perceiver, and interaction with the environment. What are the implications for music education?

Planned experiences will include both the cognitive and affective domains. The goal of music education is to develop in students a greater capacity for aesthetic experience and thus to enhance the quality of their lives. Exactly what constitutes an aesthetic experience seems to defy easy definition. For our purposes, it is enough to say that there is a heightened awareness which creates a special feeling response, an excitement, a discovery. The teacher cannot approach this goal directly. While aesthetic experiences cannot be guaranteed or dictated, they are more likely to happen more frequently and provide greater satisfaction if students have become more sensitive to the artistic medium, in this case, sound.

What do music teachers do? They provide opportunities for students to perceive what is happening in the music; the students form concepts or understandings upon which they can build in future experiences, and they respond to what they have heard. The outcome of these experiences is the possibility of aesthetic experience. The following diagram outlines the process:

**perception (————> concept formation) + response = aesthetic experience**
             **(mind)**                              **(feeling)**

---

[1] The discussion in this section is based on the absolute expressionism position described by Bennett Reimer in *A Philosophy of Music Education*. 2nd ed. Englewood Cliffs, NJ: Prentice Hall, 1970.

[2] This manner of describing the musical experience was presented by Suzanne K. Langer in *Philosophy in a New Key,* New York: Mentor Books, 1942.

[3] Gardner, H. *Frames of Mind.* London: Heinemann & Paladin Books, 1985.

A caution is necessary. Teachers do not teach feelings: feelings are a subjective phenomenon, a private concern. Rather, they focus on the music, its expressive qualities (such as rhythm, melody and harmony) and the students' understanding of musical concepts as demonstrated through singing, playing, active listening, composing, and so on, allowing students their personal response.

The evaluation of musical experience and learning by the teacher and student plays an important role in the student's growth. Motivating and encouraging students to think about their activities whether performance or composition or other musical endeavours in order to determine their level of success in solving the musical problem or reaching an objective is an essential part of a music education which strives for increasing student independence. Especially in the arts, students must be fully engaged in the learning if they are to grow. A desired outcome of the described program is that students will value their experiences - not necessarily "like," but value or appreciate.

To summarize, in this view, the non-musical benefits may often be a bi-product of planned learning strategies, but the focus is primarily on the musical experience. The quality of any experience is enhanced by an expanding perception and deeper understanding. In our schools, through music education and arts education, we have a unique opportunity to deepen the awareness and sensitivity of all students so that their lives will be richer.

> **Does this last view of music education match or conflict with what you believe education to be?**
>
> **What would you expect to see happening in a music classroom where the teacher believes in providing an aesthetic music education?**

## What Will You Teach?

The main focus of the music lesson is on the music itself, its elements and expressive qualities. Students are given opportunities to perceive how the elements of music are used and interrelate so that they can form concepts or understandings. Musical experiences take many forms: active listening, singing, playing, moving, conducting, charting, analyzing, notating, reading, composing, improvising, discussing, evaluating.

A wide variety of musical styles are made available so that students can discover how the raw ingredients of music remain constant but the products vary, and how social context and technological advances affect music. Musical selections should not include just the "classics", nor should the criterion for acceptance be what the students like. "Liking" does not determine what will be taught in any other subject; why should it in music? One purpose of education is to refine discrimination. This purpose will not be achieved if students are presented only with what they already know (probably better than the teacher). Yes, we hope students will like what they are learning, but students will most likely "like", and, more importantly value what is presented to them in a challenging way which stimulates their imagination and curiosity and gives them a feeling of success because there has been achievement. Students will tire of a diet of favourites if they experience no sense of growth or discovery.

Students will be given opportunities to develop skills in singing, listening, playing instruments, creating music and music literacy. However, improving these skills is not the primary purpose of the music program. Rather, these skills are tools to help students realize the chief aim of music education: increased sensitivity to music.

Music is but one of the arts, sharing some characteristics and purposes, yet having unique features. Placing music in a larger context helps clarify its special qualities while at the same time encouraging comparison and analysis.

It would be unwise to neglect some of the concerns raised in the non-musical discussion. Topics such as noise pollution, the power of music to influence people, the role of music in our lives, what musicians do and even less-shaking but socially helpful, what is expected of audiences in a variety of settings deserve discussion.

### SUMMARY OF GOALS FOR A MUSIC PROGRAM

To explore and develop an understanding of:

1. the elements and expressive qualities of music;
2. musical styles and their social and technological contexts;
3. the roles of music and musicians;
4. music as one of the arts; and
5. topics about music.

## Who Should Teach Music?

You may be wondering how you fit into the scheme of music education. If you agree that music is important for your students you may feel overwhelmed by the scope of the musical content and the musical skills needed by the teacher. Should music only be taught by specialists or are classroom teachers capable of teaching their own music?

The qualifications to teach music are not so very different from those to teach any other subject: knowledge and understanding the elements of music, skill in performing (singing, playing) an ability to perceive musical events, a love of music, and the skills to teach a subject which deals with an aural art. Where does that leave you? Before you get too downhearted, remember that you don't need to be a mathematician, a scientist, or a poet to teach math, science or language arts in the elementary school. Admittedly, there is a difference between teaching the "academic" subject and music. The majority of our high school graduates are at a disadvantage because they have not received adequate music education throughout their years in public school: they lack basic knowledge, understandings and skills which are taken for granted in other subject areas. There are two reasons for this deplorable state. The first should be obvious: music is not really considered important (will it help you earn a dollar?), so if students go without it, few complain. The second reason is a little more subtle. Our western cultural bias has perpetuated the notion that only the talented can do music; the majority must settle for a vague enjoyment through listening and certainly cannot be initiated into the "mysteries" of music. Thus, many believe they can't sing, can't learn to read music, can't understand aural events much beyond knowing what they like, and can't learn to play music! So we are not surprised when only a few students opt for music classes which are mainly performance oriented once a choice is available. However, studies in ethnomusicology have shown that in social groups where all are expected to be musical there are no unmusical individuals.[4] One conclusion to be drawn from research in other cultures is that our emphasis on talent has led us to "disenfranchise" the many. The latter contention does not deny the existence of or the need to nurture those with special gifts, but it does suggest that all have a capacity at some level to go beyond the passive reception of sound waves. The talent myth has too long served as an excuse for doing nothing.

As a non-specialist what are your alternatives? You may be working in a school district which employs specialists. If this is so, you could opt to remain aloof and be content to let someone else do the teaching, or you might choose to learn as much as you can, informing yourself of student progress and learning, observing classes, and enthusiastically supporting the music teacher. Even if you lack skill and knowledge, your interest and desire to learn would serve as a good model for your students. A positive attitude on your part would also help reduce one of the drawbacks of having specialists–the lack of integration of the special subject with other classroom learning.

You may, however, be working in an area where the classroom teacher is expected to teach music. If you believe that music is valuable for your students you won't skip music class at the smallest excuse (giving, of course, the impression that it's not important anyway) even though you are pressured by the many responsibilities of teaching and the unyielding twenty-four hour day. You will probably seek help from more knowledgeable teachers, consultants and musicians in the community and do your best to provide meaningful learning experiences for your students, often learning with your students.

> **As a teacher interested in the well-being of your students, do you feel a continued responsibility to grow musically throughout your professional career?**
>
> **If you honestly feel that you will harm students by attempting to provide them with a music program (this may be true in a small number of cases), what could you do to support the program?**

In conclusion, there is no reason why minimally you should not know what a quality music program is. Don't perpetuate the problem! The course you are taking will give you an initial understanding. If you can erase all the "I can't do it" messages lurking in your brain and give an honest effort, your ability to progress in this course will surprise and delight you.

---

[4] Kingsbury, H. *Music, Talent, and Performance*. Philadelphia: Temple University Press, 1988, p.60-62.

## FURTHER READINGS

Reimer, B. *A Philosophy of Music Education.*, 2nd ed. Englewood Cliffs, NJ: Prentice-Hall, 1989.
Swanwick, K. *Music, Mind and Education*. London: Routledge, 1988.

# Lesson Planning

Both long and short term planning for teaching are normally based on broader curriculum goals which, in turn, reflect some philosophical stance on the part of curriculum supervisors for the music program as a whole. Philosophy and program goals have been addressed in the previous section of this book under the title **Why Teach Music in the Schools**. Here we will consider the practical aspects of planning for implementation of curriculum goals in the daily routine of teaching music to children in elementary classrooms.

A useful and much used strategy for providing focus for daily lesson plans is the UNIT OVERVIEW — a kind of game-plan for breaking down curriculum content into manageable and meaningful chunks of teaching/learning events in a developmental sequence over given periods of time. Unit overviews are usually subdivided into smaller units called Lessons which represent what is planned for each period of instruction. A sample Unit Overview will be included at the end of this section.

This resource book is intended primarily for the future use of general classroom teachers who will teach music to their own classes on a regular basis or assist the itinerant music specialist in implementing program goals. Therefore, the following comments on lesson planning are made with this specific cadre of teachers in mind.

Lesson planning serves two general functions for all teachers:

1. It enables them to keep a record of progress towards curriculum goals in a music program.
2. It facilitates their ongoing assessment both of pupil progress and teaching effectiveness.

For beginning teachers lesson planning serves three additional functions:

1. It provides a vehicle for clear articulation of concepts and skills to be taught and specific learning objectives or outcomes for each lesson. If a teacher cannot make a clear statement of the concept(s) to be taught and the outcomes anticipated for each lesson, there is a real probability that that teacher does not fully grasp the concept(s) in question, is unable to express them in terms that children will understand, and therefore, is not quite ready to teach. This is especially true for the non music specialist. The discipline of careful lesson planning forces the beginning teacher to be thoroughly prepared. Early teaching experiences, therefore, should always be accompanied by detailed written lesson plans. With time and experience teachers will gradually be able to function effectively with less detailed written plans and move to day book entry-type preparation.

2. Good lesson plans provide evidence for school principals and curriculum supervisors that teachers are taking their task seriously and conscientiously.

3. Well prepared lesson plans provide clear guidance for substitute teachers, thereby ensuring continuity and consistency in instruction during teachers' absences.

The kind of planning that is done for units of study and individual lessons will depend greatly on a number of factors, namely:

1. attitudes about the value of music instruction in the schools on the part of district administrators, parents, school principals, and staffs;
2. the predisposition of the classroom teacher in relation to musical background knowledge and skill;
3. entry levels of students in the areas of physical, social, emotional and cognitive development;
4. available resources; and
5. the instructional schedule.

Let us look at these factors briefly to see how each one affects the quality of planning for music instruction.

1. **COMMUNITY ATTITUDES:** The extent to which music instruction is valued by the community as an essential element in the curriculum usually determines the level of support in terms of human and material resources. Where music programs are greatly valued, more hours of instruction will be offered at a higher level of professional expertise. The role of the general classroom teacher will be minimal. Where such endorsement by the community does not exist, classroom teachers are more likely to be burdened with more responsibility for music instruction and, therefore, will bear the full responsibility for planning of instructional sequences.

2. **THE CLASSROOM TEACHER:** The attitudes and motivation of classroom teachers relative to music instruction will be affected directly by the teacher's musical knowledge, background and experience. Many non-specialist teachers, although they have had little formal training in music education, bring to their teaching some previous training or experience in singing or instrumental playing. Such teachers can work quite successfully in supporting and reinforcing the work done by the itinerant music specialist. Left to their own devices, they can use graded texts and other resources with relative success. Many other teachers, however, have little or no musical background and find music instruction very inhibiting and stressful. For these people, graded texts are of little value on their own. They need the regular support and direction of a music specialist in order to use programmed materials successfully. For this category of teachers, the best hope of success is for lesson planning to be done by the specialist with specific guidelines for follow-up activities by the classroom teacher.

3. **ENTRY LEVELS OF STUDENTS:** Entry levels of students will also vary greatly according to socio-economic factors in the local community. Home background and the cultural environment, individual personal learning characteristics all impose limitations on what can be taught in the classroom. Learning disabilities, visual/aural impairment, physical and neurological limitations are all realities of modern classroom life, especially with the current move towards mainstreaming. No single approach to music instruction can serve the needs of all children in such heterogeneous groups. Individualization of instruction is becoming a very real concern for all teachers. Therefore, planning must be done on the basis of the prevailing conditions in each classroom.

Before deciding what to teach, then, be sure you know the entry level knowledge and skills of your pupils. Early in the first term, a repertoire of songs, games and movement ideas will provide opportunities for pupils to demonstrate singing, playing and coordination abilities. The teacher's first role is to observe the kinds and quality of children's responses. Such activities combined with some written and oral/aural testing can quickly generate a profile of the entry-level behaviours of pupils. Only then is the teacher ready to plan a meaningful sequence of instructional events.

4. **AVAILABLE RESOURCES:** The market in Canada and the U.S.A. abounds with graded texts for musical instruction organized by grades from K to Grade 7. Prominent examples are *Silver Burdett Music*, *MusiCanada*, *Music and Me*, *The Music Book*, and *Canada is Music*. Each series provides its own scope and sequence and detailed lesson plans. Classroom teachers rely greatly on such materials, especially when they are accompanied by records and tapes which provide better models of singing and instrumental performance than the classroom teacher feels able to provide. Unfortunately, because of variations in economic conditions and funding priorities, there appears to be little consistency among or even within school districts both in the amount of material resources and the quality of music instruction in schools. Consequently, teachers are often frustrated when even the most highly recommended texts do not work for them. Changing conditions, therefore, demand that individual teachers assume responsibility for instructional planning for their own classes.

5. **THE INSTRUCTIONAL SCHEDULE:** Instructional schedules vary greatly from district to district and even from school to school. A typical schedule might be one 30-minute lesson each week by an itinerant music specialist followed by one or more follow-up practice sessions by the classroom teacher. In some schools children receive regular instruction in general music (say, twice weekly) by a music specialist in the primary grades and move into beginning band or choir in the intermediate grades. In other schools all teachers are obliged to teach their own music program once or twice a week regardless of qualifications or motivation to do so. In such situations the amount of time allotted for music instruction varies greatly and the quality of instruction is affected accordingly.

Varying conditions, then, preclude total dependence on curriculum guides and graded texts series in a music program. The classroom teacher bears the ultimate responsibility for the quality of instruction and must, therefore, develop sound professional strategies for planning music lessons in the classroom.

The format used for lesson planning will vary from instructor to instructor and from classroom to classroom. The format itself, however, is not as important as the awareness on the part of teachers of what constitutes a good music lesson. Certain key components are outlined below for your consideration. Some samples of frequently used formats will follow.

## KEY COMPONENTS OF A QUALITY MUSIC LESSON

### 1. Motivational techniques.

Teachers usually plan opening activities that help establish a "mind set" for pursuing the concept(s) being studied. A lesson will either introduce a new concept or reinforce one already introduced. One general approach for introducing a new concept is to move from the children's previous knowledge of the concept in a non-musical context to the application of that concept in the musical context; e.g. a lesson introducing the concept of REGISTER (relative highness or lowness of pitches in a song) might be introduced through discussion of HIGH and LOW in a spatial context. This particular approach addresses current concerns amongst educators for integration of subject matter across the curriculum by relating concepts that are common to more than one content area. Where a concept is being reinforced, the teacher builds on what children already know and introduces the lesson with some kind of recapitulation or review of previous lesson content.

## 2. Bridging the gap between the known and the new:

This can be a crucial stage in lesson development. An example building on the one outlined in 1. above would be: When children point to something that is HIGH in the classroom (e.g. skylight) play a resonator bell in the upper range of a set; when they point to something LOW, play a low-pitched bell. Later, they will be asked to respond to a HIGH pitch by pointing to something high (a ceiling light) or something low (a waste basket on the floor) in response to a low pitch.

Use of iconic devices is important where literacy elements are involved, e.g., before introducing symbolic elements for rhythm notation (e.g., | | ⊓ | ) use more realistic visual representations ( __ __ _ _ __ ). Iconic representation is an important part of the BRIDGING process.

## 3. Concept/Topic development:

A good lesson plan articulates clear, step-wise presentation of new concepts and systematic review of previously taught elements. In this phase of the lesson a teacher should employ many ways of reinforcing meaning, e.g., body movement, singing, playing instruments, visual representation such as mapping and iconic devices leading to symbolic representation. The techniques will vary from lesson to lesson. What must be avoided is the practice of always teaching concepts in the same way. The basic motto is "feeling precedes understanding." Teachers should find many ways for children to respond to questions and tasks so that every child can find at least one way of responding (e.g. a particular child might be able to demonstrate the melodic contour of a song by movement much more readily than he/she could verbalize it).

## 4. Closure:

In closure, teachers plan for a clear link-up with the lesson objectives. At the primary level this usually means fairly focussed questioning; an activity that relates fairly directly to the motivational activity at the beginning of the lesson, e.g., "What did we talk about at the beginning of the lesson today?"; or an activity that provides opportunities for children to respond to listening experiences that incorporate the focal point of the lesson. Written, oral/aural tests can be part of the closure procedure at the intermediate level.

## 5. Questioning techniques:

Questioning is a crucial ingredient of any lesson. Music lessons can easily become too activity-based; questioning helps children think about what they do, e.g. "What did you hear when we were reaching up?" (a high note played on the bells). Questioning should be distributed across all levels of the class; questions should be suitably worded for different cognitive levels, and allow for multiple responses rather than just right/wrong ones. Key questions are part of essential teaching/learning dialogue and must be planned with care. It is always wise to write down key questions in a lesson plan along with the desired response. Teachers also need to give thought to using children's responses to clarify meanings and remediate errors, e.g. "How did you find that answer?"; " Tell us more about that so we can discuss it." The idea is to help children discover their own errors and correct them without feeling "put down."

## 6. Balance between teacher-centered and pupil-centered activities:

The accompanying Lesson Plans, numbers 2, 4, 5 and 6, provide examples of what is intended here. There is a tendency amongst some classroom teachers who teach their own music to resort to teacher-directed activities (singing games, for example) that do little to promote musical learning. The concern here is to avoid overteaching on the one hand and knowing when to "butt out" on the other. This issue is best addressed by articulating in the lesson plan those activities that will be performed by the teacher and those that will be performed by the children.

## FORMAT FOR LESSON PLANNING

Several different formats are presented below for your guidance. You are encouraged, however, to develop a format that meets the needs of your own particular teaching situation. Lessons for early primary will focus more on perceptual stages of learning — developing awareness of elements in music (e.g., presence or absence of sound as an introduction to the durational value of rests in notation). Lessons for upper intermediate classes, on the other hand, may focus very specifically on conceptual development (e.g., fractional value of notes in a divided beat). Consequently, lesson plans for primary tend to be less structured and less detailed than lesson plans for the intermediate levels. In all cases, however, teachers must be aware of the learning objectives. This means articulating learning outcomes as these relate to the program goals. Otherwise, today's lesson can easily become solely activity-based without any real relation to what was taught/learned yesterday and what will be taught/learned tomorrow or one month from today. The chart on the next page provides the scope and possible sequence of concept learning in an elementary music program. Two basic questions can serve as check-points for evaluating the integrity of your lesson plan:

(a) What will pupils KNOW when this lesson has been taught? The assumption is that each lesson either presents some new concept or reinforces a concept already presented.

(b) What will pupils be able to DO when this lesson has been taught? It is only by doing (e.g., singing, playing, answering questions, solving problems) that pupils can demonstrate knowledge of a new concept and integration of new concepts with concepts already learned. Therefore, the teacher must plan activities that serve as appropriate indicators of pupil's integration of knowledge and skills.

# Scope and Sequence Chart

| Melody | Rhythm | Timbre | Harmony | Texture | Dynamics | Form | Tempo |
|---|---|---|---|---|---|---|---|
| **Pitch**<br>•higher/lower | **Beat**<br>•steady<br>•strong/weak | **Sound/silence**<br><br>**Found sounds** | **Harmony/<br>no harmony**<br><br>**Tonal center**<br>•doh/la<br><br>**No tonal center** | **Accompaniment/<br>no accompaniment**<br><br>**Density**<br>•thick/thin | •louder/softer<br><br>•getting louder/<br>getting softer | **Same/different**<br><br>**Phrases**<br>•same/different<br>•long/short | •faster/slower<br><br>•getting faster/<br>getting slower |
| **Register**<br>•high, medium, low | **Duration**<br>•longer/shorter<br>•rhythm pattern<br>•silence<br>•even/uneven<br>•fermata | **Classroom instruments**<br><br>**Voices**<br>•children<br>•male<br>•female<br>•solo/choir | **Mode**<br>•major/minor<br><br>**Scale**<br>•pentatonic, major, minor<br>•key | **Types**<br>•monophonic, homophonic, polyphonic | | **Parts**<br>•introduction<br>•motive<br>•theme<br>•section<br>•coda | |
| **Direction**<br>•upward, downward, horizontal | **Accent**<br><br>**Anacrusis**<br><br>**Meter**<br>•beats in sets of 2<br>•beats in sets of 3<br>•beats subdivided in 2<br>•beats subdivided in 3<br>•irregular<br>•changing | **Orchestral Instruments**<br>•strings<br>•brass<br>•woodwinds<br>•percussion | **Chords**<br>•same/different<br>•major/minor<br>•I, IV, V, V$^7$, i<br><br>**Chord Progressions**<br>•1 chord (I)<br>•2 chord (I, IV: I, V)<br>•3 chord (I, IV, V)<br>•blues | | | **Forms**<br>•call/response<br>•verse/chorus<br>•AB<br>•ABA<br>•rondo<br>•12-bar blues | |
| **Melodic movement**<br>•skip, leap, repeated<br>•chord outline | | **World Instruments**<br>•aerophone<br>•membraphone<br>•electrophone<br>•idiophone<br>•chordophone | | | | **Repetition/<br>Contrast**<br>•unity/variety | |
| **Melodic contour** | **Syncopation** | **Instrumental groups** | | | | | |
| **Intervals**<br>•whole step, half step<br>•size | | | | | | | |
| **Range**<br>•wide/narrow | | | | | | | |
| **Cadence**<br>•ending<br>•complete/<br>incomplete | | | | | | | |
| **Melodic extension**<br>•augmentation<br>•sequence | | | | | | | |

# Unit Overview

**SUBJECT AREA:** *Melody*      **GRADE:** 3

**NUMBER OF LESSONS:** 4     **TIME PER LESSON:** *30 mins.*

**TEXT:** *Making Music Meaningful*

**SONGS:** pages 58, 59, 69, 72, and 76.

**OBJECTIVES:** *Children will recognize/identify melodic elements of:*
  (a) *Register — high/low pitches.*
  (b) *Direction — movement up/down/same.*
  (c) *Movement — steps, skips, leaps.*
  (d) *Contour — melodic shapes (mapping).*
  *Children will develop auditory discrimination of pitches, melodic movement and contour.*

*NOTE: One lesson may require more than one 30-minute period.*

| # | TOPIC | OUTCOMES | INTRODUCTION | VOCAB | MATERIALS | INTEGRATION | EVALUATION |
|---|---|---|---|---|---|---|---|
| 1 | **Melody** *(register)* Pitches in a song may be high or low. | *Recognition/ identification of pitch levels relative to one another (auditory discrimination)* | High/Low guessing game | Register Pitch Higher Lower | Song: "Clap Your Hands," page 69 | Spatial concepts High, Low — reinforcement Language: vocabulary development — register | *PUPIL: Individual responses* |
| 2 | **Melody** *(direction)* Pitches in a song move up, down or stay the same (repeated pitches). | *Awareness of melodic direction.; movement response to melodic direction* | Song: "Barnacle Bill," page 58 Melodic directions ↑ ↑ ↗ in song ending | Up Down Same | Song: "Barnacle Bill," page 58 Resonator bells | –higher/lower –pitch | *PUPIL: Call for individual vocal responses* |
| 3 | **Melodic Movement** Melody may move in steps, skips or leaps. | *Awareness of melodic interval.; visual/aural discrimination* | "I'm a Little Candle" (song with movement steps down); "Elevator" (song with steps up); "Barnacle Bill" (steps, skips, one leap) (direction, contour) | STEP SKIP LEAP | Songs: "I'm a Little Candle" p. 76, "Elevator" p. 72, "Barnacle Bill," p. 58 Resonator bells | Language and aesthetic development; use of imagery to dramatize a song and enhance internatilizaation of concepts | *PUPIL: Call for individual vocal responses* |
| 4 | **Melodic Contour** The shape of a melody may be represented by a map. | *Visual representation of melodic contour – mapping of: Steps: m–r–d Skips: m–s Leaps: d–s Repeated: m–m* | "Barnyard Song," page 59 | CONTOUR | Song: "Barnyard Song," page 59 Resonator bells | | *PUPIL: Response Sheet – Visual oral/ aural test "What did you hear?" TEACHER: Analyze test results.* |

# SAMPLE LESSON FROM UNIT OVERVIEW

**UNIT:** Melody

**LESSON:** #3 of 4 from UNIT OVERVIEW

**CONCEPT:** Melodic Movement — melodies may move in steps, skips or leaps.

**OBJECTIVES:** Children will learn to identify intervals in a song as steps, skips or leaps, by:

a) identifying steps, skips and leaps in staff notation
b) responding to steps, skip and leaps in a melody with appropriate body movements.

**INTRODUCTION:** Review known song: "I'm a Little Candle" (p. 76) acting out the "melting" activity as suggested.

**DEVELOPMENT**:

1. As children sing and act out the song, accompany their movement with downward scale sequence $d^l$ — d on resonator bells or keyboard.

    "How did you move as you sang?" (downward)
    "Did you hear how the melody moved?" (downward)
    "Listen as I play on the bells" (Teacher plays scale)
    "Do you recognize that melody?" (Scale)
    "Did I skip any notes in the scale?" (No)
    "The scale melody moves by steps – downward."

2. Review another known song: "Elevator" (p. 72). Act out the ascending elevator, as suggested, with Curwen hand signs.

    "This time, did the scale move up or down?" (Up)
    "Did we skip any notes?" (No)
    The scale melody of "Elevator" also moves by steps. Repeat "I'm a Little Candle" and "Elevator" as necessary to allow children time to feel the stepwise movement of the melodies.

3. Introduce a new song: "Barnyard Song" (p. 59)

    Teach by rote.

    Using resonator bells G, E, D, C, accompany singing of :

    | **fid - dle - i - dee** | then | **his - sy** |
    |---|---|---|
    | E—E—D—C | | E—G |

Display bells so all can see; then allow individuals to take turns accompanying the above melodic patterns. Several sets of bells would permit participation of several accompanists simultaneously.

Questions: for each pattern:

"Do you see a step, skip or leap?"
"Close your eyes." (Teacher plays patterns, alternating between steps, skip, leaps, repeated pitches.)
"What do you hear?" (Children identify step, skip, leap.)

**CLOSURE:** Distribute Response Sheet.

"Think about what we learned today."
"Tell me some words to describe the ways a melody may move." (steps, skips, leaps)
"Close your eyes." (Teacher plays four different 3- or 4-note melodies on resonator bells or keyboard. Children identify the melodic movement in each case by circling the appropriate word.)

---

**Response Sheet**

Name: _____

| | | | |
|---|---|---|---|
| Melody 1. | Steps | Skips | Leaps |
| Melody 2. | Steps | Skips | Leaps |
| Melody 3. | Steps | Skips | Leaps |
| Melody 4. | Steps | Skips | Leaps |

SOME EXAMPLES OF LESSON PLAN FORMATS:

# LESSON PLAN #1

**GRADE LEVEL:** Kindergarten

**CONCEPT:** Steady beat: some songs move to a steady beat, just as our bodies move to a steady heart beat.

**OBJECTIVES:** Children will develop a feeling for steady beat in a song and will demonstrate this by appropriate body movements.

**MOTIVATION:** When you visit the doctor, sometimes he feels your pulse. Sometimes he uses a stethoscope. Why?

> Can you feel your heartbeat?
> Can you feel a friend's heartbeat?
> Can you tap out the heartbeat that you feel on the floor?

**DEVELOPMENT:** Songs have a heartbeat, too. We also call it the PULSE or STEADY BEAT.

> What is your favorite song?
> Can you sing it for me?
> Together let's tap out the **Pulse** or **Steady Beat** of your song.
> With our hands? With our feet? Any other suggestions?

Introduce some small percussion instruments (hand drum, claves, rhythm sticks). Can you tap the **Steady Beat** with an instrument as we sing?

**CLOSURE:** Here's a new song — "Old Brass Wagon" (p. 80).

Teach song by rote.

Help the children find ways to **feel** and **show** the steady beat as they sing.

**EVALUATION:** By observation.

Which children do not seem to feel the steady beat with ease?

How can I help them?

One way would be to take a child's hands in yours and sway together to the beat of the song. Repeat on different occasions until child can feel/show the beat independently.

# LESSON PLAN #2

**LEVEL:** Early Primary

**SONG:** "Hot Cross Buns" (p. 75)

**MUSICAL LEARNING:**

Phrases in music can be repeated or varied to create interest. The way the phrases are organized is called the FORM of the song.

**INTRODUCTION:** Teacher sings song through once, then echo sings phrase by phrase asking children to repeat each phrase until all can sing song together.

**CONCEPT DEVELOPMENT:**

Teacher sings song again inviting children to "Watch my hand moving as I sing this time." Teacher moves hand and arm in arc-like formation to proscribe each phrase of the song as follows:

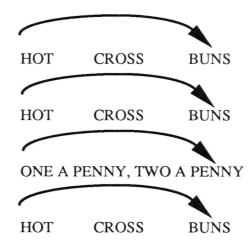

| TEACHER | CHILDREN |
|---|---|
| How many times did I make this movement with my hand (demonstrate) | Four times. |
| Why? | There are four parts in the song. |
| Are all the parts the same in length? | Yes. (Some children might think the third phrase is longer because there are more words. However, all phrases have the same number of beats.) |

| | |
|---|---|
| We have a special name for these parts; they are called PHRASES. How many PHRASES are there in our song? | Four phrases. |
| Let's sing the song together and this time let's all show the PHRASES with our hands in the air. | All sing the song and again proscribe the phrases in the air as demonstrated. |
| Can you find another way to show the PHRASES in our song? Teacher encourages individual ideas, intervenes as necessary to help children develop their ideas. | Children experiment with body movements, walking to the beat and changing direction at the beginning of each phrase, drawing the phrases on paper or chalkboard. |

CLOSURE:

| | |
|---|---|
| What new musical word did we learn today? | PHRASE |
| How many PHRASES are there in "Hot Cross Buns"? | 4 PHRASES |
| Are the phrases all the same length? | Yes. |

# LESSON PLAN #3

**GRADE:** 3

**CONCEPT:** DURATION — Melodies are made up of long and short sounds.

**SONG:** "Long-legged Life" (p. 79) [For the purpose of this lesson the song should be presented without the fermatae on the opening two notes.]

**LEARNING OUTCOMES:**

Children will recognize long and short notes in a song and will demonstrate visual and aural discrimination in relation to these durational elements ( | and ⊓ ).

**PROCEDURE:**

1. Teach action version of song by rote with appropriate interpretive movements for words ***long, short, one,*** and ***no.*** Encourage children to imitate teacher's movements first; then invite suggestions for other verses. Sing song again (several verses) using clap/patsch pattern to articulate the duple beat pattern.

2. Teaching/learning dialogue:

   How many different things do we do with our hands as we sing? (2)

   Why? (Because the beat of the song moves in 2s)

   Is one beat louder/stronger than the other? Which one? (The first)

   Still keeping the beat in the same way, let's put the words of the song in our feet.

   Now let's step out the words – I'll do it first – watch my feet. Are all my steps the same length? (No, some are shorter than others.)

   Which words in the song occur on long steps? ("long," "life," "wife")

   Are the notes we sing on these words also longer than the other notes in the song? (Yes)

   As we keep the beat going, can you tell whether these long notes get one whole beat each? (Yes, they do.)

How many notes do we sing on all the other beats? (Two)

3. Iconic representation

   Let's try to draw a BEAT PICTURE for our song: Teacher involves children in constructing on the chalkboard the following BEAT PICTURE:

   Have you ev-er, ev-er, ev-er  in your long  leg-ged life,  seen a...

   Have you  ev- er, ev- er, ev- er  in your long  leg-ged life,  seen a...

   An overhead transparency could be used for each of the pictures above. Then, superimpose the RHYTHM PICTURE on the BEAT PICTURE to produce a composite BEAT/RHYTHM PICTURE as follows:

   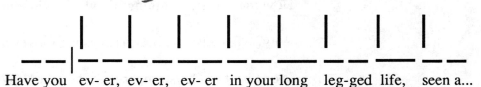

   Have you  ev- er, ev- er, ev- er  in your long  leg-ged life,  seen a...

# LESSON PLAN #4

**GRADE:** 4/5

**TOPIC:** An exploratory activity to identify readiness levels in reading and writing of melodic and rhythmic notation; review and testing of aural skills recognition, identification and vocal reproduction of intervals in the pentatonic scale.

**CONCEPT(S):** Aural recognition, identification and vocal reproduction of intervals in the pentatonic song "Weavily Wheat" (p. 91); visual recognition and reading of the same intervals in staff notation. (By this time children have already learned how to read m-r-d-l-s and $s_|$–$l_|$ in key of G on recorders.)

**OBJECTIVES:** **Cognitive:** Children will recognize and identify the staff notation for the tones of the pentatonic song "Weavily Wheat" in the key of G; later, they will transpose using the principle of movable doh.

**Behavioral:** Children will read and sing "Weavily Wheat" from staff notation in the keys of G and F major.

**PROCEDURES:**

A. Motivation
—Repeat game-song "Weavily Wheat."
—Review: What did we learn to do with this song last week? Identify and sing parts of the song in solfa (m-d-m-s-s; m-d-$s_|$-$l_|$-$s_|$-$l_|$-$s_|$; m-r-d)
—Sing song one more time; substitute the various tonesets for words of the song.

(One possible strategy: Teacher sings solfa version of a toneset — ask children to identify the appropriate part of the song using the words; then have children substitute the solfa for the toneset).

B. Development

| Teacher activities | Pupil activities |
|---|---|
| What are the last three tones of the song in solfa? (m-r-d) | Recall. Identify. |
| Display staff notation of melody on overhead and ask: Where is doh? Show me; it's the last note in the song, isn't it? Can you find a doh in the first measure? (second note) | Scan notation. Find doh. Scan first measure. |
| | Find doh. |
| What is the name of the first note? | mi |

| | |
|---|---|
| What is the name of the third note? | Recall previous learning. |
| How do we find out? Recite the scale tones backward as we descend, making sure not to skip any lines or spaces. | Reading of staff notation in key of G using solfa syllables. |
| Continue to lead children through reading of entire song from the staff notation. Read and sing. | Read and sing from staff notation in key of G. |
| **Extension** (time permitting) – What happens if I change the position of doh from the first line to the first space? Will the solfa names change? No – only their position on the staff. | Transfer learning of G scale to new key — F. Transpose. |
| When we change the position of doh we **TRANSPOSE** (may be a new word in their musical vocabulary). We just transposed our song from one key to another. | Add new word to musical vocabulary. |
| Note: Some children will be able to identify the key from the key signature (one sharp or one flat). For the benefit of all, help them identify the # as ti and ♭ as fa. | Learn about key signatures.<br><br>Identify and understand the meaning of same. |

C. Closure –

| | |
|---|---|
| Today we learned an important (new) skill — reading the notation for a familiar song. Would it have been so easy to read a song we had not already known by ear? Why is it important to be able to read music? | Think about what we learned today.<br><br>Think about the value of being able to read music.<br><br>Suggest answers to questions. |
| We also learned how to transpose. What use is transposition? (adapts melody to range of voice or instrument) | Think about the purpose and value of transposition.<br><br>Suggest answers to questions. |

# LESSON PLAN #5

**GRADE:** 5

**CONCEPT:** m-r-d, m-s-l, and d-m-s tonesets
These tonesets may be found in many songs; we can recognize them in songs and sing them on the tone ladder.

**OBJECTIVES:** a) Cognitive: Children will: (i) reinforce awareness of the tonal pattern m-r-d in songs and; (ii) become aware of the d–m-s and s-m-l patterns on the tone ladder (modulator) and in songs.

b) Behavioral: Children will identify and sing/sight read the 3 tonal patterns from the tone ladder and in songs.

**SONGS:** "Rocky Mountain" (p. 152)
"Long Legged Life" (p. 79)
"Who's that Yonder" (p. 94)
"Great Big House" (p. 121)

**PROCEDURE:**

| Teacher activities | Pupil activities |
|---|---|
| MOTIVATION: Teach game song "Great Big House." | Learn by rote:<br><br>words,<br>melody, and<br>movements (dance). |
| DEVELOPMENT:<br><br>Isolate m-r-d ("Pumpkin pie"). What are the last 3 notes in solfa? Can you show me with hand signs? | Identify aurally the m-r-d ending.<br>Sing the ending in solfa, substituting m-r-d for the words "Pump-kin pie."<br>   m   r   d |
| Where is "doh"? Can you put a marker at the beginning of the music? | Find "doh" and place a marker on overhead at beginning of notation. |

| | |
|---|---|
| ⎡ Alternate route if song in key of F or G    Look at key signature.<br><br>What is the solfa name for the last flat or sharp? | Apply previous learning about finding "doh." ⎤ |

| | |
|---|---|
| Can you read the rest of the song and sing it in solfa? | Apply previous learning. |
| Have children take turns developing the solfa notation measure by measure (reading, then singing). | Using "doh" as a reference point, discover the solfa names for all notes in the song. |
| Reinforce with practice on the tone ladder. | Practice singing in solfa. |
| Work with other songs on list as time allows to develop awareness of the d–m–s and s–m–l–r patterns (aurally and visually). | Develop ability to sight read different melodic patterns. |
| Reinforce with work on tone ladder. | Develop and reinforce awareness of pitch/ intervals on tone ladder. |

CLOSURE:

| | |
|---|---|
| We learned 2 important skills today. What were they? | Recall lesson content. |
| 1. finding the starting note of the song using "doh finder" and | Focus on important new learning. |
| 2. finding tonal patterns within a song and sight reading them. | Integrate new learning. |
| What new tonal patterns did we discover today?<br>     —d-m-s<br>     —m-s-l-(r)<br><br>Can you sing them if I give you the starting note? | Develop tonal memory by recalling the patterns out of context. |

# LESSON PLAN #6

**GRADE:** 4/5

**CONCEPTS:**
1. Steady Beat
2. Meter

Music moves with an underlying beat. Beats are grouped by accent to create meter. We can feel the meter and show the beat pattern by the way we move in response to a song.

**OBJECTIVES:**

a) Cognitive: Children will develop an understanding of the functions of beat and meter in a song ("Great Big House" p. 121).

b) Behavioral: Children will learn to articulate beat and meter through appropriate body movement and body percussion ideas.

c) Creative: Children will extend their repertoire of movement ideas through exploration, thereby increasing their sensitivity to the rhythmic elements in the song "Great Big House."

N.B. Many other things are happening too, for example practice in singing, pitch matching, socialization, memory sequencing of movement ideas, and so on. No concept is ever learned completely in isolation.

**LESSON ELEMENTS:**

1. Motivation: Game Song "Great Big House." Children learn game by rote, teacher modeling.

2. Development: Teach by rote the following body percussion ostinato.

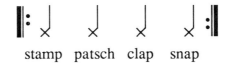

stamp   patsch   clap   snap

How many parts are there in this movement idea? (4)

Which count is accented (sounds loudest?) (1)

Which count is next loudest? (3)

What we have here is a 4 beat pattern which describes the meter of our song. Can you accompany the song with our body percussion pattern? Demonstrate and lead class in performance.

-29-

When we repeat a pattern in this way to accompany a song, we call the pattern an **ostinato**. An ostinato can be clapped, sung, or played on instruments. Let's look at an ostinato for instruments. To prepare, let us do this:

(a) Body Percussion, preparatory exercise:

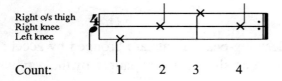

(b) Transfer to Alto Xylophone:

(c) Ostinato 2

Prepare

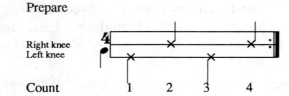

Play (Bass Xylophone)

(d) Bordun

Prepare

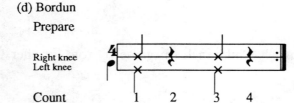

Play (Bass or Alto Metallophone)

(e) Ostinato 3

Prepare

Play (Glockenspiel)

3. Closure: Combine singing, movement (body percussion and playing instruments) in whole-class performance.

What is the beat pattern (meter) of our song? (4 beats per measure)

Who played the beat pattern? (xylophones)

How many ostinati did we have (four, 3 instruments and 1 body percussion)

What did they all have in common? (They played the same melodic/rhythmic pattern continuously throughout the song.)

Could you make up (compose) your own (or a different) body percussion ostinato? A different instrumental ostinato? A vocal/melodic ostinato? and present it in class next time?

4. Evaluation: By observation:

i) Were children able to articulate the appropriate body percussion patterns? If not, perhaps a simpler pattern may be devised at first, for example:

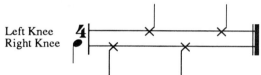

ii) Were instrumental parts easily learned (sufficient time allowed for preparatory body percussion exercises?)

Written or oral test to review definition of terms (beat, ostinato, meter, *D.C. al fine*, and so on) once these terms have been discussed and explained.

EXTENSION: N.B. You cannot do everything in one lesson. Choose your focus for each time-bound lesson period and be content with extending learning piece by piece from lesson to lesson, shifting focus as required. What is paramount is that in each lesson children develop a feeling for the wholeness of music rather than become immersed in a rigorous academic exercise.

# LESSON PLAN #7

**GRADE:** 6

**TOPIC:** Singing — providing opportunities for children to expand their range of singing experiences and to develop their singing ability.

**CONCEPTS:** Form — $aa_v bb_v$ Phrases in a song may be similar or different. We can label phrases to help us identify these similarities and differences.

Rhythm — Review of steady beat and melodic rhythm: A song may move to a steady beat or pulse that recurs throughout the entire song (4-beat pattern). Within this beat structure, the melody has a rhythm of its own determined by the words (melodic rhythm).

**OBJECTIVES:** Cognitive — Children will learn to analyze the form of the song "Jack was Ev'ry Inch a Sailor," isolate the beat pattern and distinguish it from the melodic rhythm.

Behavioral — Children will demonstrate their recognition of the form $aa_v bb_v$ with appropriate hand and/or body movements; they will articulate the beat and the rhythm patterns by tapping/clapping or other appropriate body movements; likewise they will "perform" the quadruple meter with body movement.

**PROCEDURES:**

| Teacher Activities | Pupil Activities |
|---|---|
| Motivation: | |
| Sing the song through (one verse). | |
| Question: Who or what is the song about? What does the song tell us about Jack? Where was he born? What kind of sailor was he? How long did he spend at whaling? | Listen to the song; remember the story of Jack and recall episodes from the story. |
| Continue questioning along these lines to elicit recall of the story of Jack. | |
| Development: | |
| Display song on overhead. | |

Invite children to sing the first verse; sing with them and ask them to tap the beat quietly.

Ask: Do you feel the beat moving in 2s or 3s? Is there anything that helps us find out? Yes! – the $\frac{4}{4}$ time signature.

Suggest a body percussion pattern to articulate this:

| 1 | 2 | 3 | 4 |
|---|---|---|---|
| stomp | patsch | clap | snap |

Invite children to practice this as we sing.

Now that we can feel the beat pattern, let's put the words in our hands. Slow down the tempo here.

Divide class:   Beat people
                Word people

Everybody sing to accompaniment of beat and rhythm pattern.

When we put the words in our hands like that we are playing what is called the "melodic rhythm."

(Time permitting, or to reinforce the concept, have them put the words in their feet, head, shoulders, and so on.)

PHRASING:

How many phrases are there in this song (4)? Does everyone know what a phrase is?

Look at the words and then decide where the first phrase begins and ends. As we sing, can you show with your hand the length of the phrase?

---

Read from overhead.

Tap the beat and decide whether it moves in 2s or 3s.

Identify the time signature. (Some will recognize this already; others will need explanation.)

Perform the body percussion pattern and feel the quadruple meter.

strong–weak–medium–weak

Put the words in hands, clapping out the melodic rhythm.

Feel and distinguish between beat pattern and melodic rhythm.

Discover new vocabulary, melodic rhythm.

Define "phrase" – perhaps drawing from their language context.

Relate the language phrase and the musical (melodic) phrase.

Lead children through examination of the phrase structure (form) of the song. Help them derive the true form through discussion of phrase length; they will likely begin by making two phrases out of the first one.

Analyze the phrase structure of the melody by relating and comparing length of language and musical phrases to derive the melodic line of each musical phrase; look for similarities and differences.

Optional activity:

If needed, use geometric shapes to represent phrases of similar and contrasting form.

Use visual aids to identify phrases as same or different.

Closure:

It is usual to label the phrases in a song with letter names; if we call the first phrase a, what should we call the second phrase? Is it the same? Identical? Slightly different? Where is it different? One way of showing that the phrase is almost the same but slightly different is by the use of a subscript $_v$. Demonstrate.

Learn a new way to identify the form of a song.

Label "Jack was Ev'ry Inch a Sailor" as $aa_v bb_v$ form.

Proceeding along these lines, help children derive the form as $aa_v bb_v$. Today we learned how to discover the **FORM** of a song. Next time we will look at a new song and see if you can discover its form.

# LESSON PLAN #8

**GRADE:** 7

## *THE WORLD OF SOUND*

**CONCEPT:** Tone-color (Timbre): Every sound source produces its own unique quality of sound. We can change the sound an instrument makes by the way we play it.

**OBJECTIVES:** Pupils will become aware of conventional and potential sound sources in their immediate environment.

Pupils will participate in group composition of a sound story.

**MOTIVATION:** How many things does it take to produce a sound? (At least 2 — an active agent and a passive agent).

How many different sounds can you produce using only your hands? Your feet, other body parts? In each case which was the sound source? The active agent? the passive agent?

Can you change the quality of the sound by the way you use the sound sources? Can you find other sound sources in your immediate environment? (pencils, rulers, desk, etc.)

**DEVELOPMENT:** Would you call these sounds musical? Perhaps not. Yet, we could make a sound composition in the same way that composers do. You've all heard electronic sound compositions (discuss).

What design elements are needed to make a composition? (Unity and variety)

Let's see if we can create a composition of our own using these random environmental sounds.

Choose 5 or 6 sounds already identified from random environmental sources. Arrange them in a sequence — stress beginning, ending, unity, variety.

Tape record the sequence and play back (10 – 15 seconds is enough).

Devise (with class input) a scoring procedure or "legend" in order to write down the composition on the chalk board.

e.g.

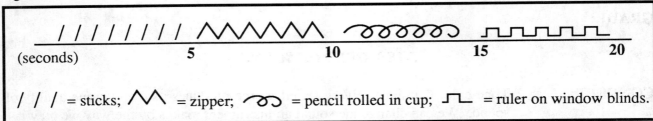

/ / / = sticks; ∧∧ = zipper; ☊ = pencil rolled in cup; ⊓ = ruler on window blinds.

EVALUATION: Form groups of 4 or 5. Allow five to ten minutes for developing group compositions.

Tape each group's performance. Have each group evaluate its performance using criteria of unity and variety and a rating scale of 1 to 10.

Refer to the section in this book on **Composing Music** (pages 187–194) for further information on composition.

# Evaluation

**Evaluation** is a term which is sometimes used synonymously for measurement, testing, and assessment. It is however a broader term implying the need for making judgments. The teacher must not only measure or observe what a student does but must also evaluate the worth and quality of the experiences the student has undergone, making judgments about each child's progress.

If curriculum goals and learning outcomes are to be achieved, systematic evaluation of student progress must be a responsibility for every teacher. Likewise, if teachers want to be assured that the methods they use are effective, they must systematically evaluate their own teaching. The two, student progress and teacher effectiveness, are therefore necessary components of evaluation procedures. To evaluate any one component without reference to the other would be meaningless. In the most practical terms, what all this means is that a teacher needs to be able to answer two questions when considering student progress: 1. Is the success or failure to meet objectives attributable to the student's strengths or weaknesses or to the teaching methods employed by the teacher? 2. In what ways might teachers gather evidence that will enable them to respond accurately to the first question? The rest of the discussion will deal with the second question, the gathering of evidence.

## STUDENT ASSESSMENT

Teaching is an interactive process requiring an awareness of what students can do. The evaluation of students can be **formative** (frequent, diagnostic) or **summative** (serving as a final report). It can be **quantitative** (involving grades and numbers) or **qualitative** (using more subjective kinds of evidence). It can be **normative** (comparing students with each other or established norms) or **criterion-referenced**, establishing what the student has accomplished with a view to determining the next learning objectives.

While in the recent past student evaluation has focussed on tests and measurements and an obsession with the attainment of objectivity in an attempt to be "scientific," the current trend is toward student assessment which is formative, qualitative, and criterion-referenced rather than measurement. **Assessment** thus involves:

1. the frequent description of student progress within regular classroom activities,
2. the use of a wide variety of methods to collect information, and
3. the incorporation of many types of data collection.

The new acceptance of more subjective methods is not an excuse for a return to the past. The teacher must still interpret, that is evaluate the data; such evaluations must be based on evidence carefully collected over a period of time. Teachers will need to develop acute observational skills. How does this theory apply to music education?

Many people think that student work in the arts should not be evaluated since the product is a matter of personal expression and taste. Such a position has indeed been prevalent in music classrooms, often resulting in grades in music being based on participation and cooperation or sometimes the teacher's unarticulated and unsubstantiated impression of a student's performance usually as part of a group. This is one of the behaviours which has given subjectivity its unsavoury reputation in scientific circles. In an attempt to be more "objective" some teachers have resorted to written theory tests usually involving lower level thinking skills or fill-in-the-blanks questions. You may recall having experienced such unfortunate methods of evaluation. Is there no alternative to these approaches? A look at the **what** and **how** of evaluation will suggest some avenues to explore.

1. The **WHAT** of Music Assessment

    What can be considered in the attempt to describe student growth in musical understanding, skills, and enjoyment?

    - perception of musical qualities
    - performance skills
    - composition/improvisation/arranging
    - response to music (that it is happening, not the specific nature of the response)
    - literacy skills
    - understanding and use of music terminology
    - interest in music activities

2. The **HOW** of Music Assessment

    How can we assess student growth? The following techniques can serve diagnostic and information purposes:

    - perception tests – showing phrases, meter... (visual data)
      – movement activities showing an understanding of concepts
      – pencil and paper (tests)
    - performance – singing
      (live or taped) – playing
      – conducting
    - pencil and paper knowledge tests
    - making listening charts (maps)
    - compositions
    - scores (small group or individual)
    - reflections (oral, in journal format) on performances, compositions, listening selections, and other musical activities
    - reading music
    - aural skills (vocal or rhythmic echoes.../dictations)
    - correct response to and use of music terminology
    - student request to take on an extra music assignment

    Many of these activities could be found occurring as part of the daily procedures in the music class; no disruption of class time is necessary. Teachers must be sensitive observers, aware of what to notice and record. Student work or samples can be regularly collected in a portfolio for which the student is responsible. A portfolio of student work is useful for your information but also so students can see how they have grown throughout the year. Such a portfolio is a good aid to self-assessment and a basis for student-teacher interviews.

One important feature of regular assessment is that the teacher is more likely to use a variety of methods of data collection thus giving students a better opportunity to show what they really know. A one-shot written test may well favour a certain type of student but disadvantage others. For example, one student may sing or play very well but not be as perceptive in hearing what happens in the music. Another student might be able to explain the meaning of 3/4 but not be able to clap a rhythm pattern in 3/4. The variety of methods gives the teacher a more accurate picture of what the student can do.

## EXAMPLES OF STUDENT ASSESSMENT

Songs and listening selections from three lessons will provide examples of how to move from strategies to assessing student learning in music.

1. The strategies for the "**Morris Dance**" (p. 181) suggest three avenues for observing student learning in small group situations or as individuals:

    - How well does the listening chart designed by students show the form of the piece?
    - Do the movements demonstrated by the students match the form of the music?
    - Does the follow-up for either activity show that students are focusing on musical qualities in the statement of their judgments?

2. "**J'entends le moulin**" (p.133) provides many opportunities for whole class or individual student assessment. All of these are not to be used in every lesson.

    - Do the students sing in tune?
    - Can they show the phrases? (rainbows in the air or on paper)
    - How many phrases are there in the song? (Have students show the answer with fingers so you can check the whole group quickly.)
    - Draw a phrase chart to show the form.
    - Circle the beats in the song.
    - Write and/or clap new rhythm patterns.
    - Add words to the rhythm patterns.

3. For "**Billy Bad**" (p.61), a primary song, the assessment could be to determine over a period of time whether individual students can sing in tune using the s-f-m-r-d and s-m patterns in the song.

The purpose of student assessment is to inform students of their progress and set directions for future learning, inform parents about what their child can do, and help teachers evaluate their teaching strategies. In order to record student progress for your files and to inform students and parents, in addition to maintaining student portfolios you may need to use a variety of record keeping devices such as checklists, selected anecdotes, inventories and interview forms. Some samples are provided.

## A) RECORDING STUDENT PROGRESS WITH CHECKLISTS

Checklists are quick devices for keeping track of student behaviour. What you will observe specifically will depend on your objectives.

1. **Sample checklist for later primary level students**

   Class –
   Time Frame –                                    Students' Names

   | | | | | | |
   |---|---|---|---|---|---|
   | Singing: | | | | | |
   |   sings in tune | | | | | |
   |   tone calls (4 and 5 notes accurately) | | | | | |
   |   inner hearing (rejoins out loud correctly) | | | | | |
   | Responds to the beat in a variety of tempos | | | | | |
   | Differentiates between beat and rhythm pattern | | | | | |
   | Reads patterns using ♩, ♫, 𝄽, 𝅗𝅥 | | | | | |
   | Explains meter signatures ($\frac{3}{4}$, $\frac{4}{4}$) | | | | | |
   | Identifies meter aurally (beats in sets of 2s and 3s) | | | | | |
   | Identifies AB and ABA forms | | | | | |
   | Shows the phrases | | | | | |
   | Identifies folk instruments (banjo, guitar, autoharp, dulcimer) | | | | | |
   | Identifies string families (violin, viola, cello, string bass) | | | | | |
   | Is sensitive to the sounds made by others in group improvisation | | | | | |
   | Listens/watches when others perform | | | | | |
   | Contributes in discussion about music | | | | | |
   | Talks about musical activities outside music class | | | | | |
   | Brings own musical experiences to school | | | | | |

       ✘ = problem area     ✚ = success     ✔ = superior

2. **Sample short term checklist** (for a lesson or sequence of a few lessons at the intermediate level. This one is for some lessons comparing two versions of a riddle song, "I'll Give My Love an Apple" and the "Riddle Song")

   Class –
   Time Frame –                                    Students' Names

   | | | | | | |
   |---|---|---|---|---|---|
   | Identifies areas of contrast and similarities between two songs | | | | | |
   | Organizes and performs in small groups an arrangement of one of the songs | | | | | |
   | Written analysis of one song | | | | | |
   | Assigned comparison of two different songs. | | | | | |

## B) RECORDING STUDENT PROGRESS WITH ANECDOTES

Select one to three students for special observation during one class. You may focus on observing one particular musical learning or skill which you determine before the class or general musical behaviour. The samples give an example of the latter and are for the teacher's use, not for reporting to the child or parent.

**Sample Anecdotes**

**Date** – Lesson - form and mood in "The Elephant" (Saint-Saëns)
**Class** – grade 3

---
Name – Mary J.

Mary was attentive throughout most of the lesson. She volunteered several times to engage in discussion about the form of "The Elephant." She noticed the return of the A section. During movement to the music she seemed to find it difficult to concentrate on the music, giggling occasionally and distracting others. We will be trying this movement again next class; I will watch for improvement. In the closing song, "The Animal Fair," Mary still has a tendency to oversing and go out of tune.

---

Name – Andy L.

Andy continues to surprise with the depth of understanding he shows in his responses. Today, he volunteered the form of "The Elephant." He seems to see pattern very well. During movement to the music Andy showed wonderful concentration. He demonstrated the feeling of heaviness by using size and slow movement and changed his body language with the music. In the concluding song Andy still did not sing out with a full voice. He continues to be reticent.

---

## C) RECORDING STUDENT PROGRESS WITH INVENTORIES

Given time limitations it is useful to develop forms which can be re-used. Base the observation points on your objectives and revise/improve the forms as needed. The grade level and experience level of your students will need to be considered in the design of these forms. Follow-up anecdotes on some of the points for some of the students would give greater depth to the record. Observe only a few of the students during one activity or all students on one point only. You could develop symbols to expedite the actual recording. For example:

✗ = problem area,  ✚ = success,  ✓ = superior,  ? = check again

### 1. Inventory for Small Group Project

| Class –  Nature of Project – | | | | | |
|---|---|---|---|---|---|
| Date –   Students' Names | | | | | |
| 1. Did student contribute to group effort? | | | | | |
| 2. Was mode of operation cooperative? | | | | | |
| 3. Was student on task? | | | | | |
| 4. Was student satisfied with results? (oral or written reflection) | | | | | |
| 5. Was learning objective met? | | | | | |
| 6. Did student go beyond the assignment? | | | | | |

## 2. Inventory for Performing (Solo or group)

| Class – <br> Date – | Work performed – <br> Students' Names | | | | | |
|---|---|---|---|---|---|---|
| Accuracy | - in tune | | | | | |
| | - notes | | | | | |
| | - rhythm | | | | | |
| Tone | | | | | | |
| Diction | | | | | | |
| Musicality | - phrasing | | | | | |
| | - expression | | | | | |
| Memory work | | | | | | |

## 3. Inventory for Moving to Music

| Class – <br> Date – | Name of Piece – <br> Students' Names | | | | | | |
|---|---|---|---|---|---|---|---|
| Concentration on music | | | | | | | |
| Expression of music | - tempo | | | | | | |
| | - dynamics | | | | | | |
| | - phrasing | | | | | | |
| | - form | | | | | | |
| | - texture | | | | | | |
| Movement | - use of space | | | | | | |
| | - fluidity | | | | | | |
| | - variety | | | | | | |
| | - appropriateness | | | | | | |
| Willingness to experiment | | | | | | | |

## 4. Inventory for Listening to Music

| Class – <br> Date – | Name of Piece – <br> Students' Names | | | | | |
|---|---|---|---|---|---|---|
| 1. Did student concentrate on the listening selection ? | | | | | | |
| 2. When class was asked to indicate a musical feature, did student give an independent answer or check others first? | | | | | | |
| 3. When asked to justify his/her response, student gave reasonable explanation | | | | | | |
| 4. Student had unusual insight into the piece | | | | | | |
| 5. Student made comparison with earlier or personal listening | | | | | | |
| 6. Student followed the listening map | | | | | | |
| 7. Student completed the listening guide | | | | | | |

## 5. Inventory for Group Composition

Class –
Date –
Names of students in group –

**Planning:**
1. Did all students contribute to the decision making ?
   Comment:

2. Was the musical problem solved ?
   Comment:

3. Did the composition demonstrate a building on music techniques/concepts/skills previously discussed or used in class?
   Comment:

4. Did the composition use musical techniques/concepts/skills the students picked up on their own?
   Comment:

**Performance**
5. Was the composition well delivered ?
   Comment:

**Reflection**
6. What was the quality of the discussion about their own work? (List ideas discussed.)

## D) INFORMING STUDENTS AND PARENTS

a) Interviews provide a student with an opportunity to select what he/she considers to be the best examples of work accomplished, to hear the teacher's assessment and to participate in the formulation of future directions. Interviews with parents include the discussion of the variety of recorded data the teacher has accumulated and student work as kept in the portfolio. Such a conversation is an excellent opportunity to get feedback from the parents about the impact the school is having on the student and to request information which might assist the teacher in helping the student.

b) Written reports can be a summary statement of the general progress of the student, could include anecdotes or could be a checklist. An example based on the primary checklist (p. 38) follows.

**Sample Report**

**Name –**
**Term –** Final
**Level –** Grade 3

This term we have been concentrating on using our singing voices more effectively, distinguishing between folk (banjo, guitar, autoharp) and orchestral (violin, cello) instruments, recognizing ABA forms, and listening to music with greater concentration and understanding. We use_____ as our text book.

|  | Not Yet | | | | Does |
|---|---|---|---|---|---|

Sings "Donkey Riding" in tune with others

Distinguishes visually and aurally between autoharp, banjo and guitar

Distinguishes visually and aurally between violin and cello

Identifies songs and listening selections in ABA form

Shows beats in sets of two or three with patsch-clap pattern

Listens attentively while music is played

Moves expressively to "The Elephant" and "The Swan"

Was attentive while others performed or spoke

Contributed to classroom discussion

Participated eagerly

Comment:

Teacher's Signature

# METHODS

Throughout this textbook you will have encountered a number of strategies for teaching music. These strategies are based on what psychologists have discovered about learning and child development, such as the need for the student to play an active role in learning (doing), the need to move from the concrete to the abstract (through enactive, iconic, and symbolic stages), and from the simple to the complex (refer to the Scope and Sequence Chart on page 16). Such research findings are reinforced by the experience of practitioners. The authors' underlying assumption is that it is important that children (and you as classroom teachers):

1. perceive musical qualities and expressive gestures,
2. explore the elements of music,
3. play an active role in the learning process (listening, singing, playing, moving, composing),
4. develop musicality,
5. respond with increasing sensitivity to music,
6. develop skills in reading and writing music,
7. become increasingly independent musicians, and
8. think about and articulate music learnings.

These assumptions translate in practice to the types of strategies presented in *Making Music Meaningful*. The "method" does not have a single founder or name but is constantly adapting to incorporate new research developments and classroom practice.

There are other methodologies which focus on a particular aspect of music teaching such as improvisation, creativity, literacy, or movement. Such methods have advocates who claim that their way gives students the best possible music education. Most require special training providing certification courses for those who wish to use the approach authentically. Since you will likely hear of Orff or Kodaly courses or specialists you should be aware of the general nature and rationale for some of the methods used in our schools. We will briefly examine three named after the founders, **Orff, Kodály, Dalcroze,** and two whose names express their underlying philosophy, Education Through Music (**ETM**), and the Manhattanville Music Curriculum Program (**MMCP**).

## ORFF–SCHULWERK
(Music for Children)

The Orff-Schulwerk approach to music education was inspired in the 1920s by Carl Orff (1895-1982), a German composer, and his colleague, Gunild Keetman. Orff established a school for gymnastics, music, and dance in Munich, where physical education teachers learned to play their own music. Later, the Bavarian radio system commissioned Orff and Keetman to prepare materials for children. The five volumes of Schulwerk contain models of their work. Today the Orff Institute in Salzburg, Austria is a teacher training centre, and Orff-Schulwerk is used widely in Canada, the United States, Europe, Japan, China, Africa, Australia and South America.

Orff-Schulwerk is not a clear-cut method; instead the participants are involved in the process of learning as they **explore**, **imitate**, and **create**; outcomes are thus not entirely predictable. Orff realized that:

> Elementary music is never music alone but forms a unity with movement, dance and speech. It is music that one makes oneself, in which one takes part not as a listener but as a participant. It is unsophisticated, employs no big forms and no big architectural structures, and it uses small sequence forms, ostinato and rondo. (Carley 1977, p. 6)

The components of Orff-Schulwerk are singing, speech, movement, instrumental play, and improvisation. A brief description of each of these follows:

1. **Speech** — the materials used are names, rhymes and chants which are familiar to children. Musical concepts (eg. rhythm, phrasing, dynamics, form) are introduced through speech. Sound gestures (clap, patsch, stamp, snap) reinforce learnings and serve as accompaniment.
2. **Singing** — initially, tonal material is restricted to the pentatonic scale. The first interval is sol-mi; then la, re and doh are added to complete the scale. This scale with its absence of semitones is ideal for improvisation with singing and instruments.
3. **Movement** — elemental or natural movement possibilities (eg. walking, running, skipping, galloping) are explored and then combined with singing and playing.
4. **Instruments** — pitched barred instruments are of three types, all with removable bars, and played with mallets:

    1. xylophone (bass, alto, soprano) – rosewood bars
    2. glockenspiel (alto, soprano) – steel bars
    3. metallophone (bass, alto, soprano) – metal alloy bars

    Recorders and unpitched percussion are also used. Harmony begins with the bordun or drone (I and V) as accompaniment and tonal support for the pentatonic melodies. Ostinato patterns emerge from melodic material and provide a "carpet" over which melodies are improvised.
5. **Improvisation** — spontaneous composition permeates all components of Orff-Schulwerk: singing, speech, movement and playing instruments. Thus, Orff-Schulwerk evolves into a total process of exploration to imitation to creation, and the child is involved in each step of the progression.

## Suggested Readings

I. Carley, ed. *Orff Re-Echoes (Selections from the Orff Echo and the Supplements).* Brasstown, NC: American Orff Schulwerk Association, 1977.

G. Keetman. *Elementaria.* London: Schott, 1974.

W. Keller. *Introduction to Music for Children.* New York: Schott, 1974.

B. Landis and P. Carder. *The Eclectic Curriculum in American Music Education: Contributions of Dalcroze, Kodaly, and Orff.* Washington: Music Educators National Conference, 1972.

# THE KODÁLY APPROACH

*Musical Education contributes to the many-sided capabilities of a child, affecting not only specifically musical aptitudes but his general hearing, his ability to concentrate, his conditional reflexes, his emotional horizon, and his physical culture.*
-Zoltán Kodály (1882-1967)

The Kodály method of music education grew out of the Hungarian composer's concern about the musical illiteracy of Hungarian children at the beginning of the twentieth century. His approach to dealing with the problem was through teacher education. He felt that through the influence of teachers, children would become knowledgeable about music — their own Hungarian heritage music as well as the works of the master composers. His objective was to establish a musically literate society in Hungary. In collaboration with his contemporary Béla Bartók, he compiled the *Corpus Musicæ Popularis Hungaricæ* — a comprehensive collection of traditional folk songs which would become the fundamental material of children's study of music. Kodály felt strongly that the folksongs of the peasant people were the best material for the children to study first because, like their spoken language, they learn this material most naturally before being introduced to other musical genres. Once children had become well versed in their folk music, they would be introduced to good composed music suitable for children's voices. Kodály himself composed much of the music that has subsequently passed into the common repertoire for Kodály programs world-wide.

For a detailed description of the Kodály method, its sequence, tools and materials, the reader should consult Lois Choksy's *The Kodály Method* (1974). In brief, the method is based on a sequence of instruction that is designed to reflect the developmental growth patterns of children. Singing the minor third interval (s-m) is the starting point since this interval appears to be one that children everywhere can produce from a very early age. Gradually, s-m songs give way to songs of a wider melodic range, adding the solfa pitches la, mi, re and doh to form the pentatonic scale. Pentatonic songs form a large part of the early singing repertoire. Eventually, the full major and minor scales are developed and children are trained to analyze melodies for their tonal characteristics. The basic tools for working in this context are the system of movable doh, a symbolic system of rhythm-duration syllables, and the Curwen hand signs.

A fundamental premise of the Kodály method is that every child can sing and must be given the opportunity to develop that natural ability. A major thrust of the method is to enable children to become fluent sight readers of musical notation at a very early age, to develop confidence in ear training, and discrimination in listening.

## Suggested Readings

L. Choksy. *The Kodály Context.* Englewood Cliffs, NJ: Prentice-Hall, 1981.
L. Choksy. *The Kodály Method.* Englewood Cliffs, NJ: Prentice-Hall, 1974.

# DALCROZE EURYTHMICS

An earlier and less well-known approach to music education is that of Emile Jaques-Dalcroze (1865-1950), often known as the Dalcroze method or Dalcroze Eurythmics. For Dalcroze, the basic source of musical rhythm is to be found in the natural locomotor rhythms of the human body, but this is only the basic foundation of his system of music education which encompasses *solfège* improvisation and eurythmics in a synthesized and inter-related experience. Dalcroze was one of the first music educators to realize, as early as 1891, that musical learning cannot be compartmentalized and that the structure of activities which lead to musical understandings must be totally integrated.

It is apparent that Dalcroze anticipated our current emphasis on conceptual learning and the spiral curriculum, as he believed that it is through numerous successive and concurrent musical experiences that true understanding and skill are developed. Thus in the Dalcroze method the sequence of musical experiences for the student is of primary importance. Rhythm is considered the fundamental activity and through rhythmic activities dynamics and tempo changes are experienced. Later pitch and texture activities are added to create a "sound palette" by which improvisational activities are introduced. The musical "internalizations" which result from these experiences are next related to aural training where sound—symbol connections are made by the student. Always related to these learnings, however, is bodily movement through which students experience the rise and fall of the phrase, the gravity-like pull of the cadence and other musical elements. Fundamental to the Dalcroze method are "the feelings of students in response to music [and] channeling these feelings into expression."[1] According to Dalcroze, before students are introduced to musical instruments, they must have a rich experience in such activities as listening, singing, dancing and composing. Only after internalizing music using the natural instruments (the voice, the body) will students have the ability to transfer these understandings to instruments.

It is not surprising that there has been little written about the Dalcroze method, since he believed that only through participation in training classes could teachers effectively learn the method.

## Suggested Reading

L. Choksy; R. Abramson; A. Gillespie; and D. Woods. *Teaching Music in the Twentieth Century*. Englewood Cliffs, NJ: Prentice-Hall, 1986.

---

[1] B. Landis and P. Carder. *The Eclectic Curriculum in American Music Education: Contributions of Dalcroze, Kodály, and Orff*. Washington: Music Educators National Conference, 1972, p. 11.

# ETM
(Education Through Music)

Inspired by Kodály and the educational theories of Piaget, Mary Helen Richards has adapted the Kodály techniques to the cultural needs of North American children by substituting songs, chants, rhymes etc. that are familiar to the children for their Hungarian counterparts. She concentrates on singing as the medium for musical education and musical education in general as a means of reaching children in order to teach them the other disciplines. In her view, any child who can speak can sing; she denies the existence of a tone-deaf child (except in the case of physical impairment). Children are taught by doing. Children will sing if they are not made to feel self-conscious about singing. Every child is special; no child is special. Song games are used as a means of involving children without "putting them on the spot." Children should not be introduced to instruments until they have become comfortable with their most primitive instruments — the voice and the body.

## Significant Features

1. The use of hand signals (developed by John Curwen in England in 1870 and used extensively by Kodály as a visual aid to facilitate the sight reading of pitches).

2. The use of familiar chants, rhymes, proverbs, jingles, and game-songs adapted to the special cultural interests of children.

3. The use of specific speech patterns and the application of numbers to proper names as a means of developing awareness of syllabication and accent in speech, and in music. e.g.

    Kevin – 7
    John –10
    Anita –11
    Jonathan – 70
    Elizabeth – Eleventy  (coined specially and deliberately)
    Christine – July (since there is no corresponding number)

4. Mapping – tracing the shape of a song as a means of developing awareness of form in music.

5. Inner hearing – a technique to teach concentration and develop rhythmic independence.

## Suggested Readings

M.H. Richards. *Aesthetic Foundations for Thinking Rethought,* Parts I and II. Portola Valley, CA: Richards Institute, 1984.

M.H. Richards. *Language Arts Through Music: A Trilogy.* Portola Valley, CA: Richards Institute, 1971.

M.H. Richards. *The Music Language II: From Folk Song to Masterwork.* Portola Valley, CA: Richards Institute, 1974.

F. Sweeney; and M. Wharram. *Experience Games Through Music.* Portola Valley, CA: Richards Institute, 1973.

# MMCP
(Manhattanville Music Curriculum Project)

In recent decades, several music education programs which stress the creative aspect of music have been developed. Through these approaches, children are treated as musicians — composers, performers and listeners. They are gradually led to a deeper understanding of all music with special attention to music of our time utilizing "discovery" techniques. Murray Schafer, well-known Canadian composer, has contributed much to this field through his booklets including *The Composer in the Classroom* (1965) and *The Rhinoceros in the Classroom* (1975). In the U.S., curriculum materials based on these innovative principles were produced by a group of leading music educators under the name Manhattanville Music Curriculum Program (commonly called **MMCP**).

MMCP produced two major curriculum guides — one for primary grades entitled *MMCP Interaction* and one for intermediate grades entitled *MMCP Synthesis*. Musical learnings are organized in a spiral fashion. This simply means that the various components of music — pitch, rhythm, form, etc., are all introduced through basic concepts and then gradually added to with further concepts that become increasingly complex. See p. 320 for an illustration of the spiral of concepts. A typical concept is "By adding accents to certain sounds, the character of the music can be changed." The suggested strategy for exploring this involves children developing their own compositions without accents, then with accents. Compositions are taped, listened to, and their differences are discussed. The music room thus becomes a laboratory in which children experiment with musical sounds, produce their own music, and learn about it through creating, performing and listening.

**Suggested readings**

A. Biasini, *et al. MMCP Interaction.* Bardonia, NY: Media Materials Inc, 1970.
R.M. Schafer. *The Composer in the Classroom.* Toronto: BMI Canada, 1965.
R.M. Schafer. *Ear Cleaning.* Toronto: BMI Canada, 1967.
R.M. Schafer. *The Rhinoceros in the Classroom.* Toronto: BMI Canada, 1975.
R.M. Schafer. *Creative Music Education.* Toronto: BMI Canada 1976.
R.B. Thomas, *et al. MMCP Synthesis.* Bardonia, NY: Media Materials Inc, 1970.

**Suggested Film**

*Bing Bang Boom.* National Film Board of Canada, 1975.

# MAKING

# MUSIC

# SONGS

The songs in this textbook have been carefully selected to reflect the following criteria:

1. Each song should provide a clear presentation of a music concept.
2. The collection should cover all the music concepts outlined in the scope and sequence chart on page 16.
3. There should be a variety of types and styles of songs (action, game, rounds, folk, traditional).

Each song is accompanied by a concept statement which identifies one or two possible focuses for a music lesson and a series of strategies which could be incorporated in a lesson plan. These strategies have been tested in classroom situations by the writers and have been refined over many years. The box highlights literacy and conceptual learnings for each song.

In order to make planning easier, the songs have been divided into primary and intermediate sections. You should realize that this division is somewhat arbitrary and that with appropriate strategy adaptations, some songs could be used at both levels.

# SONGS for the Primary Music Class

# Ah, Poor Bird

© Waterloo Music Company. Used by permission.

**CONCEPT:** Canons can be sung and shown with movement.

## ACCOMPANIMENT SUGGESTIONS:

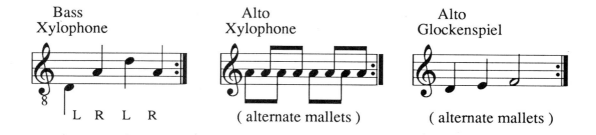

**STRATEGIES:** a) The melody is shown as a two-part canon. (If singers are secure, try in four parts.)
b) Instruments can play 2 bars of introduction and also interludes between verses.
c) Encourage children to compose additional verses (an opportunity to encourage positive attitudes towards animals!).

**MOVEMENT:** a) Divide the children into 3 groups. Each group depicts movement suggested by the words in their verse.
b) Movement could also be done in canon.

( round )

# Barnacle Bill

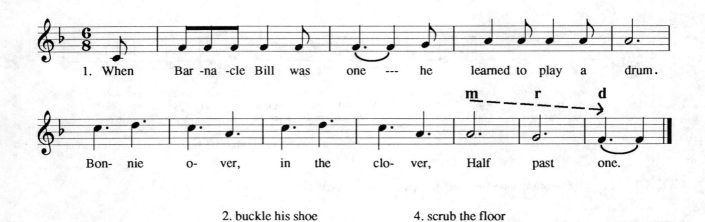

2. buckle his shoe
3. climb a tree
4. scrub the floor
5. swim and dive

**CONCEPTS:**

1. Beats in music are organized in sets. The first beat of the set feels stronger than the others.
2. Melodies move in pitch patterns which go upwards, or downwards, or are repeated.

**STRATEGIES:**

a) *Barnacle Bill* has beats in sets of two. To feel the strong beat, bounce a ball so that the ball hits the floor on the strong beat and you catch the ball on the weak beat. Another way of feeling the strong beat is to use *patschen* (slap your knees) on the strong beat and clap your hands on the weak beat.

**Can you think of other strong/weak actions which could be used to show beats in sets?**

b) Listen to *Barnacle Bill*. Here are some ways to show melodic direction:

i) On the words "half past one" show with your hands whether the sounds are moving **upwards** ↗ or **downwards** ↘ or **remain the same** → ;

ii) Use one, two or three fingers to identify the patterns you hear

i. ↗ ii. ↘ iii. → ;

iii) When you have learned to sing *Barnacle Bill*, take the resonator bells **F, G** and **A** and explore the various combinations of these three notes to discover which one matches the melody of "half past one."

**m-r-d**

**doh pentatonic**

# Barnyard Song

NOTE: Sing "Cat goes fiddle-i-dee" at the end of each chorus.
Think of other animals to sing about.
Be sure to repeat what each animal does, each time through.

**CONCEPT:** Melodies can move in steps, leaps or repeated pitches.

**STRATEGIES:**
a) Sing the song, shaping the animal sounds in the air.
b) On the chalkboard draw melody shapes as follows:

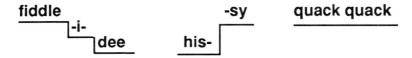

and have a student point to them as the class sings.
c) If step bells are available they are an excellent teaching aid to illustrate steps and leaps.
d) Do some aural quizzing playing and/or singing steps, leaps and repeated pitches.

> steps – m-r-d
>
> leaps – m-s
>
> repeated pitches—m - m

# Bee, Bee, Bumble Bee

Bee, bee, bum-ble bee, Stung a man up-on his knee,

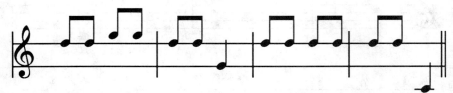

Stung a pig up-on his snout, I de-clare that you are out.

**CONCEPTS:**
1. Melodies move in steps, leaps or repeated pitches.
2. A song may be made to sound complete when it ends on **doh** (the **tonic**).

**STRATEGIES:**

a) Play the game song as follows:

"IT" is a bee in the center of the standing circle. "IT" sits on floor blindfolded or hands covering eyes. Children in circle move around as they sing as far as ...*snout*; "IT" sings the last phrase pointing at one of the children on the last word *OUT*. Person pointed "OUT" is new "IT."

b) Discover the new note **doh** (assuming children already know **s-m-l**) as follows:

Sing song through using hand signs and solfa names **s-m-l**; when you come to the last note, simply hum or sing the word *out*. Add the new name **doh** and its hand sign, and sing the song entirely in solfa.

c) Practice rhythm patterns **ti-ti ta**; **ti-ti ti-ti**.

d) Add ostinati as follows:

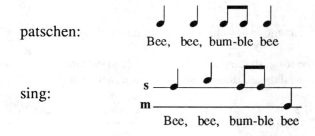

e) Sing song again adding the new note **doh** and using the hand sign.

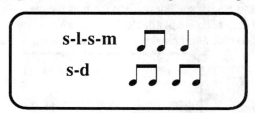

# Billy Bad

**CONCEPT:** Melodies can move in a downward direction.

**STRATEGIES:**   a) Play game song as follows:

Children take turns being "Billy Bad." Billy faces front of the room, back to class, while class sings as far as *sad*. "Billy" sings last phrase, and then "Mystery voice" sings:

b) Listen to the last line — *'Cause my name is Billy Bad.* Billy tries to guess name of singer using **s-m** interval. If guess is correct, "mystery singer" becomes new Billy Bad. If guess is incorrect, everyone sings: Try again. Billy gets three tries.
  **s   s   m**

**Is the melody moving upwards or downwards?**
**Can you move your hand to show the direction of the melody?**

c) Sing the entire melody in solfa, moving hand in downward direction on last phrase.

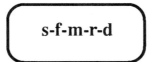

# Bingo

**CONCEPTS:**  1. Most songs have an underlying **steady beat** or pulse, very much like our own heartbeat.
2. The words in a song have a special rhythm of their own.

**STRATEGIES:**  
a) Teach song by rote, echo singing one phrase at a time. Clap/patsch beat while singing.

b) Sing song through "putting the words in our hands."

c) Divide the class into two groups. Group one claps the words while group two claps/patschen the beat; everybody singing the song. Switch roles several times.

d) Play elimination game to develop inner hearing: starting with "B," eliminate one letter of BINGO each time the song is sung until all the letters are clapped instead of sung.

NOTE: Inner hearing activites of this kind help children internalize both the beat and the rhythm. The activity should be extended to include many songs.

beat/rhythm

# Blue Bells

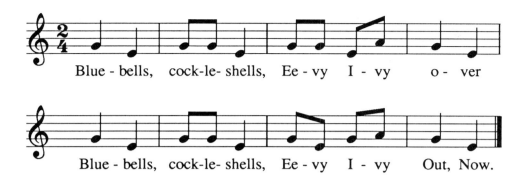

**CONCEPTS:**
1. Many children's songs use simple melodic patterns consisting of three pitches.
2. The beat is steady throughout most pieces of music.
3. Beats that are grouped in sets of two are said to be **duple** meter.

**STRATEGIES:**

a) Reinforce | | ⊓ | through clapping hands and stepping feet.

b) Feel the beat (pulse) by dividing the class into two groups:

       Group 1—claps the melodic rhythm;
       Group 2—steps the beat.

c) Reinforce **s-m-l** through the use of hand signs.
d) Sing **s-m-l** while the teacher directs with hand signs.

e) Coordinate pitches and rhythms using **s-m** with | | and ⊓ | .

f) Sing the song with words.
g) Sing the song and act out the words.
h) Play group skipping game.

    Two children swing rope; third child skips. Skipping rope swings back and forth on each beat as person skips. On "over," rope swings over the person's head. On "Out, Now," skipper goes out. New skipper moves in and song repeats.

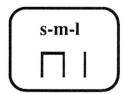

# Bluebird

**CONCEPT:** S-m and s-l-s-m are melodic patterns that may occur within melodies.

**STRATEGIES:**
a) Listen for the **s-m** intervals on such words as *bluebird*.
b) Listen for the **s-l-s-m** intervals on such words as *thro' my window* and *take a little friend*.
c) Teach the song as a singing game:
  i) Make a circle, joining hands to form a "window."
  ii) During the verse, one child who is chosen as "Bluebird" goes in and out the windows and stands behind the nearest child when the verse ends.
  iii) During the chorus, the Bluebird taps lightly on the shoulder of the partner who now becomes a Bluebird too.
  iv) Repeat the game with the two Bluebirds, then with four, eight, and so on, until all the children are Bluebirds.
  v) Finish the game by repeating the chorus as the Bluebirds skip around the circle with their partners.

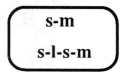

# Bounce High

Bounce high, bounce low, Bounce the ball to Shi - -loh!

**CONCEPT:** Music is organized into strong and weak beats.

**STRATEGIES:**
    a) Sing the song. Ask students to show beat. All sing the song and step beat.
    b) Ask a student to bounce the ball to the song. Use a large ball. Bounce of ball should be heard on each **"bounce"** and **"Shi—."**
    c) Have students draw the beat in the air and then on the board while everyone sings the song. Have a student bounce the ball while another puts a line under the beats with the bounce. Identify these beats as strong beats.

    All bend knees on the strong beat.
    d) Explain that instead of putting lines under the strong beats, musicians use **bar lines** to show the strong beats.

    e) Clap beats showing strong beats. Say with **ta**. The parts between the bar lines are called **measures**.

**How many measures are there? (4)**
**How many beats are in each measure? (2)**
**The beats are in sets of 2.**

**The double bar line indicates the end of a piece of music.**

> **strong-weak**
> 
> **duple meter**
> 
> **s-l-s**

# Bow, Wow, Wow

**CONCEPT:** Melodies are made up of musical intervals.

**STRATEGIES:**
    a) Play game song as follows:

        Children are in two circles, face to face. Sing to partner opposite shaking finger at partner on first two phrases; stamp feet on phrases 3 and 4; everybody moves to the left on the last phrase; repeat performance to new partner.

    b) Isolate **s-m-d** and **m-r-d** passages to sing in solfa; sing rest of song using words.

    c) Add ostinati:

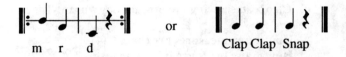

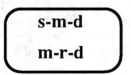

-66-

# Categories

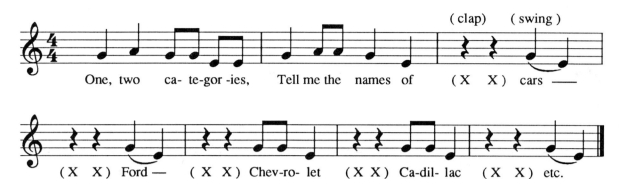

**CONCEPTS:**
1. Many melodies are composed of sound and silence.
2. The beat in music can de divided into smaller units, thus forming different rhythmic patterns.

**STRATEGIES:** a) Reinforce the following rhythmic patterns through clapping:

b) Say the rhythmic syllables for the song.
c) Clap the beat and say the rhythmic syllables being aware of the quarter rests.
d) Say the rhythmic pattern and clap only on the rest as indicated.
e) Review **s-m** and integrate with rhythmic patterns.
f) Discuss the text—the relation of syllables in the words to rhythmic patterns.
g) Sing the song and clap on the rests.

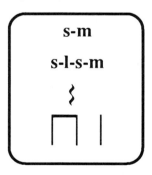

# Charlie Over the Ocean

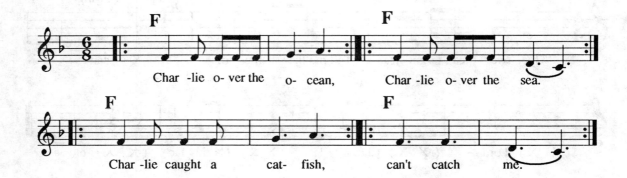

**CONCEPTS:**
1. The beat can be divided in two.
2. The beat can be divided in three.
3. The top number of the meter signature indicates the number of beats; the bottom number indicates the kind of note which gets the beat.

**STRATEGIES:**
a) Teach the song by rote. Divide class in 2 halves. One half claps/patschen the beat in 2s. Other half "put words in their hands" (i.e. clap the melodic rhythm).
b) Teacher:
**How does the beat move in this song?** (in 2s).
**Can you feel it as you clap/patsch?**
**Do you remember another song that has the same beat pattern?**
 ("Rain, Rain;" "Old Brass Wagon").
Look at the music for "Old Brass Wagon."

**What sign tells us how the beat moves?** ( $\frac{2}{4}$ ).

The 2 tells us that the beat moves in 2s and the 4 tells us that ♩ = one beat or count. Now look at notation for "Charlie Over the Ocean." The meter sign says $\frac{6}{8}$ but we felt the beat moving in 2s, didn't we. Actually, it still does, only this time we count 6 and every ♪ gets one count. Now if ♪ = 1 count, then ♩. gets 3 counts. So 2 sets of ♩. = $\frac{6}{8}$.

Another way of counting $\frac{6}{8}$, then would be:

♩.   ♩.  |  ♩.   ♩.  |
1    2      1    2
 23   23    23   23

When a dotted note gets one beat, we call the meter **compound**. So $\frac{6}{8}$ is the compound equivalent of $\frac{2}{4}$. $\frac{6}{8}$ can also look like this:

$\frac{6}{8}$ ♩ ♪ ♫♫  or  $\frac{6}{8}$ ♫♫ ♫♫

$\boxed{\frac{6}{8}}$

# Clap Your Hands

① 
```
    s    s  s    s  s       s
    m    m       m  m       m
```

②
```
s m  s s m  s s m m  s m
```

③
Clap, clap,  clap your hands,  Clap your hands to-geth-er.
Stamp, stamp, stamp your feet, Stamp your feet to-geth-er.

**CONCEPTS:**  1. Many children's songs use simple melodic patterns consisting of two pitches.
2. The beat is regular (steady) throughout most pieces of music.

**STRATEGIES:**  a) Reinforce | | ⊓ | through clapping hands and stepping feet.
b) Feel the beat (pulse) by dividing the class into two groups:
   Group 1 — claps the melodic rhythm;
   Group 2 — steps the beat.
c) Reinforce **s-m** through the use of hand signs.
d) Sing **s-m** while the teacher directs with hand signs.
e) Coordinate pitches and rhythms using **s-m** with | , ⊓ .
f) Sing the song with words.
g) Sing the song and act out the words.
h) Use transparency overlays to show progression from **s-m** notation to standard notation.
i) Create new verses.

> **s-m**
>
> **high/low**
>
> ⊓ |

# Eency Weency Spider

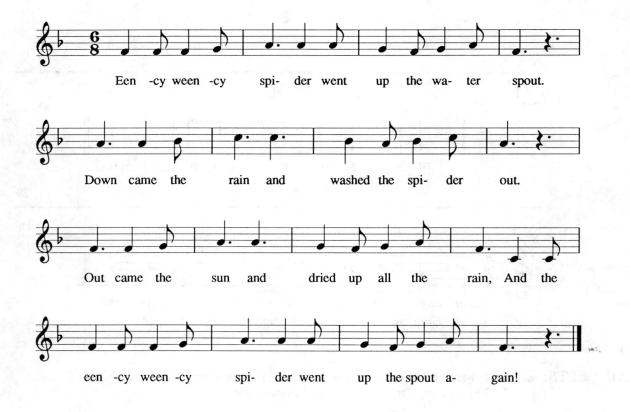

**CONCEPT:** A nursery rhyme can be expressed as a sound story.

**STRATEGIES:** Arrange an instrumental accompaniment as follows:

| INSTRUMENTS | ACTIVITIES |
|---|---|
| Soprano Xylophone and/or Glockenspiel | Using fingers or rubber-headed mallets, make spiral movements from lowest to highest bar |

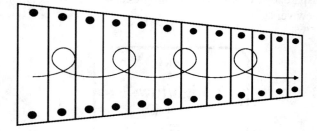

*Eency weency spider went up the water spout*

(Eency Weency Spider, cont.)

Alto Metallophone and/or Alto Xylophone     Make downwords movements in straight lines—from low to high.

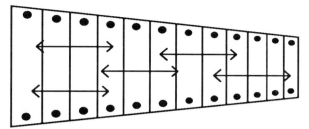

*Down came the rain and washed the spider out*

Alto and Soprano Glockenspiel     Using random pitches, tap lightly on bars with rubber-headed mallets.

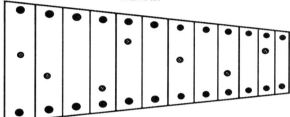

*Out came the sun and dried up all the rain*

Soprano Xylophone and/or Glockenspiel     Repeat spiral movements as for first line.

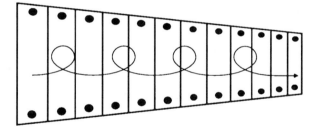

NOTE:     If Orff instruments are not available, autoharps and resonator bells may be substituted.

# Elevator

**CONCEPT:** A song may use all the notes of the **scale** in an upward step-wise movement.

**STRATEGIES:**
a) Using Curwen hand signs, teach song by rote. Emphasize direction by starting with arms fully stretched downward for **low doh** and fully stretched upward for **high doh**.

b) *Express to the basement* should be spoken in a high-pitched voice.

c) On *Zoom*, everybody slides quickly to the floor (teacher may play an accompanying **glissando** on piano or bells).

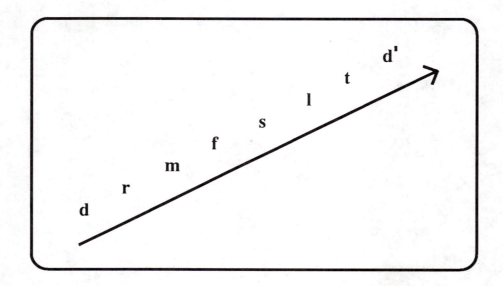

# Engine, Engine Number Nine

Engine, Engine number nine, Going down the Island line.

If the train goes off the track, Do you want your money back?

**CONCEPTS:**
1. The tempo of a song may change from **slow** to **fast**.
2. A song can be made up of just two notes.

**STRATEGIES:** a) Play train game as follows:

Choose a station-master, individual children to be carriages and a caboose. Start singing slowly to imitate train leaving station, moving feet in time to the rhythm. Train gathers speed as feet move faster and faster.

b) Add **ostinati** as follows:

i) Rhythmic

♫ ♫ ♫ ♫
chug-a chug-a chug-a chug-a
(moving feet or patschen)

ii) Melodic:

♩ ♪ ♩ ♪ ♩ ♪ ♩ ♪
s-m  s-m  s-m  s-m
(play on melody bells or xylophone)

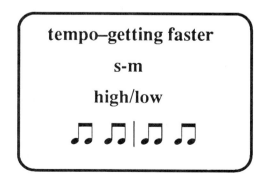

# Hey, Hey, Look at Me

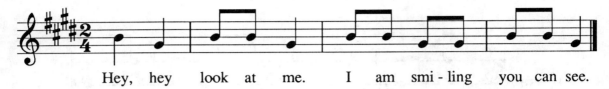

Hey, hey look at me.   I am smi-ling you can see.

**CONCEPTS:**  1. Melodic patterns can move upwards and downwards.
2. Words used to describe music are sometimes comparative rather than absolute terms (faster/slower, louder/softer, higher/lower).

**STRATEGIES:**  a) Teach the song by rote. Ask children for other facial expressions or body actions to replace *smiling*.
b) To **review** the comparatives, ask individual children to sing the song faster or slower, louder or softer, higher or lower, than the preceding model. The rest of the class listens to determine if the instructions are being followed. When the children are familiar with the activity, one soloist could request the next kind of performance.
c) Place eight beat icons on the board. Proceed measure by measure and have the children name the rhythm pattern and write the symbols under the appropriate beat.

Proceed two beats at a time (singing first the words, then to loo, high/low and **s-m**). Write the solfa names under the rhythm pattern.

You could show how these pitches appear on a two-line staff.

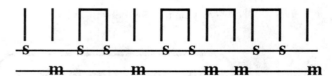

Another day, you could place **s** in a space so children would realize that notes can be placed on lines or in spaces.

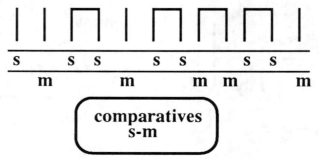

comparatives
s-m

# Hot Cross Buns

Hot cross buns. Hot cross buns.

One a pen-ny, two a pen-ny, Hot cross buns.

**CONCEPT:** Phrases in music can be repeated or varied to create interest. The way the phrases are organized is called the **form** of a song.

**STRATEGIES:**
a) Sing the song. Ask students to clap the beat and the melodic rhythm pattern. Ask students to show the phrase in the air ( ⌒➔ ). Repeat but ask how many phrases there are in the song (4). Sing the song again.
b) Ask for a volunteer to take on a shape to represent the first phrase. Sing the phrase.
c) Ask a volunteer to be the shape for the second phrase. **Will the shape be the same or different?** (the same) Sing to check.
d) Repeat for the third phrase (different). Check by singing the first three phrases.
e) Repeat for the fourth phrase (the same as 1 and 2).
f) Sing the whole song. Label phrases as: **a a b a**.
g) **What would happen if you jumbled the phrases?**

   Try **a a a b, a b a a, b a a a**.

**Which sounds best? Why do you think so?**

> phrases
> form
> m-r-d

# I'm a Little Candle

**CONCEPT:** A song may use all the notes of the scale in a downward step-wise movement.

**STRATEGIES:** Begin with hands joined over head, palms flat together to resemble a candle. Teach song by rote. As scale descends, hands separate and body slowly melts until the singer lies in a "puddle" on floor as he/she reaches "doh".

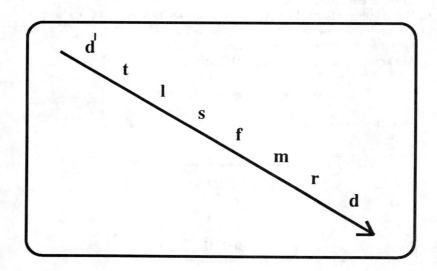

# Ich-a-back-a

Ich - a - back - a  so - da crac- ker  Ich - a - back - a  boo!

Ich - a - back - a  so - da crac- ker  Out  goes  you!

**CONCEPTS:**
1. Music can have periods of silence among the sounds.
2. A period of silence in music is called a **rest**.

**STRATEGIES:** a) Teach song by rote, echo singing one line at a time; clap/patsch beat pattern while singing.

b) Focus on the quarter rest (assuming children already can read/recite the rhythm units ♩ and ♫ )

Teacher: **Does "boo" sound on the first or second beat of that measure?** (first)

**What happens on the second beat of that measure? Is there any sound?** (no)

**The sign 𝄽 tells us there is no sound on that beat.**

**When we clap the rhythm we have a special action for the rest.** (Turn both palms up and forward in gesture of throwing away the sound.)

Lead children in clapping the melodic rhythm for the whole song using the newly learned gesture for the quarter rest.

# If You're Happy

**Other Verses:** If you're happy and you know it stamp your feet
........... snap your fingers
........... slap your sides
........... shout "Hurray!"

**CONCEPTS:**
1. Phrases have endings.
2. The words of songs can suggest actions.

**STRATEGIES:** a) Ask children to join you in doing the actions the song suggests. Children learn the song either from just listening or phrase by phrase if they are having problems learning the tune. They must clap etc. at the right time so they must listen to the music. (The claps occur at phrase endings although children do not need to know this information in Kindergarten or Grade 1.)

b) Have children suggest alternative moods or states (eg. "If you're hungry...") and appropriate actions.

**How would facial expressions change?**

**Would tempo and dynamics change?**

> phrase endings
> tempo
> dynamics

# Long-Legged Life

1. Did you ev-er, ev-er, ev-er in your long-leg-ged life
   Meet a long leg-ged sail-or with a long leg-ged wife?

   No, I nev-er, nev-er, nev-er in my long-leg-ged life
   Met a long leg-ged sail-or with a long leg-ged wife.

2. ... short-legged...   3. ... bull-legged...   4. ... no-legged...

**CONCEPT:** Some beats or parts of beats can be lengthened using the **fermata** sign ( 𝄐 ).

**STRATEGIES:** (a) Sing the first verse showing the actions:

| | |
|---|---|
| *Did you* | Face your partner with hands above your head, palms extended to meet your partner's on one side. Together on *did you*, move arms to other side. (This action helps students "feel" the fermatas.) |
| *ever, ever,* | Clap hands together, clap partner's hands. |
| *ever in your* | Repeat. |
| *long-legged life* | Spread hands apart. |
| *life* | Right hand over heart. |
| *sailor* | Salute. |
| *wife* | Cross arms over chest. |
| *short-legged* | Hands close together. |
| *bull-legged* | Stand with legs in "bull-legged" formation. |
| *no-legged* | Hop |

(b) Ask students to imitate the actions, all having you as a partner. Repeat as necessary.
(c) Without any actions, have students sing song.
(d) Sing and do actions. Learn the whole song. Perform with partners.
(e) Ask students to clap the beat of the song.

**Is there any place where the beat does not seem steady? Where?**

Look at the music to discover the symbol which tells that the sound has been lengthened and identify it as a **fermata** ( 𝄐 ).

Experiment with **fermatas** in other parts of the song. Are they as effective elsewhere? Why? Why not?

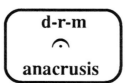

# Old Brass Wagon

Cir-cle to the left, Old brass wag-on, cir-cle to the left, Old brass wag-on
Cir-cle to the left, Old brass wag-on, You're the one my dar——ling

2. Do-si-do
3. Into the center
4. Allemande left

5. Grand right and left
6. Swing, oh, swing

NOTE: Make up your own words, or have the children make up words to suit the needs of your class.

**CONCEPT:** A beat may contain more than one sound.

**STRATEGIES:**  a) Teach the song by rote.
    i) Ask students to tap beat while you sing the first verse;
    ii) Sing the song again while children show phrase .
    iii) **How many phrases are there?** (4)
    iv) Teach the song phrase by phrase. [CAREFUL! each phrase begins on a different pitch.]
    v) Have the children sing the first verse.

  b) Once the melody has been mastered, have the children try some of the following concentration skills:
    i) sing and step beat;
    ii) sing and clap rhythm pattern;
    iii) sing, step beat and clap rhythm pattern;
    iv) clap rhythm pattern only;
    v) "turn" the phrases (moving clockwise, change direction for each phrase while stepping the beat);
    vi) step the rhythm pattern;
    vii) use inner hearing except for *darling*;
    viii) vary the activity for each phrase,
        eg. phrase 1–inner hearing
            phrase 2–clap beat
            phrase 3–step rhythm pattern
            phrase 4–sing

  c) Teach dance.

  d) Make conscious:

(Old Brass Wagon, cont.)

Place four beat icons on board.

**How many beats do you feel in the first phrase?** (4)
Step beats and sing. Begin with the last two beats of first phrase.
**How many sounds do you hear on the third beat?** (2)
Repeat for fourth beat. Step beat and sing to *loo*. Step beat and clap rhythm pattern.
**What do you call two even sounds in one beat?** (ti-ti)
Draw the rhythm patterns under the hearts.

Use the process described above to determine the number of sounds on second beat (1) and first beat (4).

**Are the sounds on the first beat even or uneven?** (even)

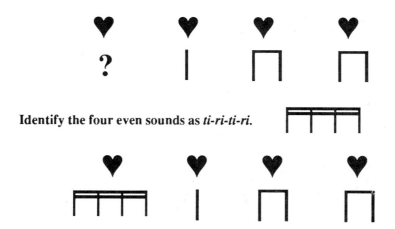

**Identify the four even sounds as *ti-ri-ti-ri*.**

**Identify the rhythm pattern of the second and third phrases.**
Notice that the first three phrases have the same rhythm pattern.
**Is the melody the same in the first three phrases?**
(It has the same contour — shape — but begins on a higher pitch for each phrase.)

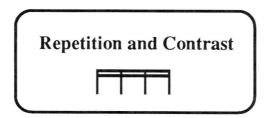

# Poor Bird

**Japanese Folk Song**

Poor bird, you are so sad, fly-ing in your bam-boo cage.

Will you sing a song for me, if I come and set you free?

All to-geth-er now fall down. "Who's be-hind you,? Can you guess?"

**CONCEPT:** Each voice and instrument has a unique sound.

**ACCOMPANIMENT SUGGESTIONS:**

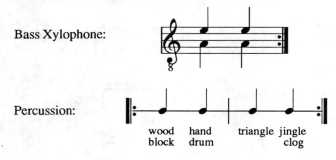

Bass Xylophone:

Percussion:

wood block, hand drum, triangle, jingle clog

(pattern is played five times; last two bars are unaccompanied)

**STRATEGY:** Game:
Formation: circle (hands joined), one child in center.
Measures 1-8: Children walk in circle around the "bird." Bird uses circle "cage" for flying movement.
Measures 9-10: All children sit down and bird covers eyes.
Teacher points to one child to go behind bird.
Measures 11-12: Child sings "Who's behind you? Can you guess?" Bird guesses who is singing. Soloist becomes new bird, and game continues.

---

vocal timbre

instrumental timbre

# Prendés i garde

Guillaume d'Amiens

Ta - ta - ta - tum - ta   ta - ta - ta   tum - ta -

ta - ta - ta - tum - ta   ta - ta - ta   tum *

[*or other alliterative syllables]

© Waterloo Music Company. Used by permission.

**CONCEPT:**
1. The beat is the steady pulse of the music.
2. Rhythm patterns interweave with the beat.

**STRATEGIES:**
a) This is a comical 13th century song about poaching for fish. "Prendés i garde" should be sung exuberantly and at a lively tempo.
b) Soprano recorders could double the melody line.
c) Try layering patterns, one by one on successive playings.

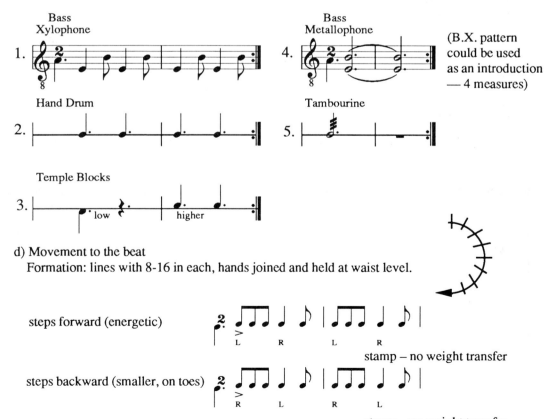

d) Movement to the beat
   Formation: lines with 8-16 in each, hands joined and held at waist level.

   steps forward (energetic)

   stamp – no weight transfer

   steps backward (smaller, on toes)

   stamp – no weight transfer

   i) lines may form circle by end of piece.
   ii) bend knees on accented beats.

# Pussywillow

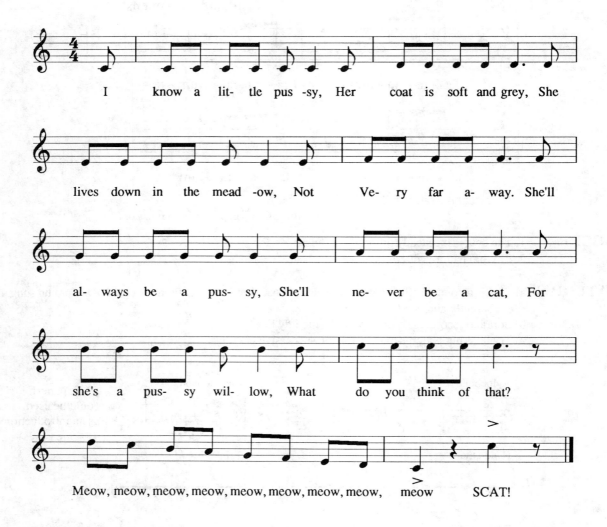

**Assignment:** The lesson plan for this song is left for students to devise concept statements and strategies.

**CONCEPT(S):**

**STRATEGIES:**

# Rain, Rain, Go Away

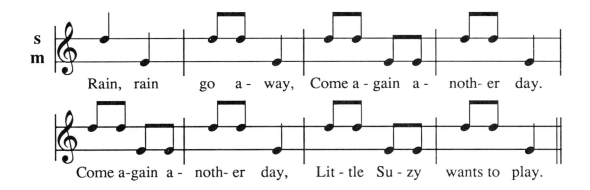

**Melodic Patterns:** so-mi; so-so-mi

**Rhythmic Patterns:**

**Dynamics:** Getting louder/getting softer

**Ostinati:**

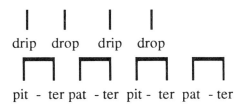

**CONCEPTS:**
1. Sometimes there is one sound (note) on a beat, and sometimes there are two.
2. A song may be made up of long and short sounds.

**STRATEGIES:**
a) Teach song by rote, echo singing two measures at a time; clap/patsch beat pattern while singing.
b) Divide class in two. One half clap/patsch beat while other half "puts words in their hands" (i.e. clap melodic rhythm). Then switch roles.
c) Teacher: Step out words (long/short pattern) while children sing song. Then change the words of song to *long, long, short-short long* to match teacher's steps (melody remains the same).

d) Display durational pattern on chalkboard or feltboard as follows (3 steps):

-85-

(Rain, Rain, Go Away, cont.)

**1. Iconic notation**

— —  — —  — —

Rain, rain   go  a - way,

— —  — —  — —  — —

Come  a -gain  a -noth-er  day.

**2. Symbolic notation**

Superimpose the ryhthm notation:

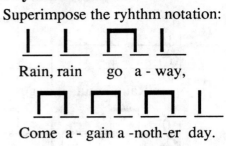

Rain, rain   go  a - way,

Come  a - gain a -noth-er  day.

**3. Juxtapose beat and rhythm patterns**

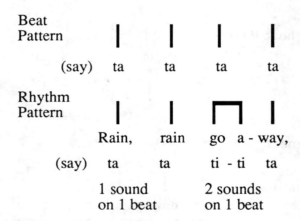

Beat Pattern

(say)   ta   ta   ta   ta

Rhythm Pattern

Rain,   rain   go  a - way,

(say)   ta   ta   ti - ti   ta

1 sound on 1 beat    2 sounds on 1 beat

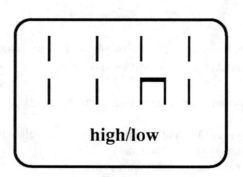

**high/low**

# Row Your Boat

Row, row, row your boat, Gently down the stream.
Mer-ri-ly, mer-ri-ly, mer-ri-ly, mer-ri-ly, Life is but a dream.

**Assignment:** The lesson plan for this song is left blank for students to devise their own concept statements and strategies.

CONCEPT(S):

STRATEGIES:

# Snail, Snail

Snail, snail,   snail, snail,   Turn a-round and 'round and 'round

**CONCEPT:** Melodic patterns can move upwards or downwards.

**STRATEGIES:**

a) Teach the song as a winding game.

Students join hands and follow the leader into a snail-like circle, moving to the beat.

When circle is tight, unwind the snail.

b) When the song has become a *friend* use the first four notes to make **s - m** conscious

i) Sing and clap the beat. Stop after four beats. Point to beat icon (  ).
ii) Sing the four beats to **loo**.
iii) Show high/low sounds with your hand.
iv) Sing using words **high/low**. Place "snails" on board under beat icon.
v) Identify high note as **sol** and low note as **mi**, showing hand signs.
vi) Sing the song substituting **s-m**. Play the game once again.

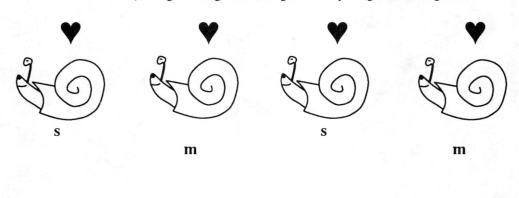

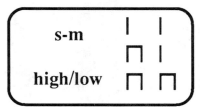

# Starlight, Star Bright

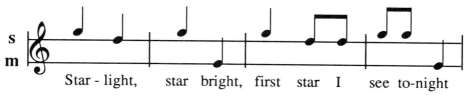

**CONCEPTS:**
1. Songs are made up of melodic patterns.
2. Songs are made up of rhythmic patterns.

**STRATEGIES:**
a) Feel the beat pattern moving in 2s by clapping/patschen as you sing the song:

clap   patsch   clap   patsch

b) Divide class in two; one half clap/patschen the beat while the other half put the words in their hands (i.e. clap the melodic rhythm)

c) Practice melodic intervals by singing song in solfa; choose individuals to sing ostinati as follows:

1.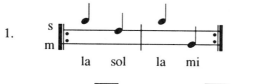

   la   sol   la   mi

2.

   la - la   sol - sol   la - la   mi

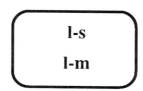

# Telephone Song

**CONCEPT:** Call/response is a musical form for solo and group.

**STRATEGIES:** Teach song by rote, one phrase at a time, echo singing. Teacher "calls" — whole class "responds." Call for volunteers to solo-sing the responses. Substitute volunteer's name for "Charlie" and "I" for "You" as appropriate.

**NOTE:** This song is particularly suitable for use with beginning intermediate music classes, to encourage singing and to allow teacher to hear and assess individual vocal efforts and learning needs. In this context, emphasis should be on participation rather than accuracy.

> major/minor mode
> call/response

# Weavily Wheat

**CONCEPTS:** Melodies are organized in phrases.

**STRATEGIES:** Teach game song as follows:

> Divide class into groups of four, each group joining hands to form a circle.
>
> Line 1 *Don't want...barley* — circle steps to the right on the beat.
>
> Line 2 *Take some...Charlie* — circle steps to the left on the beat.
>
> Line 3 *Five times...thirty* — on the beat, stack right hands, then left hands until all hands stacked in the center.
>
> Line 4 *Five times...forty* — remove hands from stack in reverse order, always on the beat

**phrases**

# What Kind of Cake

**CONCEPTS:**
1. Children can create their own music in an informal setting.
2. Songs nearly always end on **doh**.

**STRATEGIES:**
a) Sing the song, having the whole class join in at the second phrase (measure 5). Ask volunteers to complete the song (last two measures).
b) In subsequent singings, invite others to complete the song.
c) Change the words to

      **What kind of pie...**
      **What time of year...**
      **What kinds of colours...**
      **What time of day...**

d) Ask children to suggest other words. Accept all song completions without negative comment. Likely all answers will end on **doh** (F). If so, discuss why (it makes the song sound complete).
e) Look at other songs to reinforce the concept that melodies normally end on **doh** such as "Who's That Yonder."

           **creating music**

           **ending on doh**

# What the Turkey Said

Words and Music by Moiselle Renstrom

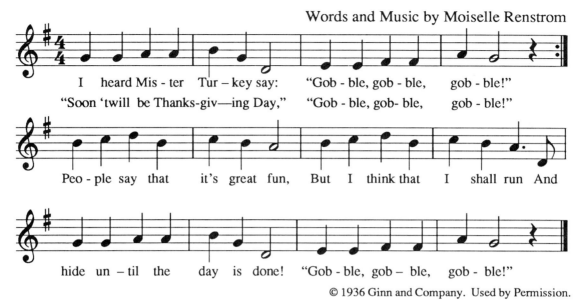

© 1936 Ginn and Company. Used by Permission.

**Variation:** An interesting variation to this song can be produced by making the "gobble" notes eighth notes, rather than quarter notes.

**CONCEPTS:**
1. Music is a part of seasonal celebrations.
2. Quarter notes can be divided into two eighth notes.

**STRATEGIES:**
(a) Teach the song prior to Thanksgiving Day.
(b) Have half the class sing the second last measure with the quarter note pattern:

while the other half sings the same measure with the eighth-note pattern:

(c) Switch parts.

—93—

# Who's That Yonder

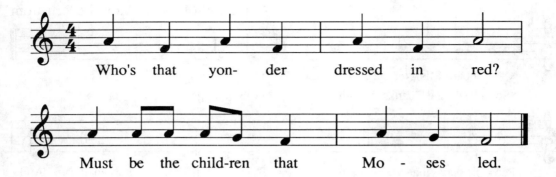

Who's that yon- der dressed in red?

Must be the child-ren that Mo- ses led.

**CONCEPTS:**
1. Melodies may contain longer and shorter tones than indicated by the beat.
2. Melodies have resting points.
3. Melodies move by skip and step.
4. Phrases can have a feeling of question and answer.

**STRATEGIES:**
a) Sing (using hand signs) patterns of **m-r-d** and **d-r-m**.

b) Sing **m-d** to reinforce the concept of **skip**.

c) Sing these melodic patterns using different rhythmic patterns, ♩ , ♫ , ♩ and so on.

d) Sing the first phrase and discuss the unsettled feeling and how this is reflected in the text (a question).

e) Sing the second phrase, discussing the final feeling of **closure** when the question is answered. (Explain that **doh** is usually a final resting place when found at the end of a song.)

> m - d
> 
> m - r - d
> 
> high/low
> 
> question/answer

# SONGS for the Intermediate Music Class

# Are You Sleeping

## *Frère Jacques*

① Are you sleep-ing? Are you sleep-ing?
*Frè - re Jac - ques, Frè - re Jac - ques,*

② Bro - ther John, Bro - ther John,
*Dor - mez vous? Dor - mez vous?*

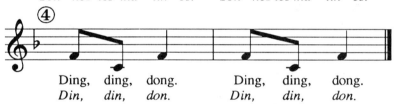

③ Morn-ing bells are ring-ing. Morn-ing bells are ring-ing.
*Son - nez les ma - tin - es! Son - nez les ma - tin - es!*

④ Ding, ding, dong. Ding, ding, dong.
*Din, din, don. Din, din, don.*

**CONCEPTS:**
1. Groupings of different rhythmic values are called "rhythmic patterns."
2. There may be many different rhythmic patterns in one song, however, all patterns must coincide with the beat.
3. Introduction of the rhythmic pattern: **ti-ri-ti-ri** and relation to **ta** and **ti-ti** (subdivision).

**STRATEGIES:**
a) Have all students clap the beat (**ta**).
b) Have the teacher clap the beat while the students clap the **ti-ti** pattern.
c) Divide the class so that some students clap the beat and others clap the **ti-ti** pattern while the teacher claps the **ti-ri-ti-ri** pattern — notice how the beat remains constant and coincides with each pattern.
d) Think up words that represent each pattern (i.e. 1 word divided into syllables)

examples:  pie         =   ♩ (ta)

ap-ple      =   ♫ (ti-ti)

hu-ckle-ber-ry  =   ♬♬ (ti-ri-ti-ri)

e) Clap the beat and sing the song.

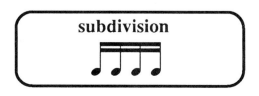

# Bonavist' Harbour

**Canadian Folk Song**

Oh! there's lots of fish in Bon-a-vist' har-bour, lots of fish right in a-round here. Boys and girls are fish-ing to-geth-er, for-ty-five from Car-bon-ear. Oh! catch a-hold this one, catch a-hold that one, swing a-round this one, dance a-round she. Catch-a hold this one catch a-hold that one, did-dle dum this one, did-dle dum dee.

Well, now, Uncle George got up in the mornin',
He got up in a heck of a tear,
Ripped the seat right out of his britches;
Now he's got ne'er pair to wear.

**CONCEPT:** The notes of the I chord (d, m, s) can form part of a melody.

**STRATEGIES:**
a) Sing this rollicking Newfoundland song.
b) Note the use of the three notes of the I chord at the beginning of the song.
c) Highlight this melodic pattern by playing it on an instrument (bells, piano, recorder) as you sing the song again.
d) Try altering the beginning motive by playing the I chord notes in a different order.
e) Do several different versions of d.
f) Discuss which versions you liked and why.

# Brave Wolfe

**Canadian Folk Song**

Come, all you old men — all, let this de-light you,
Come, all you young men all, let naught a-fright you.
Nor let your cou-rage fail when comes the tri-al
Nor do not be dis-mayed at the first de-ni-al.

© 1933 Harvard University Press. Used by Permission.

2. I went to see my love,
　　Thinking to woo her;
　I sat down by her side,
　　Not to undo her;
　But when I looked upon her
　　My tongue did quiver;
　I could not speak my mind
　　While I was with her.

3. "Love, here's a diamond ring,
　　Long time I've kept it
　All for your sake alone,
　　If you'll accept it.
　When you this token view,
　　Think on the giver;
　Madame, remember me,
　　Or I'm undone forever."

4. Then forth went this brave youth
　　And crossed the ocean;
　To free America
　　Was his intention.
　He landed at Quebec
　　With all his party,
　The city to attack,
　　Both brave and hearty.

5. Brave Wolfe drew up his men
　　In a line so pretty,
　On the Plains of Abraham
　　Before the city.
　The French came marching down
　　Arrayed to meet them,
　In double numbers' round
　　Resolved to meet them.

6. Montcalm and this brave youth
　　Together walked;
　Between two armies they
　　Like brothers talked,
　Till each one took his post
　　And did retire.
　'Twas then these numerous hosts
　　Commenced their fire.

7. The drums did loudly beat,
　　with colours flying,
　The purple gore did stream,
　　And men lay dying.
　Then shot from off his horse
　　Fell that brave hero.
　We'll long lament his loss
　　That day in sorrow.

(Brave Wolfe, cont.)

8. He raised his head
   　　Where the guns did rattle,
   And to his aide he said,
   　　"How goes the battle?"
   "Quebec is all our own,
   　　They can't prevent it."
   He said with a groan,
   　　"I die contented."

**CONCEPTS:**
1. The phrases of a song are repeated or contrasting to create a form.
2. The endings of phrases (cadences) may sound complete or incomplete.

**STRATEGIES:**

a) Explain the historical background of the song. Throughout the Seven Years' War (1756-1763) the French and British fought over European concerns, but some of the skirmishes between the two powers took place in North America. The French, who held Quebec, sent Louis Joseph, Marquis de Montcalm-Gozon to defend their extensive North American territories. Montcalm was initially successful against the ill-prepared British forces. When William Pitt became British Prime Minister, he appointed capable officers who launched an invasion of French strongholds in 1758 and again in 1759 when Fort Niagara was taken. Montcalm, lacking reinforcements and supplies from France and hindered by the intendant, Bigot, and the Governor General of New France, the Marquis de Vaudreuil-Cavagnal, retreated to Quebec. Major-General James Wolfe, commander of the British forces against Quebec effectively blockaded the city and New France. The Seige of Quebec lasted for twelve weeks, ending on September 13, 1759 when Wolfe surprised the French troops at the Plains of Abraham. After a short battle during which Quebec fell to the British, both Montcalm and Wolfe were mortally wounded. New France officially came to an end in February 1763 with the signing of the Treaty of Paris in which most of France's possessions in North America became British.

Teach the song by rote. {The song is on the recording *Maple Sugar* (Springwater, S1/B2).} Focus on the narrative. Notice the changing point-of-view? (Verse one is an invitation, verses 2 and 3 in the first person, and verses 4 to 8 in the third person.)

b) **What is the phrase form of the song?**

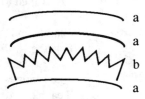

**Are all the phrases the same length?** ( yes )
The melody is quite repetitive and straightforward.
**What holds you attention?** ( the story? )

c) **Describe the cadences.** (complete, complete, incomplete, complete)

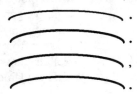

(Brave Wolfe, cont.)

For a more detailed explanation of cadences, see "Rocky Mountain" (page 152).

d) **How could you make the performance of this song more interesting?** (use of instruments; vary the vocal sound — different group, soloist; add introduction, interludes)

NOTE: For more information about this Canadian folk song, especially historical references, consult the following work: E. Fowke.; A. Mills; and H. Blume. *Canada's Story in Song* (rev. ed.) Toronto: W.J. Gage, 1965.

> **phrase form**
> **cadence**
> $m_1 \; l_1$

# Canoe Song

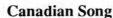

1. My pad- dle's keen and bright, Flash-ing with sil- ver.
2. Dip, dip and swing her back, Flash-ing with sil- ver.
   Fol- low the wild goose flight, Dip, dip and swing.
   Swift as the wild goose flies, Dip, dip and swing.

**CONCEPT:** A repeated melodic or rhythmic pattern can be used with a song to create harmony. The repeated figure is called an **ostinato**.

**STRATEGIES:**
a) Teach "Canoe Song."
b) When all have mastered the melody, you may add a new element by separating the melodic fragment *dip, dip and swing* while the children sing the song. Ask them to identify what has been added. Call the repeated pattern an **ostinato** (from the Italian word *obstinate* meaning "stubborn").
c) Let the children sing the ostinato while you sing the melody.
d) Divide the class in half. Have half the children sing the ostinato and the other half sing the melody. Ask the children to listen to both parts as they sing.
e) Another time, use a different pattern from the song as your ostinato.
f) You can experiment with using the ostinato as an introduction to the song and a **coda** (or ending). If the children can sing melodies with ostinati well, then the move to singing a successful round should be easy.

NOTE: Learning to hold a vocal part while attending to other melodic or rhythmic lines is an essential musical skill. However, it is important to develop solid unison singing before moving on to rounds and other part songs.

> **la pentatonic**
> **syn-co-pa**

# Come to the Land

Romanian Folk Song

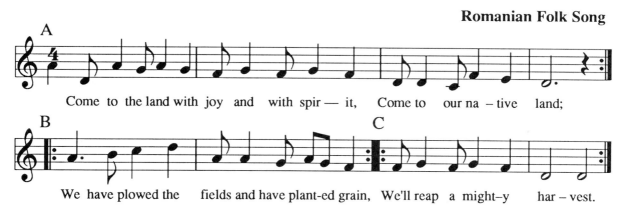

Come to the land with joy and with spir — it, Come to our na – tive land;

We have plowed the fields and have plant-ed grain, We'll reap a might–y har – vest.

**CONCEPT:** A melody consists of phrases which define its musical form.

**ACCOMPANIMENT SUGGESTIONS:**

Bass Xylophone    Alto Xylophone    Timpani

**STRATEGIES:** a) Movement should be developed by the students, as a class or in small groups.
b) One possibility: (formation: circle, hands joined, on hips or on neighbours' shoulders)

- A step-close to L (x4)
- A step-close to R (x4)

- B to center L R L R (arms gradually raised)
- B back to circle L R L R (arms gradually lowered)

- C step on L, swing R diagonally in front of L
  step on R, swing L diagonally in front of R
- C repeat

For C section, you can add a clap or snap on "swing" beat. Body turns slightly to follow direction of movement.

> phrases
> syncopation

# Der Hans

Swiss Folk Song

Literal Translation: Hans in the snail-shell has everything he wants.
And what he has, that wants he not,
And what he wants, that has he not,
Hans in the snail-shell has everything he wants.

Pronunciation Guide:
Der Hahns im Schnack-geh-loh (back of throat) het ah-les, vas er voht.
Oont vahs er het, dahs voht er nit,
Oont vahs er voht, dahs het er nit,
Der Hahns im Schnack-geh-loh het ah-les, vas er voht.

**CONCEPTS:**
1. Melodies can outline chords.
2. A melodic motive can be extended through sequence.

**STRATEGIES:** a) Look at the notation. **How many phrases do you see?** (3) **Are any repeated?** (1 and 3) **Which phrase moves mostly by step?** (2) **How does the melody move in the 1st and 3rd phrases?** (by leap)

Explain that this song is about a snail named Hans who is never satisfied: what he has he doesn't want, and what he wants he doesn't have. Sing the song. Children listen and watch the notation to see/hear the melodic movement. Teach the song phrase by phrase, practising the Swiss-German pronunciation.

(Der Hans, cont.)

b) The up-beat (anacrusis) and the first two measures outline the d-m-s chord. Sing the section to solfa syllables with hand signs (s d s m m d). Tell the students that some melodies have segments which **outline chords**. How can you tell by looking at the music?

(The three notes, d-m-s, are all on lines,

or spaces 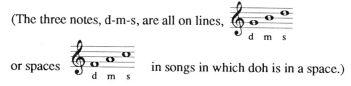 in songs in which doh is in a space.)

Sing the song using solfa syllables and hand signs when the chord outline occurs.

c) **How is the second phrase constructed?** (The first two measures are repeated.) There is also a different kind of repetition. How does [music] compare with [music]?

(They have the same contour, but begin on different notes.) The first one is the melodic idea or **motive**. The second one is the same idea repeated a step higher: the technique is called a **sequence**. A sequence is one way of making a phrase longer.

d) Add a harmony part by playing the root of the two chords in the song (G and D) when the chords change. Play a note for each beat. There are two beats per measure. ¢ represents $\frac{2}{2}$ meaning 2 beats per measure with the half note, ♩, the unit of beat.

e) Play the chords on the autoharp, strumming on the beat.

## Additional Experiences:

a) Make a work-sheet asking students to build chords on different notes.

b) Ask students to write the chord notes in different orders, repetitions allowed, and then play the arrangements on a melody instrument. Use the chord on C (C E G), G (G B D), and F (F A C). Example: C C G E G E. Students will become familiar with the sound and formation of a chord.

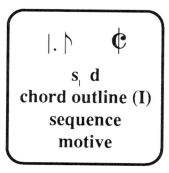

# Donkey Riding

**Canadian Folk Song**

1. Were you ev- er in Que- bec Stow- ing tim- ber on a deck, Where there's a king with a gol- den crown, Rid- ing on a don- key?
2. Were you ev- er off the Horn Where it's al- ways fine and warm, See- ing the lion and the U- ni- corn, Rid- ing on a don- key?
3. Were you ever in Car- diff Bay Where the folks all shout "Hur- ray! Here comes John with his three months' pay," Rid- ing on a don- key?

Hey, ho! A- way we go! Don- key rid- ing, don- key rid- ing.
Hey, ——— ho! A- way we go! Rid- ing on a don- key.

**CONCEPTS:**
1. A song can have contrasting sections (**A** and **B**). Sometimes these sections are called **verse** and **refrain**.
2. Phrases may be similar but not identical (a a₁ b b₁ etc.).

**STRATEGIES:**
a) Sing the song asking students to listen for answers to questions dealing with the lyrics.
b) Discuss the words.
c) Put two patterns on the chalkboard:

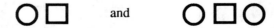

d) Sing the verse and chorus and ask students which pattern matches the song, and why.
e) Label each section **A** as verse and **B** as refrain.

**How does the refrain differ from the verse?**

(melody, rhythm pattern, accents, 3 verses — 1 refrain, text, and so on)

(Donkey Riding, cont.)

    f) Teach the song by rote.

        **How will ♩ be sung?**

    g) **How many phrases do you feel in the verse?** (2)

        Draw the phrases in the air and on the board.

        **Are the two phrases the same or different?** (You may get both answers. Ask students to explain their choices.)

        Discover that the phrases are similar but not the same. They can be described as **a** and **$a_1$**.

        Repeat the process for the refrain or B section.

    h) Have students record the form in their music notebooks.

## ADDITIONAL EXPERIENCES:

    a) Play recording of selections as performed on *Canada's Favourite Folksongs for Kids*. Ask how students' recorded version differs from class manner of performance.

    b) Teach a dance to go with the recorded version:

    Circle Formation

        **Introduction**    Stand in place.

        **Verses 1, 2 and refrain**
        1st Phrase    Walk to left.
        2nd Phrase    Walk to right.
        3rd Phrase    Walk to center, raise joined hands.
        4th Phrase    Walk backwards to circle formation.

        **Interlude**    Each student does own improvised "soft shoe."

        **Verse 3 and refrain** (see above)

        **Coda**    Stand in place.

    c) If you do not have access to this particular recording you could still make up a dance which will show the form of the piece through movement. Movement is another way of helping children feel and understand musical concepts.

# Eggs and Marrowbones

**Irish Folk Song**

1. There was an old wo-man in our town, in our town did dwell, She loved her hus-band dear-ly but an-oth-er man twice as well, With your right ta-lour-a lad-die and your right ta-lour-a — lee.

2. She went to the doctor's house for some medicine for to find;
   "Oh, won't ye give me something that will put the old lad blind?"

3. "Go boil him eggs and marrowbones and make him sup them all,
   And it won't be so very long after that, 'till he can't see you at all."

4. So she boiled him eggs and marrowbones, and made him sup them all,
   And it wasn't so very long after that, 'till he couldn't see her at all.

5. Says he, "I'd go and drown myself, but that would be a sin.
   Says she, "I'll come to the water's edge and help to push you in."

6. So they jogged and jogged and jogged along till they came to the water's brim;
   Says she, "Ye come here to drown yourself, and I push you in."

7. The old woman made a rush for to push the old lad in;
   But he stepped calmly to the side, and she went trundling in.

8. How loudly did she yell and how loudly did she bawl;
   "Oh, hold your tongue," the old man said, "Sure I can't see you at all."

**CONCEPTS:**
1. In compound meters the beat is divided in three.
2. Songs can tell stories.

**STRATEGIES:** 
a) Listen to the song for the story. (The song may be performed by the teacher or on a recording. *Music Builders* VI has Bram Morrison narrating the tale.) Discuss the story.

   **How does the singer help tell the story?** (Such devices as dynamics, tempo, dialect and character dialogue could be used.)

b) If the song is performed by the teacher, after a few verses without stopping the song, invite the class to sing the repeat of the refrain. If a recording is used note the class response. This type of singing which has a soloist tell the story while all join in on an easy chorus is a popular device in folk songs.

(Eggs and Marrowbones, cont.)

    c) Teach the song and sing it. Try to dramatize the story. When the song is well learned, experiment with volunteer soloists. Discuss the devices they use to make the story interesting.

    d) Sing the song and pat the beat.

**How are the beats are organized?** (In sets of 2 = patsch, clap.)

Sing and clap rhythm pattern.

**Do the beats divide in two ♪♪ or three ♪♪♪ ?**

Try clapping ♪♪ ♪♪ to the piece, then ♪♪♪ ♪♪♪ .

**Which fits the music?** ( ♪♪♪ ♪♪♪ )

This piece has beats which divide into 3 parts. Look at the meter signature ($\frac{6}{8}$).

**What does it tell us?** (A response might be: six beats in a measure and ♪ gets the beat.)

It is true that there are six eighth notes per measure [ ♪♪♪ ♪♪♪ ] but we found out earlier the piece has 2 beats in every measure. Each ♪♪♪ is one beat. The meter signature should be $\frac{2}{♩.}$; that is, two beats in every measure with the dotted quarter note getting the beat. When the beat normally divides in threes, the result is **compound meter**.

    e) Practice clapping $\frac{6}{8}$ patterns.

$\frac{2}{♩.} = \frac{6}{8}$   ♩.   ♩.   |   ♪♪♪ ♪♪♪   |   ♩.   ♩.   etc.

Add another typical rhythmic figure ♩ ♪ (long short).

$\frac{2}{♩.}$   ♩ ♪ ♩ ♪ | ♪♪♪ ♪♪♪ | ♩.   ♩. | etc.

**How many measures like ♩ ♪ ♩ ♪ can you find in "Eggs and Marrowbones?"** (5)

**How many like ♪♪♪ ♪♪♪ ?** (1)

Challenge the students to circle the beats in "Eggs and Marrowbones."

## ADDITIONAL EXPERIENCES:

    a) Dramatize the story using pantomime. The challenge is to keep action developing during the chorus.

    b) Analyze the song.

        i) Write out all the notes in the song from low to high.

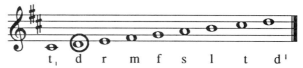

Circle the tonal center.

(Eggs and Marrowbones, cont.)

**Is the song doh or la centered?** (doh)

**Is the song in a major or minor mode?** (major)

**What is the range?** (9th)

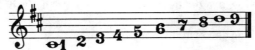

ii) **How many phrases are there?** (4)

Label the phrases and describe the cadences.

iii) Compare the song with "I'll Give My Love an Apple" (page 131) for mode, range, form, meter, melodic contour, lyrics.

**How do the differences contribute to the overall experience of the songs?**

---

**compound meter
(beat divides into three)**

**6
8**

# Ezekiel Saw the Wheel

**Traditional Spiritual**

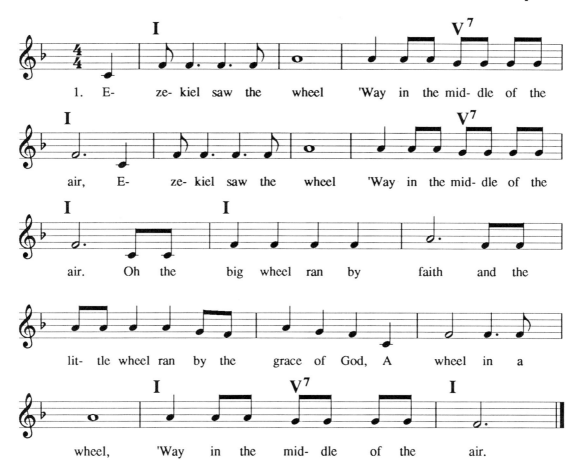

2. One of these days about twelve o'clock, 'way in the middle of the air,
   This old world goin' to reel and rock, 'way in the middle of the air.

3. Ezekiel saw the wheel, 'way up in the middle of the air,
   Ezekiel saw the wheel, 'way up in the middle of the air.

**CONCEPT:** Some songs can be accompanied by 2 chords which can be sung or played on an instrument.

**STRATEGIES:**
a) Learn song by rote.

b) Divide class in 3 groups (high, middle and low voices). Teach the following chord sequence by rote

(Ezekiel Saw the Wheel, cont.)

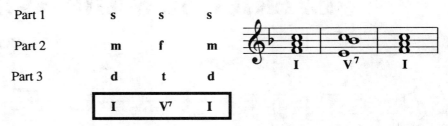

| Part 1 | s | s | s |
| Part 2 | m | f | m |
| Part 3 | d | t | d |
|        | I | V⁷ | I |

Following the chord symbols **I, V⁷** on music, use index finger to indicate **I** and 5 fingers to indicate **V⁷** as choral group sings chords, first in solfa, then using neutral syllable "loo" or humming. Sing chords against solo voice or another group singing the song.

# Fish and Chips

Camp Song

(Fish and Chips, cont.)

**CONCEPT:** Songs which share a harmonic progression can be sung together to make harmony (**partner songs**).

**STRATEGIES:**  a) Teach the four songs separately to the entire class. When all songs are well learned, make a tape recording of each.

b) Play back tape of song #1 and lead children in singing song #2 simultaneously; likewise, lead singing of song #1 during play-back of song #2. Repeat for the other songs. Try different combinations.

c) Children should now be able to sing both songs together as **partner songs.**

d) Add to the harmonic effect by playing the D (**I**) chord and $A^7$ ($V^7$) chords on the autoharp while singing.

---

**partner songs**

$I \quad V^7$

# Five Hundred Miles

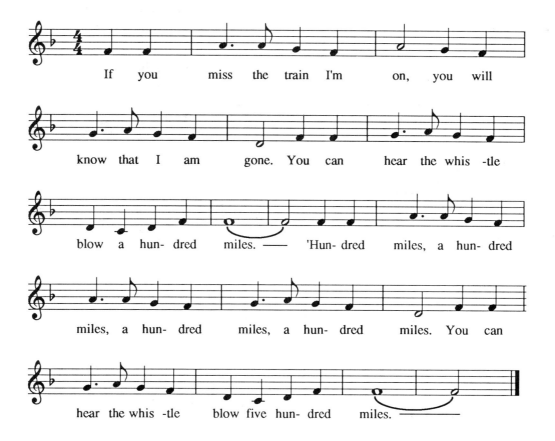

If you miss the train I'm on, you will know that I am gone. You can hear the whistle blow a hundred miles. 'Hundred miles, a hundred miles, a hundred miles, a hundred miles, a hundred miles. You can hear the whistle blow five hundred miles.

**CONCEPT:** There are a very few songs based upon only the **I** and **IV** chords.

**STRATEGIES:**
 a) Begin by accompanying the song on strong beats (1st & 3rd in each measure) with the **I** chord.
 b) When students' ears tell them that the **I** chord no longer "fits," try the **V⁷** chord. If this does not fit, try the **IV** chord (on *know*).
 c) When the **IV** chord no longer fits, revert to the **I** chord.
 d) Write (in pencil) the chord symbols **I** and **IV** (or **F** and **B♭**) where the chord changes were indicated by the sound.

> **I, IV chords**
>
> **anacrusis**

# The Ghost of John

**CONCEPTS:**
1. Some melodies can be sung as rounds to produce a **polyphonic** texture.
2. A piece can be performed twice as slowly. The device is called **augmentation**.

**STRATEGIES:** a) Model the song being careful to perform the first phrase very smoothly (*legato*), as a cellist would bow, the notes on *gone*; getting gradually louder (*crescendo*) on ♩ (*oooh*) in the third phrase and singing the **staccato** notes on *no skin* being careful not to punch the two notes. (Staccato notes are detached and about half the written value.) Teach the song by rote or note. Using the solfa version will help establish accurate pitches.

(The Ghost of John, cont.)

To teach by rote, one method is:
  i) Sing the whole song.
  ii) Sing first phrase. Students echo.
  iii) Sing second phrase. Students echo.
  iv) Sing first and second phrases. Students echo.
  v) Continue until the whole song is learned. If errors occur, correct immediately.

b) Discuss texture in concrete objects as felt, as tasted, as seen. Music has texture which is heard. When everyone sings "The Ghost of John" together there is a single melody or **monophonic** (one sound) texture which could be drawn:

This song can also be sung as a round.

**What happens in a round?** (One melody is sung but not at the same time by everyone.)

The texture is no longer **monophonic** but **polyphonic** (several sounds). It could be drawn:

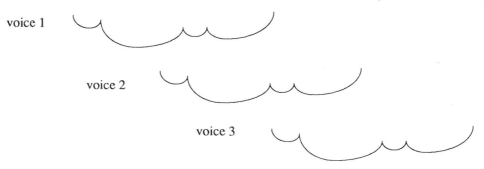

Sing the song as a round.

c) Another day, use the same song to make a polyphonic texture in a different way using **augmentation.** One group of students sings "The Ghost of John" at the regular tempo, the other, twice as slowly. Begin together.

**How many times will the first group have to sing the song for both groups to finish together?** (2)

**What is the effect created?**

> **monophonic / polyphonic**
>
> **augmentation**
>
> **minor mode (la centered)**
>
> **staccato**

# God Rest You Merry, Gentlemen

**English Carol**

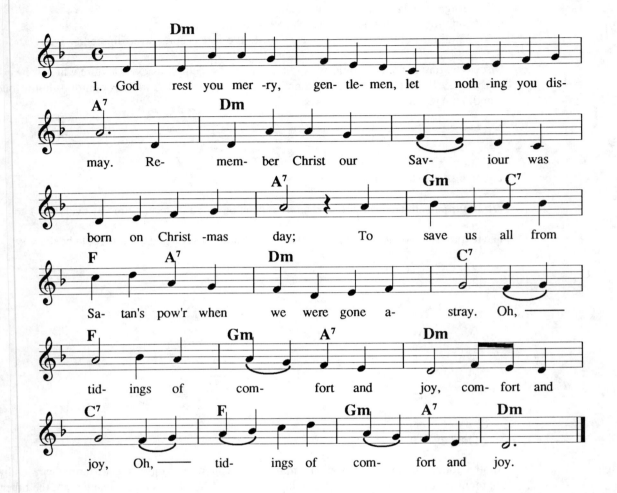

1. God rest you merry, gentlemen, let nothing you dismay. Remember Christ our Saviour was born on Christmas day; To save us all from Satan's pow'r when we were gone astray. Oh, tidings of comfort and joy, comfort and joy, Oh, tidings of comfort and joy.

2. From God our heavenly Father
   The blesséd Angels came
   Unto some certain Shepherds,
   With tidings of the same
   That there was born in Bethlehem
   The Son of God by name:

Chorus:
   O tidings of comfort and joy
   O tidings of comfort and joy.

3. God bless the ruler of this House
   And send him long to reign
   And many a merry Christmas
   May live to see again
   Among your friends and kindred
   That live both far and near.

Chorus:
   And God send you a Happy New Year, New Year,
   And God send you a Happy New Year.

(God Rest you Merry, Gentlemen, cont.)

**CONCEPT:** Some songs are **la-centered** rather than **doh-centered**.

**STRATEGIES:** NOTE: This song may be taught by rote, sung or played on the recorder and accompanied on the autoharp or guitar.

Assuming children have learned to identify major key signature, ask:

> **What does the key signature tell us?** (where **doh** is)
> **Does the song end on** doh? (no)
> **Which note of the scale is the final note of the song?** (la)
> **But the key signature is the same, is it not?** (yes)

We have discovered something new about key signatures. (The same key signature stands for 2 keys — the major or **doh-centered** key and its relative minor or **la-centered** key). This song is **la-centered**. La-centered songs have a special character of their own that is different from **doh-centered** songs. La-centered songs create a special mood.

> ( **major/minor tonality** )

# The Grand Old Duke of York

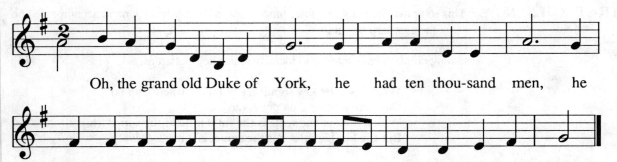

Oh, the grand old Duke of York, he had ten thou-sand men, he marched them up to the top of the hill, and he marched them down a - gain.

    2. And when they were up, they were up
       And when they were down, they were down,
       And when they were only half way up,
       They were neither up nor down.

    3. Oh, a-hunting we will go,
       A-hunting we will go,
       We'll catch a fox and put him in a box,
       And then we'll let him go.

**CONCEPT:** The beat is the steady pulse of music.

**STRATEGIES:** In moving to music, students often respond to the beat.

Formation — 2 lines, partners facing

**verse 1:** One side advances towards the other (3 steps and touch), returns to place. Repeat. (Other side advances.)
**verse 2:** Head couple joins hands, side gallops down set, returns to place.
**verse 3:** Head couple separates; each leads own line to foot. At foot, they form an arch for others. The first couple through the arch is the new head couple.

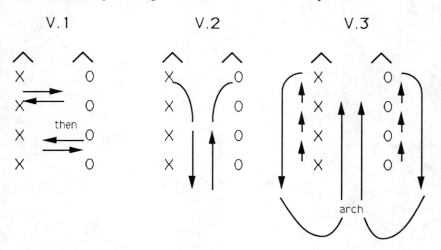

# Great Big House

2. Went down to the old mill stream to fetch a pail of water,
   Put one arm around my wife, the other 'round my daughter.

3. Fare thee well my darling girl, fare thee well my daughter,
   Fare thee well my darling girl with the golden slippers on her.

**CONCEPTS:**
1. Music is organized in **measures** and musical sentences called **phrases**.
2. Sounds may last longer than one beat.

**STRATEGIES:**
a) Teach the song by rote.
b) Using the first verse only, tap the beat. Put beat in feet.
c) Tap rhythm pattern.
d) Show the phrases using rainbow gestures with arm.
e) Sing the song (all verses). Have children listen for phrases. Children show phrases using rainbow gestures with arm ⌒ ⌒ while teacher sings first verse.

**How many phrases are there in verse one?** (4)

**NOTE:** A phrase is usually easily identified in vocal music because the singer normally breathes after a phrase. Like sentences which we speak, musical phrases have a feeling of beginning and ending. You will acquire a greater sensitivity for musical phrases as you focus on how music is put together.

If some students answer 2 phrases, indicate that their answer is also correct but that you would like them to use 4 phrases because of the dance which you will be learning.

f) Using verse one only, tap the beat. Put the beat in feet. Clap the rhythm pattern while stepping the beat for the first three phrases. Write the rhythm patterns and say them.

For the last phrase, sing to *loo*.

**How many beats are there on "pie"?** (2)

( Great Big House, cont.)

Identify the new value as  ta–a. Write the fourth phrase

♫ ♫ ♩

    g) Sing the song using rhythm syllables as the text.
    h) Play inner hearing and memory games:
       i) memorize rhythm pattern phrase by phrase, and
      ii) change activity for each phrase (eg. show phrase, step beat, clap rhythm pattern, sing).

**DANCE:** The dance reinforces the feeling of phrasing and beat.
Arrange children in even-numbered groups and count off 1, 2.

    **Verse 1** — measures 1 & 2: strut clockwise to the beat.
                 measures 3 & 4: strut counterclockwise to the beat.
    **Verse 2** — measure 1: "Ones" join hands.
                 measure 2: "Twos" join hands under the "Ones."
                 measure 3: "Ones" loop arms over and behind "Twos."
                 measure 4: "Twos" loop arms over and behind "Ones."
    **Verse 3** — Moving clockwise, arms still looped, cross right foot behind left on the first beat, then step left on second beat so that entire group dips on strong beat.

# Hallowe'en Night

**CONCEPT:** Tone colour and dynamics can be used to enhance the mood of a piece.

**STRATEGY:** Clap the rhythm pattern. Say the words rhythmically.
> **What mood should the performance create?**
> **What can be added to make the performance more effective?**

Accept and work with suggestions. Here are some ideas:
- i) dynamics — gradual and sudden changes;
- ii) a swing feeling;
- iii) vary pitch of voices;
- iv) use higher and lower voices;
- v) use solo voices in places;
- vi) tempo changes;
- vii) add a body rhythm (turn into a rap);
- viii) add sound effects (scary, preferably) either vocal or instrumental;
- ix) add Orff accompaniment; and
- x) make a melody.

tone colour
dynamics

# Hebrew Round

in B minor or C minor

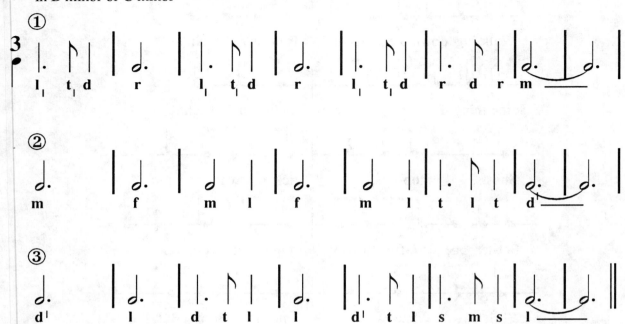

**CONCEPTS:**
1. Some melodies can be sung as rounds to create **harmony.**
2. **Contrast** and **repetition** are devices used to create interest in musical compositions.
3. Duration of notes may be lengthened by means of a **tie**.

**STRATEGIES:**
a) Sing the song. Ask students to note number of phrases. (3) Are the phrases long or short? (long)
b) Sing the first phrase.

> How many beats are heard on the last pitch, mi ( 𝅗𝅥. | 𝅗𝅥. )? (6)
> How many beats does 𝅗𝅥. get? (3)
> How does the composer get a six beat sound? (Accept and discuss suggestions.)

Composers use ties ( 𝅗𝅥. | 𝅗𝅥. ) to lengthen sounds.

> How many sounds do you hear? (one long one)
> How many beats do you feel? (six beats)
> How many notes do you see? (two joined together)

c) Learn song being careful to hold last pitch for the required six beats. Two helpful devices for feeling the six beats are:
> i) conducting the beat for the piece.

(Hebrew Round, cont.)

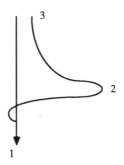

ii) showing the meter by patsch clap-clap patterns.

d) **What is the function of the tie?** (The tie joins two notes to lengthen its duration)

Examples: ♩‿♩ has one four beat sound.

♩‿♩ has one three beat sound.

e) Examine the first phrase to see how it is constructed. Have students notice that the first two bar motive is repeated three times with the last time lengthened for the cadence (resting place/ending). The same approach is used in the second phrase.

f) A look at the melodic contour of each phrase shows that phrases 1 and 2 move upwards in short sweeps.

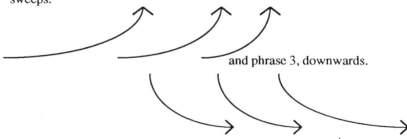

and phrase 3, downwards.

g) Sing the piece as a three-part round. Remember to hold ♩.‿♩. for six beats. Harmony is created when a round is performed.

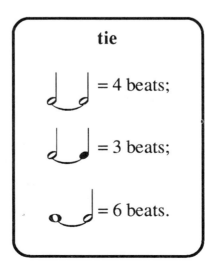

# Hoosen Johnny

**CONCEPTS:**  1. Whole steps occur in melodies and can be highlighted by such devices as ostinati.
2. Melodies may be accompanied by a repeating rhythmic or melodic figure (**ostinato**).

**STRATEGIES:**  a) Sing the song.
b) One or more students may play **C D** on the piano, resonator bells or Orff instruments as an **ostinato**.

c) One group of students may sing the ostinato while the other group sings the song.
d) Add words to the ostinato, such as *black bull* or *Johnny*.

( ostinato )

# Hungarian Dance

Words by J. Haines & S. Loveland

**CONCEPTS:**
1. Half-steps occur in melodies and can be highlighted through **ostinato** patterns.
2. Tempo affects the expressive character of a song.

**STRATEGIES:**
a) Teach the song as a singing game, doing the movements the words suggest.
b) Use *Join your hands* as a vocal ostinato for the first and last 8 measures.
c) Play the ostinato on piano, bells or Orff instruments.
d) Listen to and contrast the **half steps** with **whole steps** in such songs as "Hoosen Johnny."
e) Try singing the song at different tempos.
   **Which tempo sounds best? Why?**

half-steps
ostinato
tempo-faster/slower

# Hurling Down the Pine

**Canadian Folk Song**

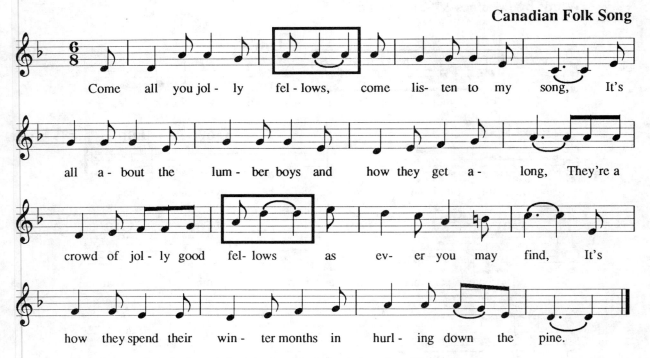

Come all you jol- ly fel- lows, come lis- ten to my song, It's all a- bout the lum- ber boys and how they get a- long, They're a crowd of jol- ly good fel- lows as ev- er you may find, It's how they spend their win- ter months in hurl- ing down the pine.

2. At four o'clock in the morning, our boss he will shout,
   "Arise, oh, ye teamsters, it's time that ye were out!"
   Those teamsters, they get up all in a frightened way,
   "Oh where are my shoes, pants, my socks are gone astray?"

3. Six o'clock is breakfast and every man is out,
   And every man if he's not sick is sure to be on the route,
   Oh you should hear those axes ring until the sun goes down,
   "Hurray, my boys, the day is o'er, a-shanty we are bound."

4. We all arrive at the shanty, cold hands and wet feet,
   We then pull off our larrigans our supper for to eat,
   We'll sing and dance till nine o'clock, into our bunks we'll climb,
   I'm sure those months they don't seem long in hurling down the pine.

**CONCEPT:** Rhythmic and melodic patterns can give a song a feeling of movement.

**STRATEGIES:**

a) Teach the song by rote, note–note, or note (see pages 203–205) paying particular attention to the altered note (B♮) in measure 11.

b) Draw from the students the musical features which help the song convey a rollicking movement. (anacrusis, repeated notes, the rhythmic pattern ♩ ♪, and the syncopated pattern ♪ ♩ ♪)

> anacrusis
> syncopation
> minor mode

# The Huron Carol

English lyrics by E. Middleton  
Canadian Folk Song

1. 'Twas in the moon of winter time when all the birds had fled, That mighty Gitchi manitou sent angel choirs instead. Before their light the stars grew dim and wand'ring hunters heard the hymn — "Jesus your King is born, Jesus is born: In excelsis gloria."

Lyrics © Frederick Harris Music Company. Used by permission.

2. Within a lodge of broken bark
     The tender Babe was found,
   A ragged robe of rabbit skin
     Enwrapped His beauty round;
   And as the hunter braves drew nigh
   The angel song rang loud and high:
     "Jesus your King is born,
     Jesus is born: In excelsis gloria!"

3. The earliest moon of winter time
     Is not so round and fair
   As was the ring of glory on
     The helpless Infant there.
   The chiefs from far before Him knelt
   With gifts of fox and beaver pelt.
     "Jesus your King is born,
     Jesus is born: In excelsis gloria!"

4. O children of the forest free
     O sons of Manitou,
   The Holy Child of earth and heaven
     Is born today for you.
   Come kneel before the radiant Boy
   Who brings you beauty, peace, and joy.
     "Jesus your King is born,
     Jesus is born: In excelsis gloria!"

(Huron Carol, cont.)

**CONCEPTS:** The meter of a song can change.

**STRATEGIES:** a) The "Huron Carol," originally "Jesous Ahatonhia" with a Huron text, was composed in 1642 by the Jesuit missionary Jean de Brébeuf to make the Nativity story meaningful to the Huron Indians. Sing the song.

**How do the words show that it is a Christmas song? A Huron song?**

Teach the verse and chorus.

b) **Is the song doh or la centered?** Look at the music to prove your answer.

    i) Check key signature. (2 flats)
    ii) What is the flat closest to the music called? (fa)
    iii) Where is doh? (third line)
    iv) Is the last note doh? (no, la — the song is in the **minor** mode).

c) Show the accented (strong) beat by patschen. Stop after the first phrase.

**Do you patsch on the first note you sing?** (no)
That first note on '*Twas* is called a **pick-up note**. Begin again and do the whole first verse and chorus.

**Are all measures the same number of beats?** (no)
**Where does the change occur?**

Repeat activity on *heard the hymn*. Look at the music. Note the meter change. Repeat activity accurately.

d) Add a rhythm pattern ♩ ♫ (patsch on ♩ and touch fists gently on ♫ ). Then play it on a drum.

**What will you do in the 3/4 measure?**

**ADDITIONAL ACTIVITIES:**

a) The verse has three phrases instead of the more usual two or four.

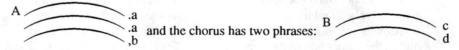

b) Try experimenting with dynamics, varying loud, soft, getting louder and softer to make the phrases more musical and to create contrast between verses.

c) The recording, *Canada's Favourite Folk Songs for Kids* has an unusual performance of the piece with tone colours creating striking effects.

---

**changing meter 2/4 3/4**

**minor mode**

**anacrusis (pick-up note)**

**dynamics**

# I'll Give My Love an Apple

**Canadian Folk Song**

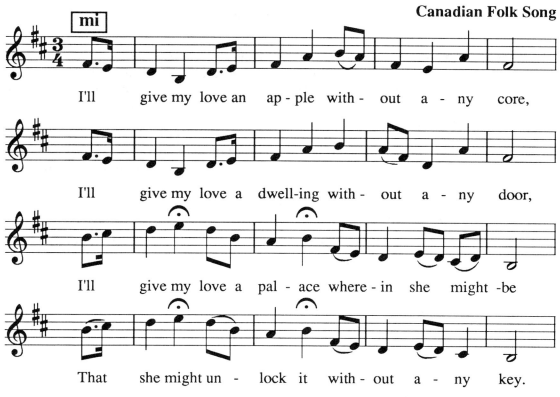

I'll give my love an ap-ple with-out a-ny core,

I'll give my love a dwell-ing with-out a-ny door,

I'll give my love a pal-ace where-in she might -be

That she might un-lock it with-out a-ny key.

© McGraw–Hill–Ryerson. Used by permission.

2. How can there be an apple without any core?
   How can there be a dwelling without any door?
   How can there be a palace wherein she might be,
   That she might unlock it without any key?

3. My head is an apple without any core;
   My mind is a dwelling without any door;
   My heart is a palace wherein she might be,
   That she can unlock it without any key.

4. I'll give my love a cherry without any stone;
   I'll give my love a chicken without any bone;
   I'll give my love a ring without any end;
   I'll give my love a baby and no crying.

5. How can there be a cherry that has no stone?
   How can there be a chicken that has no bone?
   How can there be a ring without any end?
   How can there be a baby with no crying?

6. When the cherry's in blossom, it has no stone;
   When the chicken's in the egg, it has no bone;
   When the ring is a-rolling, it has no end;
   When the baby is a-getting, there's no crying.

(I'll Give My Love an Apple, cont.)

**CONCEPTS:**
1. Many musical elements are interconnected in a melody
2. The melodies and lyrics of folksongs take different forms over time.

**STRATEGIES:**

a) Talk about riddles. What are they? Ask the students for examples. This song has six riddles. Write the six for the students (an apple without a core, a dwelling without a door, and so on). Can the students solve the riddles? Teacher sings the song. Discuss the solutions and the form of the riddles (one verse to state the problem, one to question, and one to solve ). Teach the song by rote.

b) A number of factors have been interwoven to make the melody of this song. Using techniques shown in other lessons, help students discover the following "facts" about the song.

    i) form — **a**   **a**$_v$   **b**   **b**$_v$

    ii) cadences —

    iii) range — 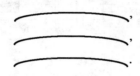 an 11th

    iv) phrase length — long, all the same

    v) meter — $\frac{3}{4}$

    vi) mode — minor

    vii) melodic movement — **a** phrase: mostly skips
                                      **b** phrase: mostly leaps

    viii) melodic contour —

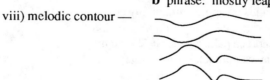

    ix) rhythmic features — ▐. (uneven), ▐ (even patterns ), ⌢ (halting flow)
    x) tempo — medium

**What is the expressive effect of these "facts" taken either in isolation or as a whole?** (The discussion might include the flowing, endless feeling promoted by the fermata, triple meter, and long phrases; the vastness of the love by the wide range; and a feeling of resolution by the descending contour of the last phrase.)

c) Compare this version of the folk song with "The Riddle Song" (page 150) to experience a different treatment of the same literary theme. A comparison will give students a better understanding of how melodies work.

# J'entends le moulin

**French Canadian Folk Song**

J'en-tends le mou- lin ti- que, ti-que, ta-que, J'en-tends le mou-lin, ta - que.

Tique, ti-que, ta-que, tique, tique, taque, ti-que, ta - que, ti- que, ta - que.

**Translation:** *J'entends le moulin* – I hear the windmill
*Tique tique* – words which sound like a windmill

**CONCEPT:** Rhythm patterns are made up of longer and shorter sounds and silences.

**STRATEGIES:** 
a) Music books are closed. Teacher sings the song asking students to listen for the phrases. Teacher sings again; children show the phrases.

**How many phrases do you hear?** Ask students to respond by showing the correct number of fingers. (4)
**How many *different* phrases do you hear?** Teacher sings again. (There are two different phrases, a and b.)

Sing once more. Ask students to raise their hands when they hear the **b** phrase.

b) Teach the **a** and **b** phrases.

**How did you arrange these two phrases so that your song will sound like the one you heard?** (The arrangement **a a b a** will be discovered.)

c) Look at the music.

**How many phrases do you see?** (2)
**How does the notation indicate the a a b a form?** (repeat sign, *D.C. al fine*, and *Fine*)

d) **What is the meter signature?** ($\frac{2}{4}$)
**How many measures can you find where each beat has only one note?** (2, the last measure in each phrase)

Look at the second measure (♩♩♩♩ ♩♩). Write the rhythm pattern on the chalkboard. Circle the beats. Clap and say the pattern. Repeat with first measure (♩♩♩♩). ♩♩♩ is a new pattern which takes place in one beat. It looks a little like ♩♩ and ♩♩♩♩ and is called ti-ti-ri. Clap and say the pattern of measure 1 several times.

-133-

(J'entends le moulin, continued)

**How many times do you find the pattern in the song?** (3 times without repeats)

Clap and name rhythm patterns of whole song. Sing to rhythm syllable names.

e) Return to words. Students should have a good grasp of the song. If they do, try a two part round. Note the quick entries: The round begins on the second beat.

f) Another day, try a three- and four-part round. When the parts are clear, it is easy to imagine the windmill because the words *tique tique* sound like the creaking of the wood.

-134-

# Jack Was Ev'ry Inch a Sailor

Canadian Folk Song

Second verse:
When Jack grew up to be a man, he went to Labrador,
He fished in Indian Harbour where his father fished before,
On his returning in the fog, he met a heavy gale,
And Jack was swept into the sea and swallowed by a whale.

Third verse:
The whale went straight for Baffin's Bay, 'bout ninety knots an hour.
And ev'rytime he'd blow a spray, he'd send it in a shower,
"Oh now," says Jack into himself, "I must see what he's about."
He caught the whale right by the tail and turned him inside out.

(Jack Was Ev'ry Inch a Sailor, cont.)

**CONCEPTS:**
1. Melodies can outline chords.
2. A song with an A B form may consist of verses and a chorus.

**STRATEGIES:**

a) Books are shut. Teacher sings the song, focussing student attention on the humorous story through the use of questions.

b) **How many sections does the song have?** (2, an A B form) **Which section, A or B, has repeated lyrics?** (B) It is called the chorus. Teach the chorus by rote.

**How does the melody move?** (mostly by leaps) Careful listening will be needed to sing the melody accurately.

c) **Look at the A section, the verse. What stays the same in every verse?** (the music) **What changes?** (the lyrics)

d) **Where is doh?** (space below the staff, D) We have been singing chords. (Sing d-m-s.) The notes from chords can be used to make melodies. **Find a chord outlined in the verse. How will you recognize the chord?** (notes move by skips:

or find d-m-s pattern).

**What chord is outlined?** (d-m-s) Ask students to sight-read the chord outline to solfa syllables.

**How many times is the pattern used?** (2)

Teach the rest of the verse by rote. Sing the verse substituting d-m-s for the words when the chord outline occurs.

e) Have students play the chord outline on a melodic instrument. You will need D, F# and A.

> chord outline
> A B form
> d-m-s

# Joshua Fit the Battle

**NOTE:** For the music of this song, see page 261 in the guitar section.

**CONCEPT:** Chords can have a **minor** sound. The chord on the tonic of **a la** mode is **minor**.

**STRATEGIES:**  a) Teach the song by rote.

b) Add the rhythm pattern 𝄽 | 𝄽 |, clapping on the off-beats.

c) **Is the song doh or la centered?** (la)
Strum the chords as the students sing.
**How many different chords can be heard?** (2)
Play the chords **Em** and **B⁷**.
**Do they sound like the familiar I V⁷ progression used in "Old Smokey?"**
Play **EM** and **B⁷** for comparison.
Sing the following progression with E as doh:

| s | s | s |
|---|---|---|
| m | f | m |
| d | t | d |
| I | V⁷ | I |

Explain that **d m s** is a **major** chord.
Major chords are symbolized by upper-case Roman numerals.

The chord on **la** is a **minor** chord. Sing

| m |
|---|
| d |
| l |

with E as la.

Sing the following progression with E as la:

| m | m | m |
|---|---|---|
| d | r | d |
| l | si | l |
| i | V⁷ | i |

The minor chord is symbolized by a lower-case Roman numeral.
Alternate between singing the **major** and the **minor** progression.

d) Practice singing the minor progression with teacher using the index finger to show **i** and all five fingers to show **V⁷**. Select a small group to sing the melody while the rest of the class accompanies with the sung chord progressions.

## Additional Experiences:

a) Play major and minor chords on the autoharp, guitar, piano or ukulele. Students identify the correct chord type by raising cards with the words **major** or **minor**.

b) Learn to accompany the song on the autoharp, guitar, piano or ukulele.

> **minor chord**

# Kookaburra

Koo- ka- bur -ra sits in the old gum tree,

Mer -ry mer -ry king of the bush is he.

Laugh koo -ka bur -ra, Laugh koo -ka bur -ra,

gay your life must be!

**CONCEPT:** There are a very few songs based upon only the **I** and **IV** chords.

**STRATEGIES:**
a) Learn the song as a round.
b) Begin by accompanying the song on strong beats (1st & 3rd in each measure) with the **I** chord.
c) When students' ears tell them that the **I** chord no longer "fits," try the **V⁷** chord. If this does not fit, try the **IV** chord.
d) When the **IV** chord no longer fits, revert to the **I** chord.
e) Write (in pencil) the chord symbols **I** and **IV** (or **D** and **G**) where the chord changes were indicated by the sound.

**I, IV chords**

**round**

# Land of the Silver Birch

Canadian Folk Song

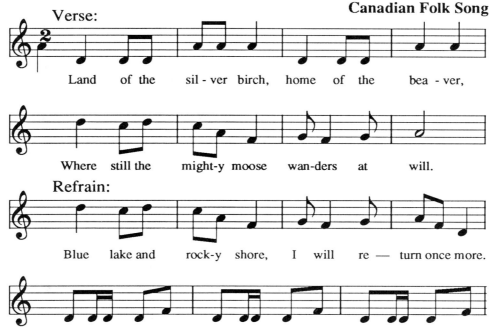

Verse 2: Down in the forest, deep in the lowlands,
My heart cries out for thee, hills of the north.
REFRAIN

Verse 3: High on a rocky ledge, I'll build a wigwam,
Close by the water's edge, silent and still.
REFRAIN

**CONCEPT:** Ostinato patterns can be used to build accompaniments.

**STRATEGIES:** 
a) Hand Drum plays 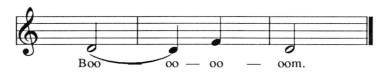 throughout song.

b) Complementary ostinato patterns on unpitched percussion instruments can be added. e.g. maracas, temple blocks.

c) Play these melodic ostinati.

ostinato
la pentatonic

# Loo-Lah

**CONCEPT:** Music can be loud or soft. It can also be varying degrees of loud and soft. The loudness or softness of music is called **dynamics**.

**STRATEGIES:**
a) Introduce informally, with teacher singing and accompanying on piano, autoharp, guitar or uke. Sing through three times:
  First time – medium loud (indicated by *mf*);
  Second time – very soft (use **Sh!** as the last word, indicated by *pp*)
  Third time – very loud (use **Hey!** as last word, indicated by *ff*).
b) Put *ff*, *pp*, and *mf* on the chalkboard and point to the appropriate dynamics sign for each verse.
c) Have a student mix up the order of verses by pointing to the dynamics signs in a different order.

( dynamics )

# Merrily We Roll Along

**CONCEPT:** Musical rhythms may be even ( ♪♪ ) or uneven ( ♪.♪ ).

**STRATEGIES:** (a) Sing and play on recorders with the music for the word *merrily* equal eighths ( ♪♪ ) and then with the dotted eighth and sixteenth pattern ( ♪.♪ ).

(b) Listen to the differences and compare (contrast) them.

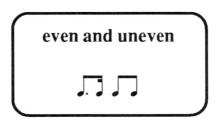

# O Canada

C. Lavallée

(O Canada, cont.)

**CONCEPT:** National songs are part of our musical heritage.

**STRATEGIES:**
1. Learn both the English and French verses.

2. Sing the national anthem regularly in assemblies and in class.

**HISTORICAL BACKGROUND:**

It was not until 1980 when "O Canada" was officially adopted by the Parliament of Canada as its National Anthem. The song, however, is quite old, having been written in 1880. The words were written by Judge A.B. Routhier and the melody is usually attributed to Calixa Lavallée. The song became very popular in Quebec and later in the rest of Canada using an English version written by R.S. Weir, which became the basis of the officially designated version appearing here. Concerts, sporting events, and meetings often begin with the National Anthem.

A 45 rpm recording of "O Canada" with English and French lyrics is available from Berandol (BER 9085).

# Old Smokey

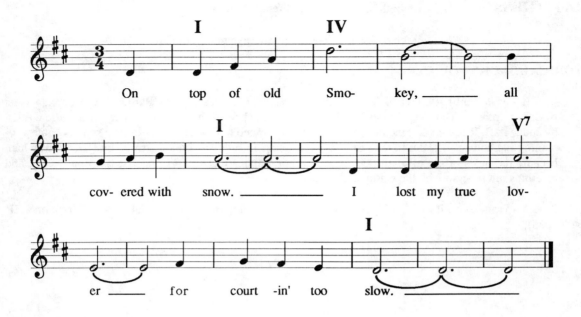

2. For courtin's a pleasure
   And parting is grief,
   But a false-hearted lover,
   Is worse than a thief.

3. For a thief, he will rob you,
   And take what you have,
   But a false-hearted lover,
   Will send you to your grave.

**CONCEPT:** Some songs require three chords for accompaniment, **I, IV** and **V⁷**.

**STRATEGIES:**
a) Start by singing the song unaccompanied.
b) Add chordal accompaniment on autoharp, piano, guitar or uke, starting with the **I** chord.
c) Ask the students to tell you when the **I** chord no longer "fits." Try the **V⁷** chord. If that does not fit, try the **IV** chord.
d) Keep playing this chord on each strong beat until our ears tell us that it no longer fits, then revert to the **I** chord again.
e) Continue in like manner until the entire song is harmonized.

NOTE: For another example of the same concept see "When the Saints Go Marching In."

( **I, IV, V⁷ chords** )

# Old Texas

**American Song**

1. I'm going to leave —— old — Tex-as now
They've got no use —— for the long horn cow. ——

2. They've plowed and fenced my cattle range,
   The people there are all so strange.

3. I'll make my home on the wide, wide range,
   For the people there are not so strange.

4. The hard, hard ground will be my bed,
   And the saddle seat shall hold my head.

5. I'll take my horse, I'll take my rope
   And hit the trail upon a lope,

6. Say adios to the Alamo
   And turn my head toward Mexico.

**CONCEPTS:**
1. Some songs require two chords for accompaniment, **I** and **V⁷**.
2. Tempo affects the expressive character of a song.
3. Singing a song in echo creates harmony.

**STRATEGIES:**
a) Sing the song, accompanying it with the **I** chord (F) on each strong beat starting on *leave* and continue as long as it "fits" the tune.
b) When students' ears tell them that the **I** chord (F) no longer sounds correct, try the **V⁷** chord (C⁷), the second most common chord in this key.
c) Return to the **I** chord (F) when the **V⁷** chord no longer "fits."
d) Try singing the song at different tempos.
   **Which sounds best? Why?**
e) Old Texas is a type of song which has a long note per phrase allowing for echo singing. Divide the class into two sections. Section one begins the song and sings all the way through. Section two begins after *leave* and sings all the way through. The echo song works much like a round except that each section ends up singing the moving melodic part while the other holds a long note. It is important that the long note be held if harmony is to result. The general scheme sounds as the following looks:

Group 1: I'm going to leave _____ old Texas now_____ .
Group 2:                      I'm going to leave_____ oldTexas now.

They've got no use_____ for the long horn cow_____
            They've got no use_____ for the long horn cow.

> **I , V⁷ chords**
> **tempo-faster/slower**

# Orthodontist Blues

Words and Music by Doug Skilling

© 1984 Gordon V. Thompson Music, Toronto, Canada. Used by permission.

2. My Daddy says my railroad tracks.
   Have cost much more than his income tax.
   But then Ma tells me that my teeth aren't straight.
   So that is why I'm stuck with these things I hate.
   (Chorus)

3. I used to play a mean trombone.
   Now I can barely talk on the telephone.
   I try to say it like I used to do.
   But both my lips and tongue seem to stick like glue.
   (Chorus)

(Orthodontist Blues, cont.)

**CONCEPTS:**
1. A song can be built upon the twelve-bar blues chord progression.
2. Melodies can be based on scales which are not major or minor.

**STRATEGIES:**
a) Sing the song or play the tape (*Canada Is... Music* 7/8), perhaps dedicating it to those whose teeth are graced by stainless steel.
Teach verse one by rote making certain that the melody is sung accurately.

b) Explain that this song is called a blues because:
   i) it tells a tale of woe;
   ii) it has a particular form called **12-bar blues**; and
   iii) it has a typical blues chord progression. Why "12 bar"? (song has 12 measures)

   **How many phrases are there?** (Students could answer 6 or 3)

The traditional 12-bar blues has three phrases.

c) Using a chordal instrument (piano, guitar, ukulele, autoharp) play the root position **chords** of the **basic** 12-bar blues progression asking students to note where changes occur. Play one phrase at a time asking questions such as:

**Did the chord change? When did it change? At which measure?**

|          |   |   |   |   |
|----------|---|---|---|---|
| Phrase 1 | C | C | C | C |
| Phrase 2 | F | F | C | C |
| Phrase 3 | G | F | C | C |

When whole **progression** has been worked out, have students play the progression on the autoharp.

NOTE:
1. As in "Orthodontist Blues," real blues players do not limit themselves to the simple chords used above. They also add notes and rhythms to make the songs more expressive. A live demonstration or recording would illustrate this point.
2. It is possible to transpose (move) the basic chord progression to any key by understanding the basic formula:

| I  | I  | I | I |
|----|----|---|---|
| IV | IV | I | I |
| V  | IV | I | I |

where **I** is the chord on the tonic (or doh) of the key, **IV** is the chord on the fourth note of the scale (or fa) and **V** is the chord on the fifth note of the scale (or sol).

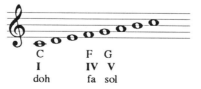

C      F   G
I      IV V
doh   fa sol

3. Budding guitar players may like to try the blues progression in an easier key.

| D Major – | D | D | D | D |
|-----------|---|---|---|---|
|           | G | G | D | D |
|           | A | G | D | D |

-147-

(Orthodontist Blues, cont.)

d) Derive the notes used in the song. Write them in scale form (low to high).

C D E♭ E F F♯ G A B♭ B

**Is the scale in "Orthodontist Blues" major? minor?**

Justify your answer. It has a unique flavour because sometimes a major sound is used, and sometimes a minor one. The mode is ambiguous. The scale is a **blues scale**.

NOTE: * is an unessential note.

e) Set up resonator bells using the notes above. Play the scale. Try some improvisation using the blues scale. Now try it over the blues chord progression.

**Do some notes sound better than other with some chords?**

Students might discover that chord notes fit better although non-chord notes can be used to make good effects.

```
CHORDS     NOTES

C     —    C E G
F     —    F A C
G     —    G B D
```

f) If students can sing **triads** (three note chords), sing the blues chord progression by performing the following triads at the appropriate places while a soloist or small group sings the melody. Practice the chords alone first.

```
 s    l    s
 m    f    r
 d    d    t
 I   IV    V
```

The teacher or a student can easily indicate chord changes by using the appropriate number of fingers (1, 4 or 5) to indicate the desired chord.

```
┌─────────────────────┐
│  12-bar blues form  │
│                     │
│     blues scale     │
│                     │
│          4          │
│          4          │
└─────────────────────┘
```

# Praetorius Round

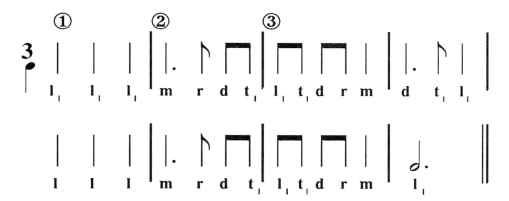

**CONCEPTS:**
1. Some melodies can be sung as a round to create harmony.
2. Contrast and repetition are devices used to create interest in musical compositions.

**STRATEGIES:**

a) Sing the song.

   **How many musical phrases can you hear?** (2)

   **Show me where you hear them.** (Use "rainbows" ⌒→ )

   In music we call musical sentences **phrases**.
   **You heard two phrases in the *Praetorius Round*.**

b) Teach the round by rote.

   **Were the two phrases the same or different?**
   Some will answer "same," some "different." Collect the answers and **the reasons**. Students will notice that both phrases start on the same note, **la**, but that one **la** is higher than the other.

   **Why did the composer use a higher la in the second phrase?**

   **The next parts of each phrase are the same, but the ends of each phrase are different. Why?**

   Some students may notice that the rhythm pattern of both phrases is the same except for the ending.

   **Composers require both repetition (to create unity) and contrast (for variety).**
   Try singing the song without the variety (i.e. phrase 1 two times) or using other variations.

c) When the song is well known, try it as a round. Sing so that you convey the musical phrase, not just every beat (the equivalent of reading sentences as a whole, not word by word). Listen to the rise and fall of the melodic lines as they intertwine.

   **You are making harmony.**

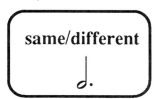

# The Riddle Song

**Appalachian Folk Song**

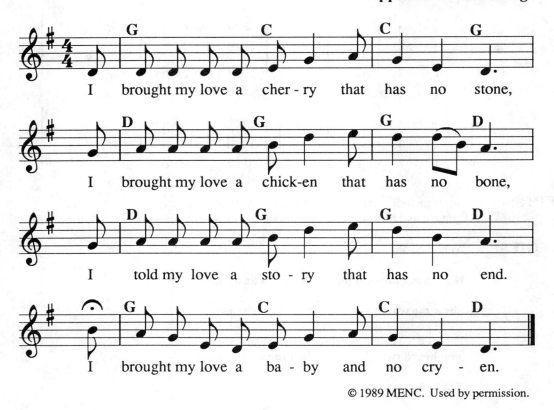

I brought my love a cher-ry that has no stone,
I brought my love a chick-en that has no bone,
I told my love a sto-ry that has no end.
I brought my love a ba-by and no cry-en.

© 1989 MENC. Used by permission.

2. How can there be a cherry that has no stone?
   How can there be a chicken that has no bone?
   How can there be a story that has no end?
   How can there be a baby with no cryen?

3. A cherry when it's bloomin', it has no stone
   A chicken in the shell, it has no bone.
   The story of I love you, it has no end.
   A baby when it's sleepin', has no cryen.

**CONCEPTS:**
1. Many musical elements are interconnected in a melody.
2. The melodies and lyrics of folksongs take different forms over time.

**STRATEGIES:**

a) This song may be taught by itself or as a follow-up to "I'll Give My Love an Apple." These suggestions will be a follow-up. Teacher sings the song. **How many riddles does it include?** (the last three of "I'll Give My Love an Apple") Teach the song by rote.

b) In order to compare the two versions, find the musical "facts" about this song.

   i) form — a  b  b$_v$  a$_v$

   ii) cadences — Students will probably feel that all the cadences sound incomplete.

(The Riddle Song, cont.)

iii) range —  a 9th

iv) phrase length — medium, all the same length

v) meter — 4/4

vi) mode — major (pentatonic)

vii) melodic movement — repeated notes, steps, and skips

viii) melodic contour —

ix) rhythmic features — one syllable per note; even patterns except for ♪ | ♪

x) tempo — medium slow

**What is the expressive effect of these "facts" taken either in isolation or as a whole? Is there a difference in the effect communicated in the two songs?**

**Which do you prefer and why?**

## Additional Experience:

i) Watch for other songs which tell a similar story but use different music.

ii) The following chord progression provides an alternative harmonization.

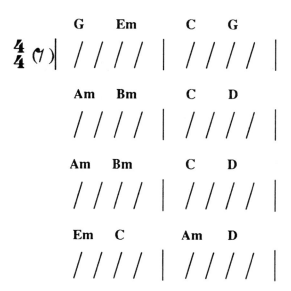

—151—

# Rocky Mountain

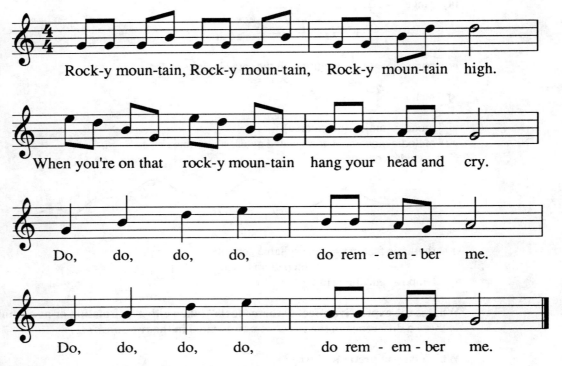

Rock-y moun-tain, Rock-y moun-tain, Rock-y moun-tain high.

When you're on that rock-y moun-tain hang your head and cry.

Do, do, do, do, do rem - em - ber me.

Do, do, do, do, do rem - em - ber me.

**CONCEPTS:**
1. Most melodies have tonal centers or home tones (keys).
2. Phrases sound complete or incomplete. The ending of a phrase is called a cadence.

**STRATEGIES:**  a)  Sing the song but omit the last note and continue as if nothing were strange. Children will no doubt respond with comments to the effect that the song is not finished. Dramatize the occasion.

> It's not finished? What do you mean? I'll sing it again. If you think it is not finished, you end it.

Students will probably sing the missing note and word. Dramatize once again.

> Well, you are right. That does sound better. I wonder why?

Let students suggest reasons (most will probably deal with words).

b) Teach the song showing phrases and counting them (there are four).

c) Let us just sing the melody without words. Follow my hand signs. Name the missing note.

        d d d m   d d d m   d d m s s

        l s m d   l s m d   m m r r d

        d m s l   m m r d r

        d m s l   m m r r <u>**?**</u> .

(Rocky Mountain, cont.)

The song needed to finish on its **home note**, its **tonic,** doh. In music, the home note is called the **tonal center**. A way of showing the tonal center is:

d) Every phrase either sounds complete (finished), or incomplete (unfinished). Let's sing each phrase and decide how each sounds. We'll show complete with a period and incomplete with a comma.

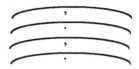

Why do some phrases sound complete and others incomplete? If we sing each phrase with solfa syllables we will find one reason. On which syllable does each phrase end?

| | |
|---|---|
| **phrase one :** | **so** |
| **phrase two:** | **doh** |
| **phrase three:** | **re** |
| **phrase four:** | **doh** |

Phrases ending on **doh** sound finished. Those ending on other notes sound unfinished.

e) Have a student lead the song with hand signs.

---

**tonal center**

**doh centered**

**cadence**

# Sakura
## (Cherry Blossoms)

**Japanese Folk Song**

Sa - ku - ra! Sa - ku - ra! Ya - yo - i - no
*Sa - ku - ra! Sa - ku - ra! Cher-ry blos-soms*

so - ra - wa, Mi - wa - ta - su Ka - ga - ri.
*mist and clouds, gent-ly float-ing in the - sky,*

Ka - su - mi - ka ku - mo - ka, Ni - o - i -
*Drift-ing far as eye can - see, fra-grance, pet- als*

i - zu - ru. I - za - ya, I - za
*ev'ry - where. Sa - ku - ra, Sa - ku -*

ya, Mi - ni yu - ka - n.
*ra, Let - all go - and see!*

**CONCEPTS:**
1. Songs may have both long and short phrases.
2. Oriental music uses different melodic organizers (scales) from Western music.

**STRATEGIES:**  a) As you sing "Sakura," ask the children to show the phrases in the air. The pattern should be:

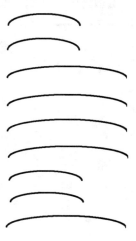

(Sakura, cont.)

Sing again. **As children show the phrases one more time, ask them to notice if all the phrases are the same length.** (No, some are shorter.) Have the phrases drawn on the chalkboard or papers. **How many phrases are there?** (9)

**Think of other songs you know. Is nine a usual number of phrases?**
(No, most songs have 4 or 8 phrases.)

b) Teach the song by rote/observation. **To get children observing the notation, ask them when the leaps occur in the melody.** (between phrases)

**Do you notice any repeated phrases?** (From this discussion, derive the phrase form of the song: **a a b c b c a a d**.)

Grouping the repetitions will draw attention to the balance (**symmetry**) of the song.

‖: a :‖  ‖: b,c :‖  ‖: a :‖  ‖ d ‖

The last phrase although different is essential to the satisfactory conclusion of the piece both melodically and structurally.

c) Derive the notes of the piece to discover the scale. Only five different pitches are used.

The scale is **pentatonic** (5 pitches) but not a variety used in Western music. This different pitch organization explains why the song sounds oriental.

d) Make some melodic and rhythmic ostinato to play with this song. **Will you use metallophone, resonator bells, or xylophones for the melodic ostinati?** Try different combinations.

**Which unpitched percussion instrument will you use for the rhythmic ostinati?**
Examples: Melodic ostinati

i)

ii)

iii)

(Sakura, cont.)

Rhythmic ostinati:

e) Have a few students play this **descant** (a melody which harmonizes with a song) on soprano recorders.

## ADDITIONAL EXPERIENCES:

a) The slower tempo of this song makes it suitable for a scarf dance. Decide on the arm movements (and body movements), to show the phrases. Using light-weight, colourful, 1 meter x 8cm scarfs, have a small group of students do the movements to show the phrases while the rest of the class sings the song.

b) Try combinations of ostinati, descant, and movement with the song.

c) Locate a recording of the piece played on a Koto (a Japanese stringed instrument).

d) Use the pentatonic scale **E F A B C** to create a melody of your own.

# The Sloop John B.

1. We came on the sloop John B., my grand-father and me. Round Nassau town we did roam. Drink-in' all night, got in a fight, oh I feel so break-up — I wan-na go home.

CHORUS: (Same melody as verse)

    So hoist up the John B. sails
    See how the mainsail sets
    Send for the captain ashore, let me go home
    Let me go home, let me go home
    Well, I feel so break-up I want to go home.

2. The first mate he got drunk, broke up the people's trunk
   Constable had to come and take him away.
   Sheriff John Sloane, please let me alone
   I feel so break-up, I want to go home.
   CHORUS:

3. The poor cook he got fits, and throw away all the grits
   Then he took and ate up all the corn,
   I want to go home, I want to go home.
   This is the worst trip, since I been born.
   CHORUS:

(The Sloop John B, cont.)

**CONCEPT:** The **triplet** is a way of changing the regular division of the beat.

**STRATEGIES:**
   a) Sing the song, patting knees on the steady beat (2 per measure).

   b) Discuss the usual subdivision of the beat (in twos) then sing again, patting knees on the beat and clapping on the half-beat.

   c) Discover the places where three equal notes are sung in the time normally taken by two notes (1 pat and 1 clap).

   d) Sing, pat and clap again, substituting three equal finger snaps instead of a pat and a clap for each **triplet** ( ♩ ♩ ♩ ).

> **triplet**
> **duple meter**
> **syncopation**

# Song for the Mira

Words and Music by Allister MacGillivray

© 1975 Cabot Trail Music Company. Used by Permission.

(Song for the Mira, cont.)

2. As boys in their boats call to girls on the shore,
   Teasin' the ones that they dearly adore,
   And into the evening the courting begins,
   I wish I was with them again.

   Chorus

3. Out on the Mira on soft summer nights,
   Bon fires blaze to the children's delight.
   They dance 'round the flames singin' songs with their friends
   I wish I was with them again.

4. And over the ashes the stories are told
   Of witches and werewolves and Oak Island gold.
   Stars on the river-face sparkle and spin.
   I wish I was with them again.

   Chorus

5. Out on the Mira the people are kind—
   They treat you homebrew, and help you unwind,
   And if you come broken they'll see that you mend.
   I wish I was with them again.

6. Now I'll conclude with a wish you go well—
   Sweet be your dreams, and your happiness swell.
   I'll leave you here, for my journey begins.
   I'm going to be with them again.
   I'm going to be with them again.

**CONCEPT:** A melodic idea can be extended through sequence.

**STRATEGIES:**

a) **What kind of place is being described? Sing the song.**

   **Do you think it is real or imaginary place? Why?**

   **Where might this place be? How do you know?**

   Tell students the song is by Allister MacGillivray and the Mira is a river on Cape Breton Island.

b) **How does the music help create the feeling of peace and nostalgia described in the lyrics?** (leisurely tempo, meter, repetition)

   Another device is the descending sequence (repeated motive) in the chorus marked by a rectangle on the score. The downward movement is relaxing. Teach the song. Explain that verses 1 and 2 are followed by the chorus, and so on.

c) Students could make a chord chart so they could learn to accompany the song on the autoharp.

(Song for the Mira, cont.)

**Chord Chart**

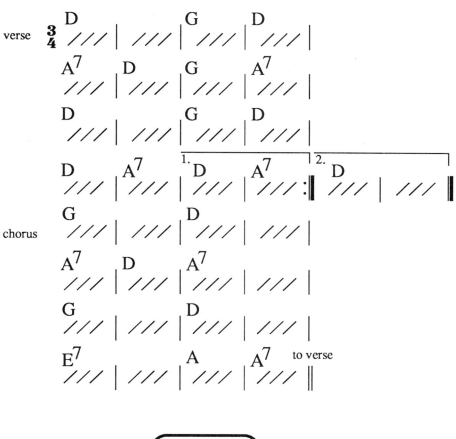

# There's a Hole in my Bucket

American Song

There's a hole in my buck-et, dear Li-za, dear Li-za,

There's a hole in my buck-et, dear Li-za, a hole.

2. Girls: Then mend it, dear Georgie, dear Georgie . . . . mend it.
3. Boys: With what shall I mend it, dear Liza . . . .with what?
4. Girls: With a straw, dear Georgie, dear Georgie . . . .a straw.
5. Boys: If the straw be too long, dear Liza . . . . too long?
6. Girls: Then cut it, dear Georgie, dear Georgie . . . cut it.
7. Boys: With what shall I cut it, dear Liza . . . . cut it.
8. Giels: With a knife, dear Georgie . . . . a knife.
9. Boys: The knife is too blunt . . . .
10. Girls: Then sharpen it . . . .
11. Boys: With what shall I sharpen it . . . .
12. Girls: With a stone . . . .
13. Boys: The stone is too dry . . . .
14. Girls Then wet it . . . .
15. Boys: With what shall I wet it . . . .
16. Girls: With water . . . .
17. Boys: In what shall I get it . . . .
18. Girls: In a bucket . . . .
19. Boys: There's a hole in my bucket . . . .

**CONCEPT:** Songs may be built upon the pentatonic scale.

**STRATEGIES:**
a) Sing song, having given starting note (**F#**).
b) As the song is sung, class listens for the rise and fall of the pitch.
c) Class "shapes" the pitches' rise and fall in the air.
d) Starting on F#, have one student find the rising and falling pitches on the keyboard (i.e. play song "by ear"). If a keyboard with earphones is available, make this an assignment that all students can do at different times of the day.
e) The teacher may wish to give them a "clue"–that the piece can be played entirely on the black notes.
f) Count up the number of different pitches used in the song. They will find that only 5 are used. This is the **pentatonic** or 5-note scale.

( pentatonic )

# Toembaï

(toom-bye)*

**Israeli Round**

Toem-baï, toem-baï, toem-baï, toem-baï, Toem-baï, toem-baï, toem-baï.

Tra-la-la, la la la la la, La la la la la la.

Tra-la-la, la la, Tra-la-la, la la, Tra-la, la la la la.

*Imitates the sound of a balalaika.

**CONCEPT:** A melodic idea can be extended through sequence.

**STRATEGIES:**
a) Clap measure three. Ask students to echo it and locate it. Repeat with measure 5, 1, and 2, 4, 6. Students will note that ♫♫ ♩♩ occurs in three measures. The pattern is a unifying principle.
b) Sing a measure and ask students to echo it and locate it. Repeat the process until all measures have been sung. **Are any melodic fragments repeated?** (no)
c) Look at the last phrase. Listen to it.

> **What does the melody do?** (It may be necessary to point out that the first two beats are a melodic motive.)

The motive is repeated at a lower pitch level. The third time, the motive is varied to lead to the closing cadence. The repetition of a melodic motive at a different pitch level is called a **sequence**.

d) Put the song together. Teach one phrase at a time. Review how the notes with accents ( > ) will be performed (with emphasis).
e) Sing in unison with rhythmic ostinato (eg ♫♩♫♩ or ♬♫♬♫) or melodic ostinato (eg. measure 2, measure 6, or make up your own: ♩ ♩ ♩ ♩ )
f) Sing as a three-part round.
g) Accompaniment suggestions:

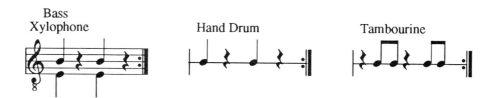

Bass Xylophone     Hand Drum     Tambourine

(Toembaï, cont.)

h) Movement should be developed by the students, as a class or in small groups. Three different sections are needed to correspond with the three musical phrases.

i) One possibility: (formation: circle, hands joined, or on hips)
Measures 1-2: grapevine to left

    step    step    step    step
    **L**     **R**     **L**     **R**
        in front of L     behind L

    step    step    step    close
    **L**     **R**     **L**
        in front of L

Measures 3-4: in to center of circle

    fw ↑ L R L close

    bw ↓ R L R close

Measures 5-6: each one turns clockwise on the spot (8 small steps) snapping fingers on beats 1 and 3, or 2 and 4.

ii) Movement could be done in a round, with 3 separate circles, or 3 concentric circles.

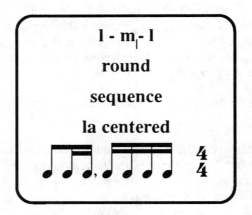

# Tom Dooley

American Song

1. Hang down your head Tom Doo-ley. Hang down your head and cry

Hang down your head Tom Doo-ley. Poor boy you're going to die.

2. I met her in the mountain,
   And there I took her life.
   I met her on the mountain,
   And stabbed her with my knife.

3. This time tomorrow
   Know just where I'll be?
   In some lonesome valley,
   Hanging from a white oak tree.

4. Hang down your head, Tom Dooley,
   Hang down your head and cry.
   Hang down your head, Tom Dooley,
   Poor boy you're going to die.

**CONCEPTS:**
1. Pentatonic songs are made up of five tones, **d-r-m-s-l**. In this song the tones **s₁ l₁ d r** and **m** are used.
2. Rhythms may contain syncopations: ♪ ♩ ♪ .
3. Songs are made up of musical phrases.

**STRATEGIES:**
a) Play on the recorder.
b) Play on the piano (transposed to G♭).
c) Have children discover **s₁, l₁,** and that **d** (the key note) as the central (pivotal) note in the piece is frequently not at the bottom of the melodic pattern, nor the beginning note. However, nearly always songs **end** on **doh**.
d) Recall other pieces with the ♪ ♩ ♪ (syncopated) rhythm. (eg. "Turn on the Sun," "Who Built the Ark?"). Note that the titles and words of a song can give you a clue to the syncopations.

# Turn on the Sun

Callender/Murray

**CONCEPT:** Some songs require three chords for accompaniment, **I**, **IV** and **V⁷**.

**STRATEGIES:**
(a) Start by singing the song unaccompanied.
(b) Add chordal accompaniment on autoharp, piano, guitar or uke, starting with the **I** chord.
(c) Ask the students to tell you when the **I** chord no longer "fits." Try the **V⁷** chord. If that does not fit try the **IV** chord.
(d) Keep playing this chord on each strong beat until our ears tell us that it no longer fits, then revert to the **I** chord again.
(e) Continue in like manner until the entire song is harmonized.
(f) Review syncopations:

(Turn on the Sun, continued)

*Turn on the* ♪ ♩ ♪

*Gather up all the* ♩ ♫ ♪ ♩ ♪

> **I, IV, V⁷ chords**
> **syncopations**

# Tzena

Words by Henry Morris  
Israeli Song

Tze-na, Tze-na, Tze-na, Tze-na, can't you hear the music playing
In the vill-age square?
Tze - na, Tze - na, join the cel-e-bra-tion,
There'll be people there from ev - 'ry na - tion,
Dawn will find us danc-ing in the sun-light,
Danc - ing in the vill-age square.

\* Second part enters here if sung as a round

**ASSIGNMENT:** Make a concept statement and design your own strategies for this song.

# When the Saints

**Spiritual**

**CONCEPTS:** Some songs require three chords for accompaniment: **I**, **IV** and **V⁷**.

**STRATEGIES:**
a) Start by singing the song unaccompanied.

b) Add chordal accompaniment on autoharp, piano, guitar or ukulele, starting on the **I** chord.

c) Ask the students to tell you when the **I** chord (D) no longer "fits." Try the **V⁷** chord (A⁷). When it does not fit, try the **IV** chord (G).

d) Keep playing the chord that fits best on each strong beat until your ears tell you that it no longer fits, then revert to the **I** chord again and follow same procedure.

e) Continue in like manner until the entire song is harmonized.

NOTE: For another example of the same concept, see "Old Smokey" (page 144).

---

**I , IV , V⁷ chords**

**harmony**

# Where the Coho Flash Silver

Lloyd Arntzen
January, 1970

In Port Hardy one morning I cast off my lines. The sea was all smooth and the weather just fine, And for Castle Rock I was headed away Where the Coho flash silver all over the bay, Where the Coho flash silver all over the bay.

2. It was just before dawn when I reached the fish ground,
   And I lowered my poles and I let my lines down,
   And I lit up my pipe and I waited and prayed,
   To see the Coho flash silver all over the bay.

(Where the Coho Flash Silver, cont.)

3. Well, the sun came up shining and so did the fish,
   All the bells were ringing what more could I wish,
   And the girdies([1]) were humming, I was making it pay
   Where the Coho flash silver all over the bay.

4. Well they bit all that morning until well after two,
   They're so hungry they'd strike at an old leather shoe,
   "This has got to be heaven!" to myself I did say,
   Where the Coho flash silver all over the bay.

5. When I tied up that night, they asked, "How did you do?"
   And I showed them silver darlings([2]) two hundred and two.
   They said, "You're the high boat, the best here today,
   Where the Coho flash silver all over the bay."

6. Now there's doctors and lawyers and bankers and more,
   And big wheels and promotors with their deals galore,
   But let me be a troller([3]) and king for a day,
   Where the Coho flash silver all over the bay.

[1] girdies: reels which hold the trolling lines.

[2] silver darlings: a coho salmon weighing ten pounds or more.

[3] troller: a fishing vessel which employs hooks and lines as opposed to a *seiner* which uses nets to catch fish.

**CONCEPT:** Phrases in a song are repeated, extended and contrasting to provide musical interest and suspense.

**STRATEGIES:**

a) Teach the song by rote or by note. If by rote, focus on the lyrics. If by note, see the method on page 204. Note that there are 6 verses but no chorus. The form of the song is A A A A A A.

b) Sing verse one together showing the phrases. **How many are there?** (5) **Are all the phrases the same length?** (no, the fourth is longer than the others.) Draw the phrases on paper while you sing a verse.

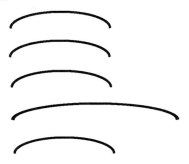

( Where the Coho Flash Silver, cont.)

**How long are the shorter phrases?** (5 measures)
**How long is the longer phrase?** (7 measures)

Most of the songs we sing have 4 or 8 measure phrases. These phrases are **irregular** in length. **What device is used to make the irregular phrases?** (long notes, $\text{♩.}\ |\ \text{♩} \text{ ξ}$ ). It is important to hold the longer sounds for their full value.

**Why is one phrase longer than the others?** Let students discuss. They may notice that

- i) the phrase form is **a b b a** (extended) **a**;
- ii) the song could have finished after the **fourth phrase**,
- iii) the composer created suspense and variety by **extending** the **a** phrase in its second hearing, especially using the upward melodic movement, and
- iv) the last phrase starts a little differently to balance the beginning of the fourth phrase.

If students do not notice these points, use questions and demonstrations of what the song would be like if it had been written differently in order to help students find the reason.

c) Sing one verse without the longer endings ( $\text{♩.}\ |\ \text{♩} \text{ ξ}$ ) for each phrase, converting the song to regular four measure phrases. **What is the difference in feeling between the two versions?**

Sing a verse leaving out the extended phrase. Discuss the difference in the effects created by the four phrases versus the five phrase version.

Sing the song as written.

**Composed Folk Songs:** Most folk songs are handed down from generation to generation and the tune and lyrics changed as people adapted them to their own needs and to the situation of the times. Musicians in modern times often compose songs in the **style** of folk songs using subjects of topical interest that appeal to a wide audience as their basis. This song was composed by Lloyd Arntzen, a teacher in North Vancouver, in 1970 and deals with fishing for coho salmon off the coast of Vancouver Island. The use of idioms specific to the subject is typical of both traditional and composed folk songs. Terms used in some traditional folk songs often have hidden meanings which are not immediately apparent to the listener and these meanings can only be determined from an examination of the historical context and location where the lyrics originated.

> **extended phrase**
> **irregular phrase length**

# Who Built the Ark

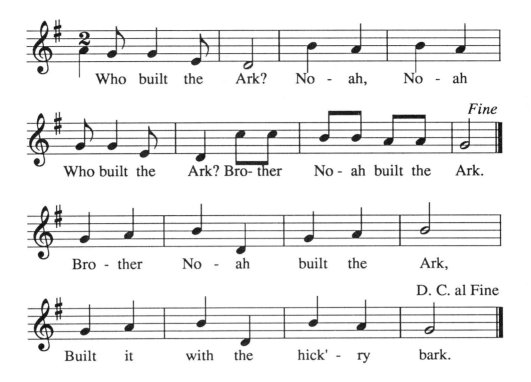

**CONCEPTS:**
1. Some songs use **syncopated** rhythm patterns to create musical interest.
2. Musical tones have names to identify them, as you and I have names to identify us.

**STRATEGIES:**
a) Sing the whole song as written.
b) All sing again using letter names for *Noah, Noah* (**B-A**).
c) Class sings whole song **except** *Noah, Noah*. Teacher substitutes new "tune" for *Noah*, such as:
   **B - G**, or **B - B**, or **A - B**, etc.

Students should note the difference, and echo new tune on their recorders.
d) The teacher may introduce a new pitch (**C**, for example) on the recorder in the music for *Noah* (**B-C**, for example) and student may echo.
e) Encourage individual students to make up their **own** settings for *Noah* (**G-B, B-C**, etc.) All students should **listen** to new patterns and echo.

> **syncopations**
>
> **note names**

# Listening

Since music is an aural art, listening is a very important part of any music program. In fact, it pervades all musical activity. However, using one's ears is a common activity even outside the music classroom. The question might be asked why it is necessary to dwell on the topic. The reason is that although most of us have ears which receive sound, we do not necessarily attend to what we hear. Constantly bombarded with sound, we often tune out. The main purpose of the listening aspects of the music lesson is to help students focus and concentrate on what they perceive, become conscious of and understand what they hear, and reflect on the experience. The intention is to help students become more aware of the soundscape and the effects which sounds have on us. Music is often used as background; the music teacher attempts to bring the music to the foreground. Greater awareness and understanding lead to greater enjoyment.

What is required of a good listener is an openness to musical experience, a willingness to attend to the music, and the ability to put preference aside for the moment. The following suggestions will help make listening experiences more enjoyable and better learning opportunities.

1. Use good quality recordings and playing equipment. Take care of your recordings and tapes.

2. Remain silent while the music is being played. Questions should be asked before or sometimes after the music. Speech during the music comes between the music and the listener. The teacher should model the appropriate behaviour.

3. In any kind of movement activity, students should understand what is expected of them.
    i) Begin when the music begins.
    ii) All movement is done quietly. No talking or sounds are allowed because these will interfere with the concentration of others on the music.
    iii) Move so as not to bump into other children.
    iv) Stop when the music stops.

4. Use visuals to show the subject matter, to illustrate concepts, or to show the notated themes.

5. The younger the student, the more clearly identifiable should be the concept on which you plan to focus in music.

6. Select pieces which will stretch the students' attention span but will not overwhelm it.

7. Listening is active engagement with music. Students should be given questions to answer, actions to do (such as show dynamic levels, follow call charts or other visual maps, plan movements, conduct).

8. Discussion about what students have perceived in the music, and the effect of musical qualities and the organization are vital to developing better listeners. The teacher

should employ such opportunities to challenge the students to think about, to reflect on the musical experience. **WHY**, **HOW**, and **WHAT IF** are key words. Students will learn from each other and be able to use the music vocabulary they have acquired. The teacher may also find occasion to present new terms as the students explain what they hear.

9. Listening lessons are not something relegated to an obligatory three periods a year. Listening skills are improved on a daily basis in the development of inner hearing and the aural discrimination needed to sing and play instruments. Listening lessons happen regularly in the form of short excerpts demonstrating a particular concept, of discussion of recorded songs used as models, of student compositions and performances, of awareness of sound in the environment, and of full-length pieces as presented in the strategies that follow. Furthermore, what has been learned through the experience of a listening selection could be applied to other aspects of the music program, for example in composition and arranging.

10. As mentioned in the section dealing with evaluation, it is possible to assess whether students are achieving the objectives of a listening strategy and to diagnose student problems, with movement, body response, call charts organized as tests, and classroom discussions but some of the ways available to the teacher.

11. Listening lessons can also include information about the composer, the social and historical context of the composition, audience behaviour, and other pertinent musical facts. The focus, however, should always be on the music.

The number of sample strategies presented in *Making Music Meaningful* has purposely been kept to a minimum. An attempt has been made to include a variety of music and approaches. Approximate grade levels have been included. Music series and other materials listed in the Resources Appendix will provide you with many other teaching strategies and suggestions of music to play for your students.

## Listening Resources

### Book

M. Rubin; and A. Daniel. *The Orchestra.* Vancouver: Douglas & McIntyre, 1984, 1988. [The book has an accompanying tape, "Peter Ustinov Reads *The Orchestra*," performed by the Toronto Philharmonic Orchestra (MRP — C107).]

### Tapes

*Beethoven Lives Upstairs.* [A&M Records — SAN1003]
*Mr. Bach Comes to Call.* [A&M Records — SAN1002]

### Listening Aid

Non-directed Listening Program — available from Karen Taylor, 22259–48th Ave., Langley, B.C. V3A 3Z7. A series of short segments of music played every day for a week with daily introductions. The program is planned for the school year.

# Air Gai

**Christoph Willibald von Gluck (1714-1787)**

**Source:** Adventures in Music. Grade I, Vol. 1.
**Grades:** 3-6
**Instrumentation:** symphony orchestra

**CONCEPT:** An ostinato is a repeated musical pattern.

**STRATEGIES:**  a) Ask students to stand. Explain that you will be playing the beginning of a piece called "Air Gai" (happy song). The piece begins with an introduction. When the students hear the end of the introduction (that is, the beginning of the theme) they are to be seated. Stop the recording after a few phrases of the theme. Most students will have sat down at the correct time.

**How did you know when to sit down?** (the rests, the build-up, nothing seemed to be happening, we were waiting for the real tune to begin)

b) Place the following rhythm patterns on the blackboard:

1) | | | |
2) | ♫ ♫ |
3) ♫ | ♫ |
4) ♫ ♫ ♫ |

Practise them.

Inform the class that they will clap one pattern until you move them to the next. You will begin the patterns when the main theme begins. Using facial and body gestures, get the students to clap louder as the music gets louder, and softer as the dynamics of the music decrease. Try to change rhythm patterns at the end of phrases (in sets of multiples of 4). Notice that the tempo changes at the end of the piece (the coda). You may stop the clapping before the coda or continue to the end of the music. The students have been clapping an ostinato to the music. (An ostinato is a repeated rhythmic or melodic pattern.)

**Were you clapping the beat or the rhythm pattern of "Air Gai?"** (Except for pattern 1 which is the beat, the rhythm patterns of the ostinati are different from the rhythm patterns of the melody.) Music is made of many layers happening simultaneously and harmoniously.

You may need to repeat the clapping activity.

c) Divide the class into four groups. Assign **one** ostinato pattern to each group. The students are to work out a body movement which will show their rhythm pattern. Their movements will begin **after** the introduction.

(Air Gai, cont.)

Allow a few minutes for planning and rehearsal. Play the recording calling to each group in turn to perform its ostinato. While not performing, the three other groups watch and evaluate. A discussion follows.

**What worked well? What needs rethinking?** (Some groups may have worked out a wonderful ostinato pattern which was too complex to maintain with the music.) Allow time for corrections. Do the movement once again, one group at a time. If all groups are working well, you could conclude this "performance" with all groups called in towards the end of the music. The effect is visual rhythm patterns. A variation would be to have the beat ostinato perform throughout with other groups alternating.

**Do you feel the other rhythm patterns happening around you?**

> **rhythm pattern**
>
> **ostinato**

-178-

# Epitaph for Moonlight

R. Murray Schafer (1933– )

**Source:** The Festival Singers of Canada (CBC Radio Canada SM274)
**Grades:** 6-7
**Instrumentation:** mixed choir with percussion instruments.

**CONCEPTS:**
1. The tone colour of voices can be used to create unusual aural effects.
2. There are different ways of notating music.

**STRATEGIES:**   NOTE: Since this piece is in a style unfamiliar to students, your preparation/motivation is extremely important. It will be necessary to get students interested in the idea of an epitaph for moonlight.

a) **What is an epitaph?** (words inscribed on a tombstone) Ask students to make one for a few imaginary or television "characters" then proceed to a more abstract character, moonlight.

**What kind of epitaph would you write for moonlight?** (Receive any suggestions, always asking why, dwelling on the feeling which would be created.)

**If you were to write an epitaph for moonlight, how would it sound?** (Make a list of suggestions on the chalkboard.)

**Here is how Canadian composer, R. Murray Schafer imagined an "Epitaph for Moonlight" would sound. As you listen, compare Schafer's composition with how you thought it might sound.** Students might mention the following, or any other points they hear:

   i) **tone clusters** — simultaneous sounds, with notes sounding very close together (not chords);
   ii) **dissonance** — the music is unsettling; only at some places is there consonance created by unison or chords;
   iii) use of unusual vocal effects like whispering, random sounds, swoops;
   iv) mixed choir — but does not have traditional harmony;
   v) no "melody" or beat making music seem ethereal;
   vi) use of high-pitched percussion instruments; ringing sounds give eerie effect;
   vii) words do not make literal sense;

The initial discussion should deal with the comparison between the class list and Schafer's use of musical qualities. It may take a few listenings and some questioning from the teacher to draw these observations from the students. The special music vocabulary (tone clusters, dissonance) may have to be provided by the teacher, as students describe the effect.

**What effect is created by Schafer's composition? How?** (The responses will be based on classroom discussion and the qualities described above.) Students might be interested in the source of the text. Schafer once gave grade 7 students the task of making up synonyms for moonlight. Such words as *lunious, sloofulp, neshmoor, shalowa, nu-yu-yul, noorwahm, shiverglowa*, and *shimonoell* appear in the work.

b) **How would you notate Schafer's composition?** (Students discuss written music.) Schafer is also a visual artist. His scores are beautiful to the eye as well as the ear. Samples of his notation should be available to the students to peruse. An example of his work in "Epitaph for Moonlight" can be seen here.

(Epitaph for Moonlight, cont.)

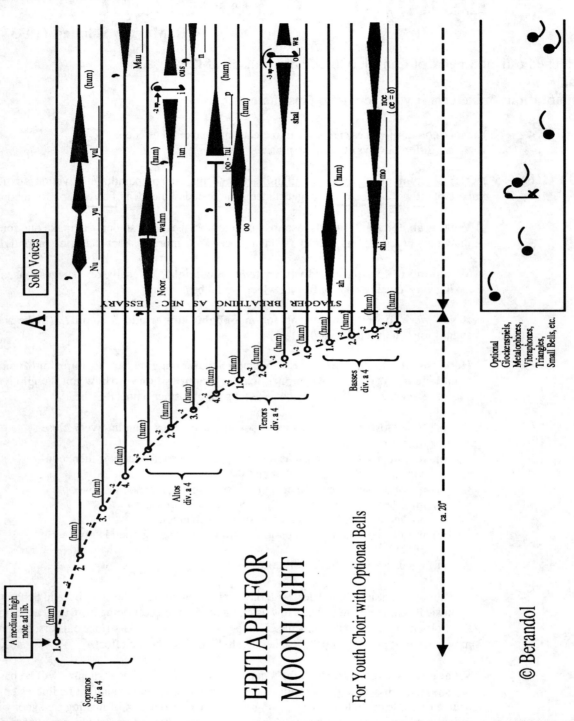

An examination of his scores will indicate how modern composers are attempting to solve the problems created by new music. Traditional notation is not adequate for some of the recent techniques. If you have enough scores, ask the students to "read" them as they listen to the music. Students may find it difficult to follow a full score, but by focussing first on one part, then another, they will develop the ability to grasp the complete musical event.

**tone colour (choir)**
**modern notation**
**tone cluster**

© Berandol

# Morris Dance
(from *Henry VIII Suite*)

Edward German (1862-1936)

**Source:** Adventures in Music, Grade 1, Vol. 2.
**Grades:** 5-7
**Instrumentation:** symphony orchestra

**CONCEPT:** Musical works have recurring themes and contrasting sections. The order of events in a piece of music is called its form.

**STRATEGIES:** The Morris dance is an English folk dance originally performed to ward off the gloom of Winter and welcome the arrival of Spring. It is traditionally performed in the street with dancers sometimes wearing bells or hitting large sticks together. Colourful flowers and streamers can be added. The steps and costumes vary across the districts in England.

a) Place the two themes before students (on overhead or chart paper). Ask students to follow the themes as they listen to the music. If students do not read music well, ask them what kinds of visual cues on the paper (acetate) will help them find their way (direction of melodic line, rhythm patterns). Play the music.

b) Ask for a volunteer to point to the themes as the music is played a second time. (The student should point to the beat. Here is an opportunity for a student who takes private lessons or who is more advanced to shine. The second playing gives those who could not follow the themes a chance to hear/see how the themes are organized.)

c) Ask for three volunteers: one to play the cymbal (with brushes) during theme 1; a second to play the claves during theme 2; and a third to play the tambourine during the other sections of the music. Play the music again (cueing if necessary). When the piece is finished, discuss whether the students identified the themes and other sections correctly, and what each played (e.g. beat, rhythm pattern of melody, a contrasting rhythm pattern, a rhythmic ostinato) and how each played (Could each be heard? Did each respond to dynamic changes?) This evaluation is an important part of the activity since students are required to perceive and make musical judgments. The activity could be repeated with different players.

(Morris Dance, cont.)

    d) The previously unidentified sections are labelled introduction, coda, and bridge.

    e) Students get into groups of four or five to produce a listening chart for the *Morris Dance,* one which will show clearly the form and one other musical quality. The chart may use words, more abstract visual symbols, or a combination. Students discuss a plan of action and then listen quietly to the music to identify the form. More discussion. The process continues until the teacher, who is circulating among the groups, thinks that the children have a good grasp of the piece (three or four times should suffice). The charts are drawn on acetates.

**Sample Listening Chart**

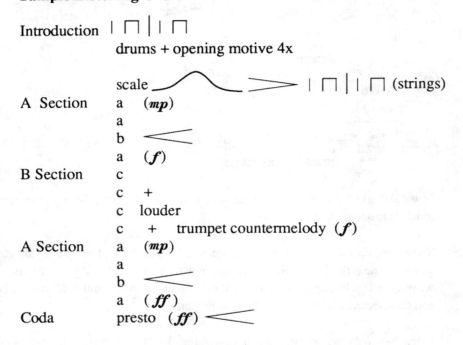

    f) Each group presents its chart to the class, pointing to symbols as the music is played. Discussion centers around accuracy of form, identification of second musical quality, and how the chart was constructed (e.g. vertically, horizontally, choice of symbols, inclusion of other dynamic features, the music).

    g) Working in groups of six or seven, students are now ready to plan a movement (dance) which will show the form. The discussion following the performances will focus on how the form was shown, why certain formations/movements were selected for the various sections, and other questions of that nature.

NOTE: The activities are not intended for one lesson, but rather will continue over a period of at least three to five lessons.

# Parade

**Jacques Ibert (1890-1962)**

**Source:** Adventures in Music, Grade 1, Vol. 1
**Grades:** 3-5
**Instrumentation:** symphony orchestra

**CONCEPT:** Music can get gradually louder or softer.

**STRATEGIES:**

a) Play the recording. Ask students to suggest titles for the piece. Discuss the alternatives. What musical qualities contributed to their decisions. If the option has not already been mentioned, identify the composer's title as "Parade." How does the music match the title? (It gets gradually louder as the parade nears, and gradually softer as it disappears in the distance. The tone of the music is joyful and festive.)

b) Ask students to show the changes in the dynamics as they listen a second time. They hold their hands together for the soft part, gradually separating them on an horizontal plane as the music gets louder. Explain that there are musical symbols and terms to express getting gradually louder ( $<$ , crescendo) and gradually softer ( $>$ , decrescendo).

c) Students now have an opportunity to "watch" a parade. They decide what character they will assume (what kind of people watch parades?) and line up on either side of the parade route. They should not tell anyone who they will be, but try to act out a role. They imagine the parade approaching, before them, and leaving. Play the recording. Afterwards, discuss whether they felt they really saw a parade. Why? Why not? What types of people were at the parade? How did they know?

It will probably be necessary to act out the parade a second time to increase the concentration and try out new ideas stimulated by the discussion. All must cooperate to create a "suspension of disbelief." Discuss the results.

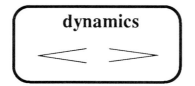

# The Swan

**Camille Saint-Saëns (1835-1921)**

**Source:** Bowmar Orchestral Library — BOL #51
**Grades:** 3-4
**Instrumentation:** 'cello and piano

**CONCEPT:** Music is made up of numerous sequences of tension and release, building in intensity until a peak is reached, at which time the music gradually comes to a close. The peak of intensity is known as the climax.

**STRATEGIES:**

a) Play the recording. While they are listening, ask students to imagine what animal the piece of music portrays. Discuss the different answers, asking what qualities in the music prompted their choices. Listen to the recording a second time. If students have not mentioned a "swan," guide them in this direction. Once the swan has been identified, ask the students for characteristics of the swan and the qualities in the music which make it swan-like. (tempo, long phrases, graceful melody for the swan, rippling water in the piano part)

b) Suggest to students that they could imitate the movement of the swan. **How will they move?** (slowly, gracefully) Play the recording and have half the class move to the music while the other students observe the response to the music. (Did the "movers" look swan-like? Why? Why not?) Let the other half of the class move to the music.

c) Ask the students if they can identify one point in the music where the swan is moving quickly with its wings widespread. Explain that this point in the music is called the **climax**. Have students move to the music one more time, showing the climax. When the music is finished, discuss whether the feeling of climax was shown in the movements. What devices did the students use to show climax?

**ADDITIONAL EXPERIENCES:**

a) Discuss the instruments that play the solo ('cello) and the accompaniment (piano).
Discuss why the composer might have chosen these specific instruments.

b) Mirror movement is particularly appropriate for this musical work. Students work in pairs with one student the leader, the other, the mirror. Movements must be slow and graceful, with both students facing each other, if the activity is to be successful. Great concentration is required. Beginners could start with just arm movements.

---

**climax**

**timbre**
**(solo instruments)**

# Walking in the Air

Lyrics from "The Snow Man," Howard Blake

**Source:** The King's Singers — "Kid Stuff" (EMI 4 DS–47870)
**Grades:** 2-4
**Instrumentation:** male vocal quintet

**CONCEPT:** The tone colour of voices can be used to create unusual sounds.

**STRATEGIES:**

a) **What would it be like to float in the air? Listen to a song called "Walking in the Air." Does it make you feel as if you are floating? How?** (high voice of solo, light sound, strumming sound, tempo)

**Listen again. What tone colours do you hear?** (Children may be surprised that only voices are used to make all the sounds, even the ones that sound like instruments. There are only five singers involved, The King's Singers, with the one who sings the solo throughout most of the song called a countertenor.) You might discuss how clever the arranger of the song had to be to create the instrumental effects and how the singers must be very capable in order to perform such difficult music well.

b) Listen to the piece again. Ask the children to close their eyes and imagine they are walking in the air. Ask half the class to show how they walk in the air to the music. The other half observes. A discussion about how convincing the movers were, and what it was they did with their bodies to convey a floating feeling follows. The other half of the class takes a turn moving to the music. A further discussion summarizes what has been learned.

```
┌─────────────┐
│   timbre    │
│             │
│   voices    │
└─────────────┘
```

# Walking Notes

**Hap Palmer**

**Source:** "The Feel of Music" — Educational Activities (AC 556)
(Activity Records, Freeport, N.Y. 11520)

**Grades:** K-3

**Instrumentation:** male vocalist and jazz combo

**CONCEPT:** The tempo of a piece may be fast or slow depending on the speed of the beat. Different tempos have different expressive effects.

**STRATEGIES:**

a) Students sit and listen to the music. When the man sings, they remain still. When the instruments play by themselves, students put the beat on any part of their bodies.

b) When the music has finished, ask students whether the beat stayed the same all the way through the piece or whether the beat changed. (It change from medium to fast, to slow, to medium.)

c) Play the piece again. This time, children will move to the beat of the music, showing that they hear the changes. As in the first listening, children will remain still "freeze" while the man sings. (This request requires children to play closer attention to the music and acts as a "cooling down period.")

( tempo )

# Composing Music

Singing, listening, playing, and moving are only some of the ways of experiencing music. Many people think that musical composition is only for great composers and possibly music students. The abundance of folk music puts a lie to this myth. Composing is arranging sounds, normally in a way which is comprehensible to others. Obviously, some results are better than others, and some people have the capacity for originality and for reaching us at deeper levels. Just as not all people write as well as Will Shakespeare, we are not all composers of the calibre of J.S. Bach. However, we can all learn more about how music works, experience the joy of playing with sound, and in the process, sometimes surprise ourselves. In the act of composition (or improvisation, if music is made up on the spot) you have an opportunity to organize sounds, select the appropriate musical qualities, make musical decisions, and evaluate the success of your venture. In the process you have the opportunity to be involved in music in a way which allows you to use what you know and feel and reflect on your experience while giving you deeper insight into the music you listen to, play, and sing. Let's examine each of these points in turn.

### Organizing Sound

You will be working with sound, organizing the elements of music which you are presently studying: melody, rhythm, harmony, form, timbre, texture, dynamics, and tempo.

### Selecting Musical Qualities

When you form a piece you will decide which qualities you will select to meet your expressive purpose.
- Will the sounds be brilliant, dull, loud, soft, high, low — and many other such decisions will be needed.

### Making Musical Decisions

How will the sounds be organized?
- How will you create variety? unity?
- How will you begin?
- How will you hold the listener's interest?
- How will you convey a sense of climax?
- How will you end the composition?

Will you piece have a program (story or mood) or be abstract (focussing on the qualities of sound)?

### Reflecting

A composition is a product which may be critiqued.

- Is the composition successful? Why? Why not?

In forming a piece of music you proceed much as you would in a English composition except that you work with sound as the raw material. You begin with a musical idea (**motive** if short, or **theme** if long). The features of this idea impact on what will happen next. Options must be examined and decisions made. So you can remember what you decided while you are composing or when the composition is completed, you may wish to notate your music. To do so you may want to use standard notation. Resulting compositions are likely to be traditional melodies requiring more formal music background than the alternative, **sound compositions,** which use idiosyncratic graphic methods to record the soundscape.

When you have a finished work, it is important that you reflect on and discuss the results of your efforts. What worked well and why? What might you improve in further refinements or future compositions?

## CLASS IMPROVISATION

One way of introducing composition is to begin with class improvisations which allow students to explore a variety of musical elements in a structured context, develop an understanding of the kind of sensitive listening needed in improvisation, experience a kind of music which may not have the melody, rhythm, and harmony to which Western ears are accustomed, and get an idea of how graphic notation can be used.

It is important in this kind of work/play to establish a serious atmosphere. This doesn't mean "long faces" but rather the intention to produce worthwhile results. Initially, some students (you too) may find it hard to accept the results as real music. Canadian composer, Murray Schafer, claims we need to do some "ear cleaning." If you persist with your improvisations, and all cooperate and concentrate on the composition, the results are often lovely.

Here are a few ideas.

1. Explore the sounds of objects in the classroom (**found sounds**). Are the sounds high/low, scratchy/smooth, soft/loud and many other categories which can be devised to classify the sounds. Would the sound be different if the source were played differently? Try a variety of ways of playing the newly discovered "instruments." Categorize the sounds into families determined by the students (e.g. long/short sounds, wood/glass). Players in the same family get into groups as do the musicians in a symphony orchestra.

   You are now ready to improvise a composition using your found sound band with you acting as composer/conductor. Remember that such pieces do not need meter, rhythm pattern, or melody in the Western sense although these could be present. As you conduct you will be making choices. Do all groups play all the time? What dynamics sound best? Will you change the tempo? How do you know when to stop? Do students just make sounds or are they listening to each other? If they are listening, compliment them. If not, the composition will probably not sound very effective. Ask students if they thought the composition effective or not. Why was it effective or not effective? You can probably draw from them the need to be sensitive to what others are doing. Next, ask for student volunteers to conduct. When a composition is concluded, ask the volunteer how he/she knew when to finish. Ask the class to identify similarities and differences among the improvisations. The purpose of this discussion is to encourage students to be aware of what is happening and to learn new strategies for future attempts. This evaluation or debriefing session is an essential part of the composition process.

2. Try number 1 with classroom instruments.

3. Plan a composition using body sounds. Have students suggest sounds and convenient symbols to represent them. A hand clap might be ( ✶ ). Dynamics could be shown by size or thickness, pitch by placement. Sounds may be singular ( ✶ ) or random:

Be as original as you wish to be. Students select an opening sound and decide how many times or how long it should last. What will follow? Since this composition is drawn of the chalkboard, change can easily be accomodated if students do not like a particular effect. What form (pattern of events) will be used? Practise intermittently and adjust as necessary. Perform the entire composition.

4. Try number 3 using vocal sounds (vowels and consonants in various combination). In music classes the only bad mistake is one from which you learn nothing.

## SOUND COMPOSITIONS

Students at the intermediate level (or lower, with careful planning) are now ready as individuals or in small groups to plan and perform sound compositions. The following steps are suggested by Regelski.[1]

1. Devise a problem based on a relevant concept.
2. Provide limitations.
3. Determine the steps to be followed and a time-line.
4. Allow students time to work on compositions and tape or perform for the class.
5. Evaluate work (a joint venture by students and teacher).

Regelski writes that sound compositions are not a special unit or one-time event but should be integrated into the other activities in the music class. Only in this manner will growth over time be evident to the students and teacher.

Here is an example of the steps worked out for an upper intermediate level class. The specific content is not suggested for a first experience with sound compositions.

---

[1] T. Regelski. "A Sound Approach to Sound Composition." *Music Educators Journal*, Vol. 72, No. 9 (May, 1986): 41-45. Some would object to the careful specification evident in the steps, arguing that such structure inhibits creativity. If there are students who can operate outside the suggested framework and benefit from the experience (because they can create their own structures) let them do so. They could help other children by explaining how they proceed. Their ideas could be explored by the class. However, for the majority of students guidelines are helpful and, in many cases necessary.

**Sample Sound Composition**

**CONCEPT**
- Unity and contrast are important design considerations in a piece of music.

**PROBLEM**
- Create, notate, and perform a piece in which contrast is achieve in the middle section by a focus on **two** musical qualities.

**LIMITATIONS**
- small groups (4 or 5)
- use classroom percussion instruments (if melodic, use C pentatonic scale)
- ABA form
- approximately 20 seconds per section
- contrast section focusses on two musical contrasts (loud/soft, high/low, fast/slow, timbre, long/short)

**STAGES** (17 minutes)

1. Decide what musical qualities you will use for your contrast.
2. Decide what instruments you will use for your first section (A).
3. Decide what instruments you will use for your B Section. Will they be the same or different?

5 min.
4. Get the instruments you will need.
5. Organize the sounds for your A section. Notate them in rough.
6. Organize the B section. Notate in rough.
7. Will your last section be exactly the same as the first (A) or will it be similar ($A_v$)?
8. Using symbols to represent your sounds, notate your composition on acetate or chart paper. Give your 1 minute piece a title.
9. Rehearse. Prepare for a taping of the performance. (If the composition is not taped it should be played at least twice, the first for listening only, the second for score watching.

**EVALUATION**
- What two musical qualities were used to establish the contrast?
- Could you hear when the B section began? How did you recognize it?
- How did the music move from one section to the next?
- Did the music keep your interest? How?
- Did you feel that the piece was finished? Why?
- What would you improve?
- What do you think worked very well?
- Does the notation show what the group played? Would other players be able to follow it? Why? Why not?

The questions under evaluation are merely samples. Many others will likely emerge from the performances themselves. It is also a good idea to ask the composers how they think their composition sounded before letting other members of the class enter the discussion.

The benefit of sound composition for student assessment will be evident. Students have an opportunity to use what they have learned in a way that shows ownership of the concepts and skills in the actual composition and in the ensuing discussion. Tapes of the performances can be a tangible record of student growth over the year. Anecdotes and checklists of comments or even written student reflections about the compositions are other ways of assessing student progress, identifying areas which will need further emphasis, and pointing out directions for new learning. Although the teacher acts as facilitator, students to a large extent are teaching each other.

## OTHER TYPES OF COMPOSITIONS

Elementary school students also enjoy making melodies and exploring harmony. Encouragements and an interest in results will often be sufficient to motivate some students. For example having the class learn a piece composed by a classmate would set the tone for further attempts. For a song (lyrics and melody) composed by three grade four students without adult assistance refer to "Being a Friend" on the following page.

In a class setting, carefully structured plans will be needed. Two strategies are provided.

1. Begin with a four-line poem, perhaps one that the children have written. Have several children sing the first line. Select one version as the one you will use for the song.[2] This is an excellent opportunity to have children give reasons for their choice of one melodic phrase over another. Ask for a volunteer to make up the second phrase. All sing the first phrase, then the one child improvises the second. Repeat until the class has found a satisfactory phrase. Repeat the process until the whole song is finished. Remember always to go back to the beginning of the song before you add the new phrase; the new phrase will probably fit better with the rest of the song than if you just ask for a phrase out of context. Record the final session. Was there any repetition? What is the form? Notate the song yourself or ask a musician to notate it if this seems appropriate.

Writing their own songs could create an interest in how other songs are constructed. Do any of the songs the students know have the same structure as theirs? Do some forms seem to work better than others? Are some forms more common? Why do you suppose this might be so? Children might start to make-up tunes of their own. Give them an opportunity to perform them for you, their classmates, or the principal.

2. If the children ( and you ) have a knowledge of I, IV, and $V^7$ chords, you could write a melody based on a chord progression. Begin with a four-line poem. You might pre-determine the meter, rhythm pattern and chord progression or allow student to work these out for themselves as they get more experience. An example follows on page 193.

---

[2] Explain to the children that you are "brain storming" and only one melody can be used.

# Being a Friend

Claire Hatcher, Laurel Patton, & Leah Stuart
arr. Betty Hanley

March 1987

-192-

i) Poem with meter and rhythm patterns.

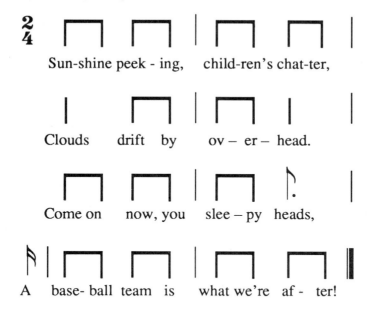

ii) Based on chord patterns you've observed in songs, you add chord progression.

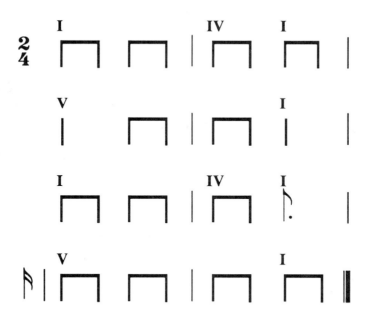

iii) Select a key. We'll use D major. Name the notes in each chord:

|     |    |    |    |
| --- | -- | -- | -- |
| I   | D  | F# | A  |
| IV  | G  | B  | D  |
| V   | A  | C# | E  |

-193-

iv) Write structure on the board.

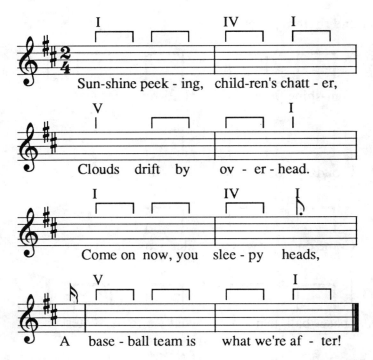

Students select notes from appropriate chords then try out the phrase. Sight reading is best but you could have help from the piano (perhaps from a student taking private lessons). Notes can be changed to improve the sound. Work phrase by phrase but always go back to the beginning to get the full effect. The first phrase might be:

v) When you are happy with the song, perform it with autoharp, ukelele, guitar, or piano chords. Have students copy the final version. They could be challenged to make up a different melody using the same chord progression.

## Suggested Readings

J. Paynter; & P. Aston. *Sound and Silence: Classroom Projects in Creative Music.* Cambridge: Cambridge University Press, 1970.

T. Regelski. *Teaching General Music: Action Learning for Middle and Secondary Schools.* New York: Schirmer, 1981.

R.M. Schafer. *The Composer in the Classroom.* Toronto: Berandol Music Ltd., 1965, 1969.

# Singing

*Music can make me soar with joy or it may bring tears — tears that can even feel good when I am overwhelmed with the sheer beauty of the sound of music. Music is as natural as sun or rain. I'd hate to imagine our world without it, for my heart is a song.*

—Big Bird

Teaching music typically involves singing, an activity which is natural and spontaneous in very young children but which, in our culture tends to become more and more inhibited in the general population as we get older. Perhaps this loss occurs because singing is such a personal act and somehow our self-concept is closely tied to how we sound. If we have been told or given the impression by people who are generally unaware of the consequences of their behaviour that our singing is in some way inadequate, our response frequently is to stop singing. Only the very brave, independent, or insensitive will persist in the face of social disapproval. Another important factor contributing to the decrease in singing as children move through adolescence is what children notice about how their world works. Above all, they seek to emulate adult behaviours. When do most children witness their parents and other adults making music, singing? If the only kind of singing valued by the important people in their lives is what is heard on records or the radio, the child soon learns that singing is something only certain (talented?) adults do and the urge to sing is soon extinguished. The result is that otherwise intelligent adults who would vehemently deny ignorance of a mathematical operation such as the addition of whole numbers blithely describe themselves as "tone deaf" even though their speech pattern belies the claim. Many in our society simply do not consider it important to be able to sing in spite of the joy expressed by those who do.

There is help for those who want to improve. Barring actual physical dysfunction (a rare occurrence) we all have the capacity to sing and experience the particular pleasure that singing can bring. While research is suggesting that it is easier to acquire pitch and rhythm skills as well as second languages at an early age, thus the importance of the primary years in school, it is possible, if the motivation is present, for improvement to take place at any age.

## YOUR VOICE

As a teacher you will be relying on your voice both in speech and song. Your overall goal should be to sing with a better tone and more accuracy. However, any work you do to improve your singing technique will help reduce the possibility of general voice abuse. In this section we will briefly examine the technical skills involved in singing (and speaking).

The two crucial areas you will need to consider are breath support and relaxation. Singing differs from speech in that sustained breath is needed. The energy for this sustained breath which supports the tone is provided by the manner of inhaling and exhaling. Poor breath support leads to muscular tension in other areas involved in voice production and amplification such as the jaw, larynx, and pharynx (see diagrams 1 and 2 on the following page).

**Diagram 1: The Voice Mechanism**

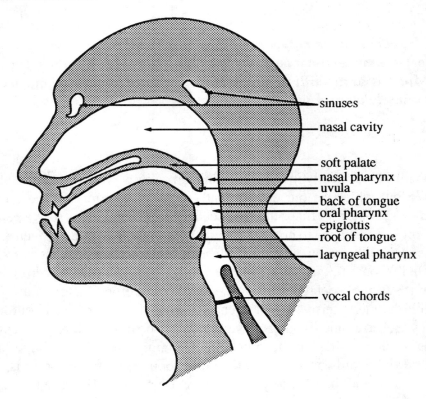

**Diagram 2: The Breathing Mechanism**

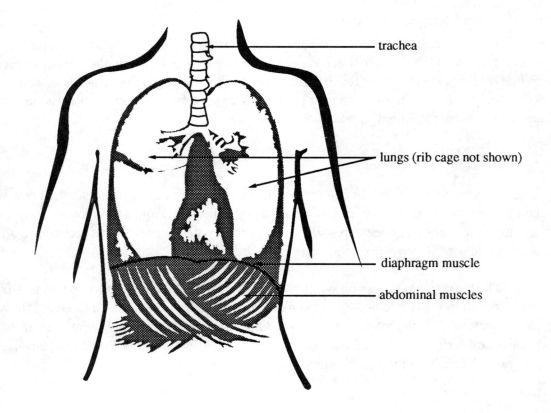

The most efficient way to breathe when singing is called deep or diaphragm breathing. There is nothing mysterious about this form of breathing except perhaps why it tends to be lost as we mature; babies use it naturally. To get the feeling, try the following activities.

1. Assume a balanced stance. "Standing like a winner" is a useful image. Shoulders are relaxed but not stooped so the rib cage can expand; the head is balanced with the chin neither reaching nor pulled back.

2. Take a deep breath. Begin by relaxing the abdominal muscles. Feel the expansion of the lower torso and rib cage. Your shoulders are totally relaxed, uninvolved. Take only enough air so your are comfortable, not feeling your throat constricting. What is really happening is that when you relax the abdominal muscles, you allow the diaphragm to lower, leaving more room in your lungs for air.

3. To exhale, purse your lips as in blowing out a candle to control the output of the air. Keep you rib cage expanded. As you gently blow out the candle you will feel your abdominal muscles moving inward and up; the diaphragm is moving back into place, helping support the flow of air.

4. Repeat the process several times. You will probably feel as if your lung capacity is expanding a little at each attempt.

5. Check for tension.

A knowledge of how breath support works will help you understand why posture is so important in singing. Unless they have already developed a superior vocal technique amateurs cannot afford to slouch when singing, whether seated or standing.

When the tone is supported by a good breathing technique, it is possible to relax other areas of the body which are often incorrectly called upon to control the tone:

- **the shoulders** — Shoulders which are relaxed and slightly back allow for unrestricted movements of the muscles and cartileges involved in producing sound in the larynx.

- **the jaw** — Much of the tension we experience daily seems to locate itself in the jaw. Many of us have developed a permanently tight jaw. Check yours now. A relaxed jaw allows the larynx and pharynx to work naturally.

- **the tongue** — helps shape the amplification chamber, form the vowels and articulate the consonants. It too should be relaxed, lying on the floor of the mouth and slightly forward.

Here are some relaxation exercises:

1. **Shoulder rolls** — Roll shoulders forward four times, back four times. At the end of the sequence, shoulders and rib cage should be in "singing" position.

2. **Head roll** — Let your head droop downwards. Slowly rotate your head to the left then the right. Repeat a few times.

3. **Jaw rotation** — Without undue force, rotate your jaw forward and sideways. You may have been asked to "open your mouth" or put two fingers between your teeth when you sing. What is really wanted is a relaxed jaw. Repeat this exercise several times a day especially when you feel tension developing in this location.

4. **Tongue loosener** — Place the tip of your tongue at the back of your lower teeth. The tongue should be flat. Move your tongue in and out as quickly as possible.

5. **Resonance (Head voice)** — Select a comfortable pitch. Sustain the note humming "mmm," feeling the tone forward in your face. You can manipulate the sound so the buzz will be more in your nose, lips, or mouth. Remember to keep the tip of your tongue down behind your lower teeth. Is your jaw relaxed? Try this exercise on different pitches going up or down by half steps.

6. Repeat the above exercise beginning with the hum but proceeding to a vowel (eg. "mmmoh" or "mmmah"). Try to keep the vowel sound in the same place as the hum, not allowing the tone to slip back to your throat. If you feel any tension, go back to some of the earlier exercises.

All these exercises are intended to be used for rather short periods of time but frequently.

Relaxation and support will correct many of your vocal difficulties. However, there are also some other psychological factors which can negatively affect your singing. Many people do not like the way they sound because they feel their voices are too feeble especially if they try to sing anything "high." These weak voices may be caused by any combination of fear of singing out, poor breath support, and a poor conception of the amount of energy needed to sing. Singing does require energy; singing is a very physical activity. The proper stance, adequate support, and energy investment will contribute to a new sound which will increase your enjoyment when you sing.

Many people are also content to live with a limited vocal range ("I can't sing that high"), unaware that they are using only their chest voice and that exploring the head register will allow them access to notes and a timbre they didn't know they had. As for those who think they "can't carry a tune in a bucket," help is at hand. More will be said about these last two points in the children's voices section.

This brief discussion will have put you on the right track to vocal health. Whether you make any progress depends on your willingness to try new techniques and work at improving your skills for your own personal development, to increase your enjoyment of singing, and for the sake of those you will teach.

## CHILDREN'S VOICES

Too many children, especially boys, grow up believing they cannot sing. There a number of reasons which have been posited to explain this phenomenon:

1. Inattention to pitch and failure to notice pitch changes.
2. Psychological inhibition toward singing.
3. Inability to coordinate the vocal mechanism.
4. Low speaking voice.
5. Lack of interest in singing.
6. Lack of practice in singing.
7. Lack of exposure to music at home.
(Gould, 1969, cited in Goetze, Cooper, & Brown, 1990, p. 17)

In the past, if personal anecdotes are to be believed, favourite tactics with "inaccurate" singers were rejection (you cannot be a member of the group) or silencing (just mouth the words). The long term effects of such strategies even if innocently practised have been devastating. Helping children would seem a more pedagogically sound approach especially since research is showing the importance of vocal development in children between the ages of four and eleven (Scott, 1989).

Children need to know the difference between a speaking voice, singing, and shouting. The difference can easily be highlighted in classroom activities and games exploring vocal sounds. For example, a nursery rhyme could be recited then sung. Ask the children to explain the difference between speaking and singing. When children sing, remind them, if necessary, to use their "singing voices."

Some children may not have discovered their "singing voices" (head voices) yet, resorting either to a low tone (chest voice) or speaking voice. These children need to feel and hear what it is like to sing, to focus on the sound. Here are some ideas:

- Make fire engine sounds as high as possible.
- Make sound of a fire cracker coming down to the ground. Start as high as possible. Note that as the pitch descends the tone stays forward, not falling back to the chest voice which sounds as if it comes from the throat.
- Tell stories requiring high sound effects.

When children have found this higher head voice tell them they have found their "singing voices." The advantages of a head voice for children are greater vocal flexibility, expanded range, and a warmer tone colour. The chest voice, while giving greater volume in the lower register limits what the children (and you) will be able to accomplish.

Like adults, children need to support their voices; however, they don't need to hear detailed physiological explanations. Imagery and metaphor are more appropriate devices. Asking children to "sit tall," "stand like a winner," or "breathe from the tummy" will often yield the desired results. The teacher needs to observe the students for signs of tension and discomfort. Watching for unnecessary shoulder movement, poor posture, facial expressions which show tension, and tense muscles in the throat will identify those students who are singing incorrectly. Usually a reminder of appropriate behaviour will be sufficient since children haven't had as long as adults to develop counterproductive habits. Comments framed in positive rather than negative terms are more effective: "Stand like a winner" is better than "Don't move your shoulders up and down."

While discovering the singing voice will solve many of the inaccurate singer problems, there will still be some singers who don't yet sing in tune. Such children have been misnamed monotones or, more appropriately, underdeveloped singers. The latter term has the advantage of suggesting that change is possible. Maturation is one of the factors which must be considered. Some children take longer to develop the listening skills and physical coordination. Nevertheless, as in other areas in education, students can be helped. The first step is diagnosis. Is the problem a lack of interest, a lack of attention, inability to discriminate between pitches (higher/lower; do the sounds go upward or downward), inability to sing what is heard, inability to tone match with others but ability to sing in tune alone, or a poor memory for auditory stimulus. Each problem would suggest a different solution. For an excellent but accessible discussion of vocal problems and solutions refer to Linda Swears' *Teaching the Elementary School Chorus* (1985). Here are a few suggestions to help children sing better.

1. Always give a starting note. Be sure the key you select is in the children's head voice range which is notated below.

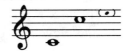

2. Do many tone matching activities (e.g. roll calls, echoes).
3. Select a number of pieces with a limited range especially if you have a number of students who are experiencing difficulties.
4. Select songs with a lot of repetition.
5. Repeat songs many times so they will become "friends." Vary the activity with the repetition; add actions; make a game.
6. Encourage the use of the "singing voice."
7. Show excitement when a child demonstrates progress, especially when the singing voice is first discovered.
8. Work to create a sharing atmosphere in which children help each other and encourage improvement.
9. Have students be the leaders in modelling activities.
10. Ask children to listen to each other, especially if they have a tendency to shout.
11. Give children opportunities to sing alone, initially perhaps in game situations such as "What Kind of Cake" (page 92).
12. To make children more aware of pitch, ask them to show with their hands the direction of a melodic phrase in a song (e.g. in "Billy Bad" the descending phrase "'cause my name is Billy Bad", and "half past one" in "Barnacle Bill") or, in a two or three pitch song, the relative high/low placement.
13. Use hand signs and solfa syllables to help children develop a better concept of repeated pitches, steps, skips, leaps, and melodic contour.
14. Listen to live performances and recordings of good children's choirs so you will know what children are able to do. Children will live up or down to your expectations.
15. Seek opportunities to let your students hear live or recorded children's choirs so they will develop a concept of the sound of children's voices.

# THE CHANGING VOICE (CAMBIATA)

One of the most frustrating situations for the inexperienced choral director, or classroom music teacher is the "changing male voice." Many teachers have little understanding of the phenomenon. Four questions must be addressed: What is the changing voice? What are the physiological concerns? What are the psychological concerns? How does one work with it?

The changing voice is the alteration, usually gradually, in the range and quality of boys' voices. The process usually begins during puberty. Most boys' voices change about twelve years of age, however, some may change as early as ten years years of age or in the fourth grade. Prior to the change process, the boy's voice is soprano in quality and range. As the voice changes it becomes lower in pitch and heavier sounding. This is caused by the lengthening of the vocal cords and the enlargement of the larynx.

## Physiological Concerns

The male voice has three stages of development — the unchanged voice (male soprano), the changing voice, and the changed voice. It is important to realize that with the physiological change there is also a psychological change. The most "fragile" period of vocal development is during the change process. This is a time when the vocal cords are lengthening and thickening, often causing the boy to lose control of his voice. Out of control "squeaks" and "squawks" are heard on a regular basis. The problem is most pronounced when the boy is encouraged to use his voice for an extended or continuous period of time as in a choir or when singing in a general music class. This does not mean that the boy should not be encouraged to sing on a regular basis. Use of the voice is important in order for it to mature; however, extended use of the voice at both soft and loud volumes as well as extended use at extreme ranges (high and low) will increase the lack of control. Appropriate vocal exercises and choice of music are essential.

## Psychological Concerns

The young male singer can become very embarrassed by his lack of vocal control. While voice change is normal, it is not often dealt with in a sensitive manner. Students must realize that all voices (male and female) change, however, the changing male voice is more obvious. Young boys will often not sing out or sing alone for fear that their voices will "break." Teachers must be on the look-out for such signs and be empathetic to the young boy if they hope to encourage him to continue singing. The changing voice is a major vocal obstacle that can have devastating effects on the child's self-image. When not handled with care, the young boy may choose to stop singing (usually on entry to high school). Lack of male singers is one of the major dilemmas facing the high school choir teacher.

## Working with the Changing Voice

Repertoire must be chosen very carefully. Music specified for SA is difficult for these young men to accept — they are becoming "men" and do not want to sing "girls" parts. However, the changing voice has a very limited range (moderate alto/tenor), hence, the majority of boys are not able to sing standard TB parts. Teachers should select music that is marked Part I, II, III; or I, II; or H (high) M (middle) L (low), or H, L. The teacher can then place male and female voices on parts that suit the individual voices. As many boys as possible should be placed on the same part, providing a sense of security for the boy and stability for the group. Also, avoid talking about soprano/alto parts when teaching young choirs.

When the voice is changing, boys should sing in the range that is most comfortable, and should avoid straining their voices. Music with a moderate range, and moderate dynamics (mf) is best. The comfortable or mid range is often known as "cambiata." The tessitura (range of the voice part) will be:

The importance of being aware of the changing voice and its uniqueness cannot be over-emphasized if we are to encourage our young male singers to continue to sing. When in doubt, choose material with a moderate range (cambiata tessitura), and exercise all voices so that all singers can develop their instruments. Remember, all children have a natural desire and right to sing.

## SELECTING SONGS

With the staggering number of old and new songs available, how does a teacher select the songs children will sing in the classroom. A good music series and *Making Music Meaningful* will already have gone through the process of selection for you, but it is helpful for you to be aware of some of the criteria for decision-making. Figure 1 summarizes the points which should be included in your deliberations.

**Figure 1**
What to consider when selecting a song

1) **variety**
   - of styles, periods, forms, and cultures
   - of musical qualities
   - of moods
   - of purpose (descriptive, story telling, patriotic, seasonal, celebration, ritual...)

2) **teaching point**
   - each song should feature one or more musical concepts which will be the learning focus of the lesson

3) **vocal considerations**
   - range of the song (should be what is best for the children, not what the adult can do)
   - register (most notes in the song are in the comfort zone— not always at high or low end of the range)
   - types of intervals (larger intervals are more difficult to sing)

4) **suitable text**
   - appropriateness for age level
   - quality of language (select some songs with poetic texts)

5) **musical quality**
   - the song should have merit

The last point is a particularly contentious issue which often deteriorates into questions of preference or taste (what I like) rather than that which is excellent. Although musicians do not necessarily see eye to eye on the specific characteristics which determine quality in music there is an agreement that some works are better than others.[1] Currently, the worth of many kinds of music is being questioned because the assumptions championed by western European tradition as the epitome of cultural progress have been severely challenged. Within each musical style, whether jazz, classical, African, or rock, it is now generally acknowledged that there exist examples of better and lesser works. Determining value has become even more complex. How are works to be evaluated within a particular style? It is important not to confuse liking or personal preference with the quality of a work. You may like a piece very much but realize that it is a rather trite composition. On the other hand, you may appreciate that a particular work is excellent for its kind but not like it. (However, it often happens that as you learn to understand and appreciate a work, you begin to like it.) The *sine qua non* of value judgments is understanding; understanding requires considerable familiarity with many representatives of a particular style and knowledge about the music. As you work with songs you will develop a better sense of what has value, lasting meaning, and be less taken in by the immediate appeal of a song. Certainly the songs which have endured for a century or more have demonstrated a lasting quality. Contemporary music is harder to select, of course, but decisions must nevertheless be made.

Songs may also integrate well with social studies, language arts, and science. Providing that musical criteria and learning are also considered, the integration of songs throughout the school day is a wonderful way of demonstrating that music is a part of life.

## TEACHING A SONG

There are different ways to teach a song: rote, rote/observation, and note. It is possible to teach a song with a recording, with the teacher as the model, accompanied or unaccompanied. Which method you will select depend on your purpose, the ability of your students, and your ability to perform.

**1. Rote Method**

a) short songs — The teacher sings the whole song giving the children something to listen for or do. After two or three performances of the song the children are asked to join in. If there are difficulties the teacher can isolate the problem phrase and have children echo the correct version. This method is particularly useful at the early primary level but can also be used with older children who have developed good memories for melodies or in conjunction with recordings.

**Examples**: "Bee, Bee Bumble Bee" (page 60), "Bounce High" (page 65), and "Clap Your Hands" (page 69) [2]

---

[1] The list of criteria includes economy of expression, unity, symmetry, and original statement. Most of these criteria are attributes of the ideals of western European music. As world music is better understood, new criteria or sets of criteria will likely emerge.

[2] Refer to the strategies provided for all the songs listed in the examples in this section for ideas about how to teach the songs.

b) longer songs — The teacher sings the whole song giving children something to listen for or do. The procedure which follows the presentation of the whole song is:

| | |
|---|---|
| Teacher sings first phrase. | Children echo. |
| Teacher sings second phrase. | Children echo. |
| | Children sing first and second phrases. |
| Teacher sings third phrase. | Children echo. |
| | Children sing first three phrases. |

Continue until the entire song has been taught.
Sing the whole song.

**Examples:** "Ghost of John" (page 116), "Donkey Riding" (page 106), and "Old Brass Wagon" (page 80)

2. **Rote/Observation Method**

In this method the song is still modelled for the students, but they look at the music and are asked to locate or identify a particular feature in the music. Examples of what to observe in the notation are:

In which phrase does the melody move by step?
Where is the longest sound?
How many times can you find m-r-d?
How many times can you find a syncopated rhythm pattern?

**Examples**: "J'entends le moulin" (page 133), and "Toembaï" (page 163)

3. **Note Method**

In this approach students actually read the song (or part of the song). There are many ways of accomplishing this goal. Here is a possible sequence. (It is important that the song contains melodic and rhythmic elements students already know or **one** new element which is to be the teaching focus.) This approach requires the most formal music background from teachers and students.

A) Rhythm pattern:
  i) Identify the meter signature.
  ii) Scan the piece for any unknown rhythm patterns (there should be none or only the new teaching point).
  iii) Using rhythm syllables, name the rhythm patterns (perhaps one phrase at a time).
  iv) Review as needed (you could do one measure per student or group of students for variety and to keep all on task).

B) Melodic pattern

   i) Look at the key signature. If there are no sharps or flats, doh is C. If there are sharps, the last tone (the sharp closest to the beginning of the musical notation ) is ti. Go up one line or space to find doh. If there are flats, the flat closest to the music is fa. Go down f-m-r-d to find doh. Check the last note of the piece. If it is doh, the song is doh centered. The absolute pitch name for doh will put you in the right key. (If doh is G, the key is G major.)
   If the last one is la, the song is la centered. The absolute pitch name for la will put you in the right key. (If la is D, the key is D minor.)
   ii) Place students in the correct key by singing d-m-s-m-d for doh centered songs and l-d-m-d-l for la centered ones.
   iii) Using solfa syllables practise reading pitches in the key of the song. Include all the different notes in a song. For the song "Five Hundred Miles" you would draw the following on the chalkboard:

   iv) Inner hear/practise the first phrase using the correct rhythm pattern. Without missing a beat, sing the phrase out loud.
   v) Repeat for the second phrase. Sing the first and second phrases. Repeat the process until the song is finished.
   Sing the whole song.
   vi) Add the lyrics. Select appropriate tempo, dynamics and phrasing.

   **Example:** "Where the Coho Flash Silver" (page 170)

## 4. Using Recordings

Many music textbooks are now equipped with dual track recordings which allow the teacher and students to listen to the vocal track, the instrumental track, or both together. While these recordings, if well performed, can provide good models and listening selections, and can be used to teach the song in the rote method described above, it is possible to rely too heavily on these soundtracks. The danger is that the recording never gets turned off and the students (and teacher) never really hear what they sound like, lulled by the electric sound they hear into believing their own output to be much better than it really is. Remember that singing takes effort; the recording sometimes camouflages this necessity. In summary, use recordings sparingly while the children are actually singing, but use them frequently to draw attention to arrangements, instrumentation, and differences in performance styles. It is important that you use the best possible sound equipment when playing music.

# THE MODULATOR (TONE LADDER)

The modulator (see Figure 2) presents all the pitches used in traditional western music. It is useful:

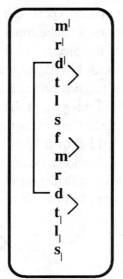

Figure 2. The Modulator

- to present or review intervals and pitch sequences used in songs
- to help with sight reading
- to introduce and reinforce harmonic concepts (eg. singing the scale as a round)
- to explain scale structures and relationships
- to sing chords and understand their structure
- to create melodies

## INTRODUCING HARMONY

One of the great joys of singing occurs when harmony is created in a vocal context. Harmony happens when two or more pitches are sounded simultaneously. It is important for singers to be aware of the combined tones, so they must listen carefully to each other. To "tune out" the other part(s) is to miss out on a good deal of the enjoyment. Before harmony is possible, however, students must have a good unison sound no matter what their ages. The following is a possible sequence for engaging in increasingly more difficult singing in harmony, beginning in middle primary years and proceeding through intermediate levels. Some examples from this book are provided where available.

| | |
|---|---|
| add an ostinato | Bee, Bee, Bumble Bee (page 60) |
| | Bow, Wow, Wow (page 66) |
| | Canoe Song (page 102) |
| | Hoosen Johnny (page 126) |
| | Land of the Silver Birch (page 139) |
| | Sakura (page 154) |
| | Star Light, Star Bright (page 89) |
| echo song | Old Texas (page 145) |
| round | Canoe Song (page 102) |
| | Hebrew Round (page 124) |
| | J'entends le moulin (page 133) |
| | Kookaburra (page 138) |
| | Praetorius Round (page 149) |
| | Toembaï (page 163) |
| | Tzena (page 168) |

|  |  |
|---|---|
| partner song | Mama Don't 'Low/This Train/Crawdad Song |
|  | Fish and Chips (page 113) |
| add chords | Ezekiel Saw the Wheel (page 111) |
|  | Fish and Chips (page 113) |
|  | Orthodontist Blues (page 146) |
|  | Joshua fit the Battle (137) |
| short harmonic section |  |
| descant | Sakura (page 154) |
| alto part |  |

## AN INTRODUCTION TO CONDUCTING

You may have occasion to work with a performing group. If such is the case you will need to know the basics of conducting. Conducting is "non-verbal" communication between the conductor of an ensemble and the ensemble. Conducting is both a physical skill and a musical art. The role of the conductor has changed over the centuries. Originally, the conductor's responsibility was to start the ensemble, indicate tempo and meter, and stop the ensemble. These continue to be some of the main responsibilities for all conductors; however, the present role involves correcting mistakes, phrasing, expression, adjusting blend/balance in the ensemble, and musical leadership. Conducting skill and artistry remain one of the weakest abilities of many music educators. Often, elementary music specialists and classroom music teachers do not believe that the level they are teaching warrants the development and use of refined conducting skills. These teachers do not realize that the quality of the ensemble will improve when their non-verbal conducting skills improve. For example, if we do not feel confident "waving our arms" in front of the ensemble, the ensemble will recognize our insecurity and perform with less security and often poor intonation. In addition, no matter what the sophistication of the repertoire, we must do justice to the composer; that is, do our best to musically present the composer's work as accurately as he/she intended. During the performance, the music must reach a level of artistic expression that can only be achieved by the immediate non-verbal communication of the conductor.

The present day conductor's role can be divided into three global areas: 1) intellectual, 2) gestural, and 3) inspirational.

1) **Intellectual:** The conductor must have a thorough understanding of the music and text of a piece prior to the first rehearsal or lesson. This is known as "score-study." This involves a great deal of thought about how the piece of music is put together and how we can best teach it. We must discover: What is the melody?; Who has the melody?; What is the accompaniment?; Who has the accompaniment?; What are the dynamics?; What is the tempo?; What is the key?; What is the meaning of the text?; How does the text relate to the music?; etc.

2) **Gestural:** This is the technical or physical act of conducting. It is important that a strong basic technique is developed so that a group of players or singers can "easily" play or sing together. Physical gestures must be refined to the point that all standard conducting patterns ($\frac{4}{4}, \frac{2}{4}, \frac{3}{4}$) appear easy and effortless. In addition, development of skill in musical expression is essential.

## Standard Conducting Patterns

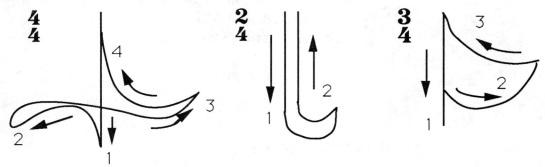

We must remember that 60% of communication is with the "face." Our facial expressions must complement the music and the gestures —we often send a facial "meta-message" which contradicts instead of compliments. Our gestures, facial expressions, and stance must be natural, so as to "invite" our young musicians to perform. As teachers and conductors we should talk less and show more. Music is emotional and we must learn to silently show all emotions. When working with children it is important to model the text of the song. First practice this by showing all emotional expressions of the text with the face. Then practice the song showing the same emotional expressions with the arms and the hands while conducting the specified beat pattern. Finally, practice the piece showing the same expression with the face, arms, and hands.

As conductors we must be able to start and stop the ensemble by a visual gesture that is in the style and tempo of the piece. The beginning of a sound is known as the "attack" and the end is known as the "release." All attacks begin with a "preparation." The preparation beat is the one prior to the initial attack. For example, if a piece of music is in $\frac{4}{4}$ and the piece begins on beat 1, the preparation beat will be beat 4. The direction of the preparation beat is determined by the starting "beat" of the piece.

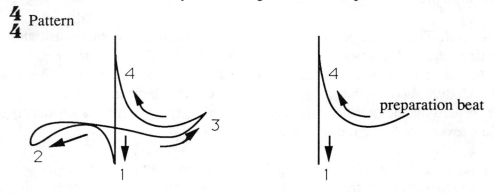

Practice all patterns, preparation beats, and facial expressions in the mirror.

3) **Inspirational:** As teachers and conductors we can be much more inspiring in front of our ensemble when we have thoughtfully considered the intellectual and gestural components. Our role is one of leadership. If we are to guide our students to enjoy and appreciate the art of music we must first guide ourselves. We can be exemplary role models only if we are well prepared.

One of the most important sources of inspiration for the teacher/conductor and the student is the repertoire. Choose music that is musically rich, and make sure that it is appropriate for the class level.

Attitude is the most important element. Your attitude is contagious whether it is positive or negative. Your attitude towards becoming an "artistic" conductor (for any grade level) is up to you. Your attitude/self-image helps to determine your style, your level of confidence, and your performance which in turn has a great effect on the ensemble you direct.

The conductor's goal is "non-verbal" communication, and the requirements are: the personal desire for lifelong learning; reflective thought; continual practice; and self-evaluation. Consult books on the subject and attend inservice workshops to upgrade your current ability.

## References

J.A. Bartle. *Lifeline for Children's Choir Directors.* Toronto: Gordon V. Thompson, 1988.

M. Goetze; N. Cooper; and C. Brown, C. "Recent Research on Singing in the Classroom." *The Bulletin*, Vol. 104 (1990): 16-32.

C.R. Scott. "How children grow musically." *Music Educators Journal,* Vol 76, No. 2 (October, 1989): 28-31.

L. Swears. *Teaching the Elementary School Chorus.* New York: Parker Publishing, 1985.

# PLAYING

# INSTRUMENTS

Recorder
Guitar
Ukulele
Piano

# The Recorder

The recorder is a woodwind instrument of the flute family. Its extensive repertoire ranges from medieval through Renaissance, baroque, and contemporary periods. Publications include works for recorder solo, duets, and quartets as well as recorders in combination with other instruments.

In the sixteenth and seventeenth centuries many composers, including Bach, Handel, and Telemann, wrote for the recorder. In 1615 Praetorius listed eight different sizes of recorders. Today four sizes are in common use: soprano, alto, tenor, and bass (see Figure 1). Soprano and tenor recorders are in the key of C (C is the lowest note) while alto and bass recorders are in the key of F (F is the lowest note).

The revival of the recorder in the twentieth century was due largely to the work of the English performer and instrument maker, Arnold Dolmetsch. Currently the recorder enjoys tremendous popularity in many parts of the world. Recorder ensembles are common in schools and in the community. Many editions of early, traditional, and modern recorder music are available to players at all proficiency levels.

## General Suggestions for Playing the Recorder

1. Hold the recorder at about a 45° downward angle away from the body. Shoulders and arms should be held loosely. The mouthpiece rests between relaxed lips in front of the teeth.

2. Hold the recorder with both hands (left hand closest to the mouthpiece), using the right thumb for balance (its position is on the back of the instrument, between the fourth and fifth holes). The holes should be covered by the soft pads of the fingers rather than the fingertips (see Figure 2).

3. Blow gently and steadily, supporting the breath from the diaphragm as in singing. Use less breath pressure for lower notes and more air for the upper register.

4. Use your tongue for a silent "duh" or "daah" in order to articulate the beginnings of notes. Thus, each note is tongued and held for its full value.

**Figure 1**
The Recorder Family

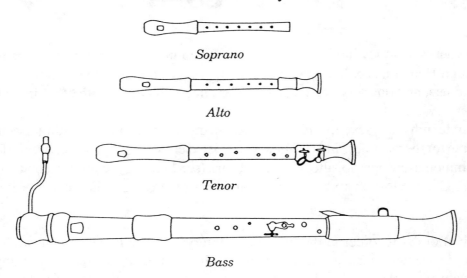

**Figure 2**
This engraving by Hotteterre (1680–1761) shows the proper holding position for the recorder.

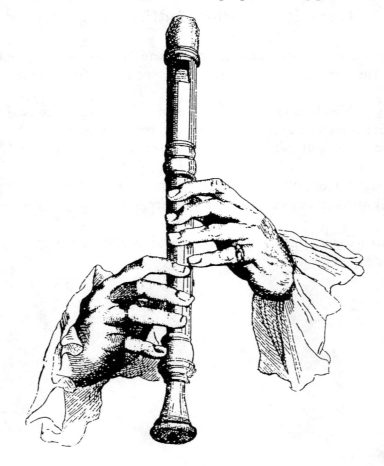

# Beginning Fingerings

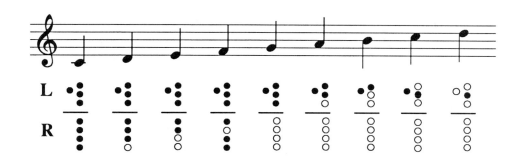

# Beginning Recorder Pieces

**1.0 Pieces Using Three Notes—B, A, G.**

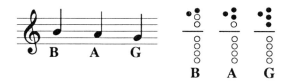

1.1 This is "B":

1.2 This is "A":

1.3 This is "G":

1.4 Down and Up:

1.5 Up and Down:

1.6 Hot Cross Buns:

1.7 Rolling Along:

1.8 Tip a Canoe:

1.9 Little Concerto for Recorder Alone:

1.10 Au clair de la lune:

1.11 Etude "à la samba":

1.12 Etude à trois doigts:

## 2.0 New Note—F

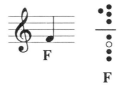

2.1 This is "F":

2.2 Old Wine in New Bottles:

2.3 Tell It All!:

2.4 Lullaby:

## 3.0 New Notes—C¹ and B♭

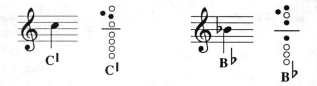

3.1 Rollin' up to "C":

3.2 Gossip:

3.3 Scale Song–I:

3.4 Waltz:

3.5 Scale Song–II:

3.6 Two Plus Three:

3.7 Little Tune:

3.8 Ballade:

3.9 Folk Song:

4.0 New Note—D¹

4.1 Roll on Up:

4.2 Lightly Row:

4.3 Folk Song (in a higher key):

5.0 Two New Notes—D and E:

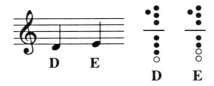

5.1 Old MacDonald:

5.2 St. Nick:

### 5.3 Dance Tune (A Duet):

### 6.0 All the Way Down to C:

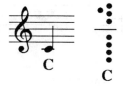

### 6.1 Brother John (NOTE: May be played as a round.):

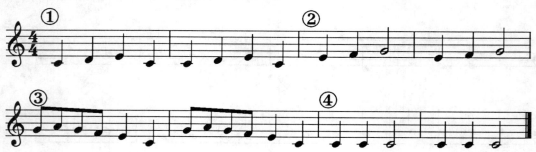

### 6.2 Rolling Down to "C":

6.3 Lightly Row:

6.4 Choral Bells (NOTE: May be played as a round):

6.5 Scale Song–III:

   – also try variations – rhythm
                         – meter

# Recorder Rhythm Reader

**1.0 Rhythms with Notation Suggested:**

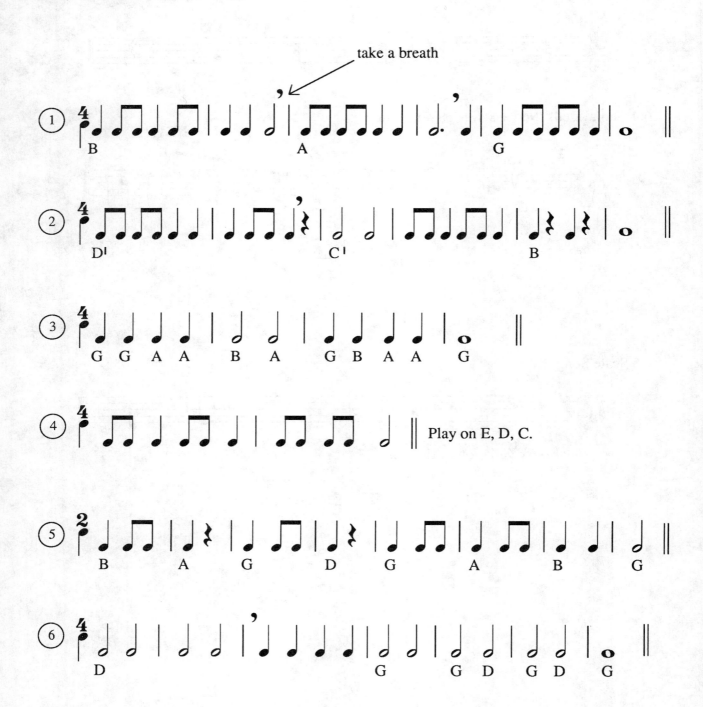

**2.0 Rhythms for Improvisation:**

# Recorder Fingering Chart

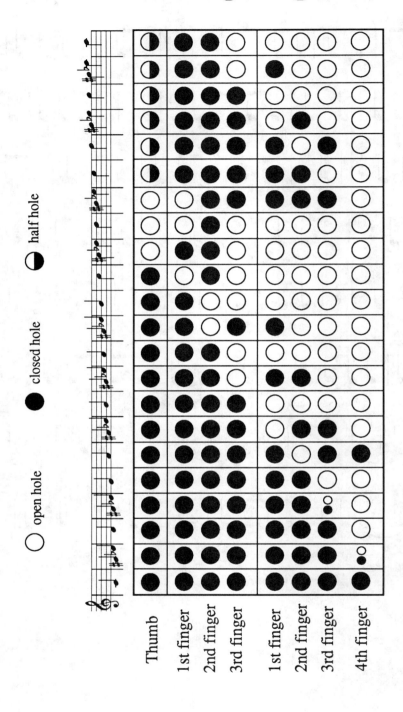

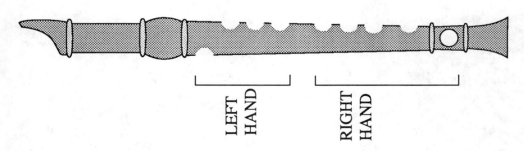

# Tunes for Recorder

**1.0 Aura Lee [Range–G-D♭]:**

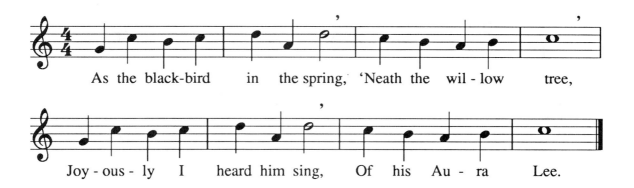

**2.0 Jingle Bells [Range–G-D♭]:**

### 3.0 Fais dodo [Range–G-D′]:

### 4.0 A la claire fontaine [Range–D-D′]:

**French Folk Song**

**5.0 Oats, Peas, Beans [Range–G-D♭]:**

**6.0 J'ai du bon tabac [Range–G-D♭]:**

**7.0 Three Farmers [Range–G-D♭]:**

Play this melody in different keys, for example, start on C, D and F.

-229-

## 8.0 Bransle [Range–G-D♭]:

**FORM: ABBA**

## 9.0 The Gypsy Rover [Range–D-D♭]:

**10.0 Ungaresca [Range–D-C♯]:**                  Anon. 16th Century

**11.0 Amazing Grace [Range–D-D♯]:**               American Song

**12.0 Ahrirang [Range–D-D♯]:**               Korean Folk Song

**13.0 Round [Range–D-D$^|$]:**

**14.0 Hey, Ho [Range–D-D$^|$]:**

**English Folk Song**

**15.0 Frère Jacques [Range–D-D$^|$]:**

**French Song**

**16.0 En roulant ma boule [Range–D-B]:**  French Song

Bass Xylophone

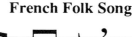

**17.0 Ah! Si mon moine voulait danser [Range–D-D¹]:**  French Folk Song

**18.0 Tallis' Canon [Range–D-D' with F#]:**

NOTE: May be played and/or sung as a round.

**19.0 Good King Wenceslas [Range–D-D' with F#]:**

## 20.0 Song for Recorder [Range–E-E']:

## 21.0 Land of the Silver Birch [Range–E-E']:

**Canadian Folk Song**

NOTE: Try this piece starting on D.

-235-

**22.0 Troubadour Melody [Range–G-F|]:**  Richard Coeur-de-Lion, 12th C.

**23.0 The Huron Carol [Range–E-E|]:**  Canadian Song

**24.0 Friendly Giant's Theme (Early One Morning) [Range–D-G| with F#]:**

English Folk Song

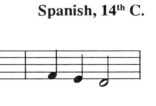

**25.0 2 Medieval Canons [Range–C-C|]:**

Spanish, 14th C.

**26.0 Traditional Round [Range–C-C$^|$]:**

( make up your own words )

**27.0 Kol Dodi [Range–C-A]:**                                                Israeli Folk Song

**28.0 Turtle Dove [Range–C-D$^|$]:**                                         English Folk Song

**29.0 Dona Nobis Pacem [Range–C-D♭]:**

**30.0 Viva la Musica [Range–C-D♭]:**

**31.0 Sumer is icumen in [Range–C-C$^|$]:**

13$^{th}$ Century

Accompaniment:

**32.0 Poor Wayfaring Stranger [Range–C-D♭]:**

**33.0 Come, Follow Me [Range–C-E♭]:**

**34.0 She's Like the Swallow [Range–D-F']:**

**Canadian Folk Song**

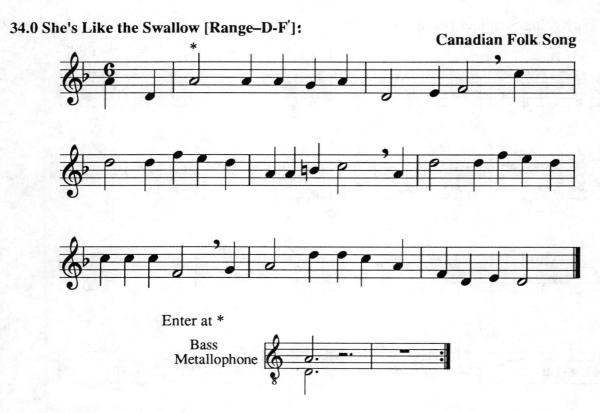

**35.0 Auld Lang Syne [Range–C-F']:**

**Scottish Melody**

-242-

**36.0 Cradle Song [Range–G-G$^|$ with F#]:**

Johannes Brahms

**37.0 Greensleeves [Range–E-G$^|$]:**

English Folk Song

**38.0 Un Canadien errant [Range C-D♭]:**

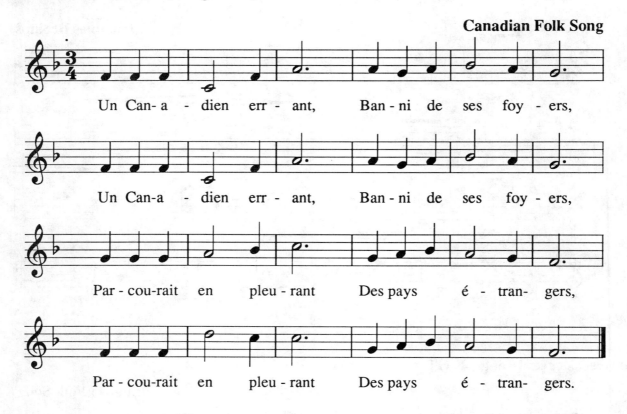

**39.0 La Bergamesca [Range–D-E♭]:**

**Suggestions:**  1. Form AABB (legato, staccato on repeats).
2. Could also be played in triple meter.
3. Use hand drum and/or tambourine on repeats.

**40.0 Edi Beo Thu [Range–D-D¹]:**

Anon. 13th C.

© Waterloo Music Company. Used by Permission.

Other songs to play on the recorder:

    Ah, Poor Bird (page 57)
    Old Brass Wagon (page 80)
    Poor Bird (page 82)
    Prendés i garde (page 83)
    Weavily Wheat (page 91)
    Canoe Song (page 102)

    Come to the Land (page 103)
    J'entends le moulin (page 133)
    Kookaburra (page 138)
    Land of the Silver Birch (page 139)
    Riddle Song (page 150)
    Rocky Mountain (page 152)

# GUITAR

This section will introduce you to the guitar as a relatively easy instrument to play. It is eminently suitable for accompanying classroom singing, is easily tuned (with practice), and is portable enough to allow the player to maintain eye-contact with the audience or class. The guitar also lends itself to easy transposition of songs to accommodate the singing range of children's voices.

This is only an introduction, intended to encourage the student to explore the usefulness and resourcefulness of the guitar for use in classroom music. You will be introduced to the basic techniques for playing chords, melodies and a variety of accompaniment styles. Song materials are suggested to illustrate the basic playing techniques, but you are encouraged from the beginning to extend your experience by looking for other songs in this book and elsewhere to complement the work done in class. By constantly looking for new materials and experimenting with your own variations on the techniques presented here, you will gradually develop your own personal style of guitar playing.

A classical guitar approach is taken in the presentation of the playing techniques in this section. However, all the techniques presented are compatible with most popular folk guitar methods.

## Anatomy of the Guitar

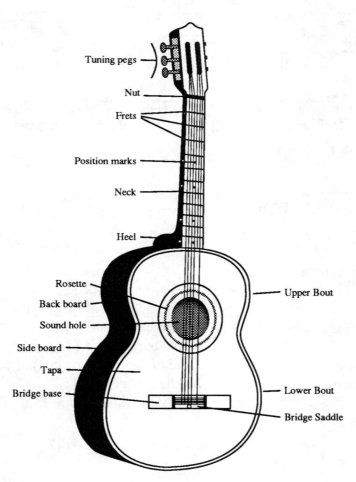

## Finger Chart

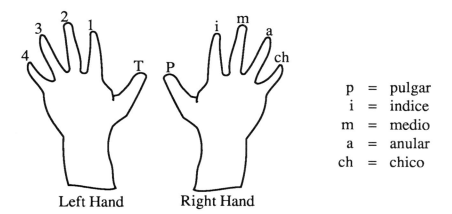

p = pulgar
i = indice
m = medio
a = anular
ch = chico

Conventional usage employs numbers for the fingers of the left hand (which is used in the formation of chords) and Spanish initials for the fingers of the right hand (used for picking and strumming melodies and accompaniments).

## Tuning the Guitar

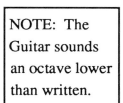

NOTE: The Guitar sounds an octave lower than written.

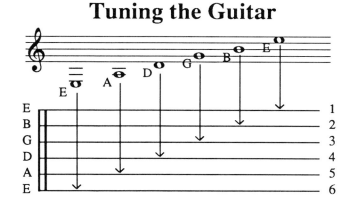

Using a well-tuned piano or a pitch pipe, sound the note **E** one ledger line below **Middle-C** and tune the 6th string to that pitch by adjusting the tuning peg for that string. Turning the peg away from the string will raise the pitch; turning it in the opposite direction will lower the pitch.

Using the index finger of the right hand (i) press on the 6th string (E) at the 5th fret and sound the note A; tune the 5th string to that pitch.

Press the 5th string (A) on the 5th fret (D) and tune the 4th string to that pitch.

Press the 4th string (D) on the 5th fret (G) and tune the 3rd string to that pitch.

Press the 3rd string (G) on the 4th fret (B) and tune the 2nd string to that pitch.

Finally, press the 2nd string (B) on the 5th fret (E) and tune the 1st string to that pitch.

# Basic Playing Techniques

## Getting to Know the Strings

Both the right hand and the left hand must be used with equal dexterity and in coordination with one another. In order for this to happen the guitarist must become thoroughly familiar with the positions of the frets relative to the pitches required to form chords with the left hand and strumming patterns with the right hand. To this end, the student must quickly memorize the names of the strings (numbers as well as absolute pitch names). The following exercises will help:

1. Place the right hand in playing position over the sound hole; the hand should hang loosely from the forearm which rests on the lower side-board. Place the tip of the index finger (i) on the 1st string (E). Using only a little pressure let the finger slide off the 1st string and come to rest on the 2nd string (B). Do this 8 times. This method of sounding a string is called the **Rest Stroke**. It is used for playing melodies with a smooth, **Legato** touch.

2. Repeat the movements in #1 with the middle finger (m). Do it 8 times.

3. Alternate (i) and (m) fingers in repeating the above exercise as follows:

Repeat several times until you achieve a smooth, clear sounding sequence of notes. The term "walking on the strings" is a good description of the technique. The technical term, of course, is the **Rest Stroke**.

4. Repeat steps 1, 2 and 3 on each of the strings in turn as follows:

-248-

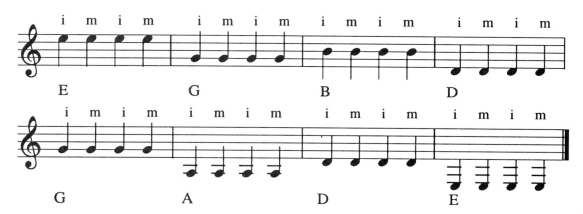

5. When you can play and name all the strings in sequence, try varying the order as follows:

Try other sequences for additional practice. Also, try using string numbers instead of pitch names while you are playing. It is important to vocalize (preferably sing) all the notes as you play them. This will help develop ear-training, an important skill that will also improve your singing-in-tune.

The above exercises should be a part of your daily practice until you become thoroughly familiar with the names and numbers of all the strings.

## Learning the First Chords

Many songs can be accompanied using only one chord. "Row Your Boat" is a good example. For a list of one-chord songs see Appendix B, page 361. Some of these songs are written in major keys (e.g. "Are You Sleeping," "Old MacDonald," and "Shortnin' Bread). Others are written in minor keys (e.g. "Canoe Song" and "Zum Gali Gali"). The accompanying chord will need to be a major or minor chord as appropriate. Here are a few major chords to get you started. You will learn first those chords that are easiest to play on the guitar.

**The D-major Chord**

This is the conventional way to illustrate chords: to interpret, hold your guitar in front of you, the neck upwards, strings facing you. The chord chart below represents your frontal view of the upper neck, fingerboard, strings and frets. The black dots indicate positions for each finger used:

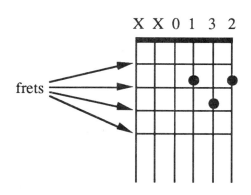

1,2,3 = left hand fingers
0 = open strings (no fingers)
x = do not play/strum these strings with the right hand.

## The Left Hand

1. The left thumb should be placed flat against the back of the fingerboard, close to the nut, allowing the fingers to be placed on the strings in front of the fingerboard. Using the thumb in this way for support, place the tip of the first finger on the 3rd string (G) close to the 2nd fret as indicated in the chord chart. Press lightly but evenly until the string touches the fingerboard beneath. Check to hear if the string sounds clearly by "walking" on the 3rd string (G) with the index (i) and middle (m) fingers of the right hand, just over the sound hole. Remember the **Rest Stroke**! Continue to alternate (i) and (m) until you get a clear, ringing tone.

2. Holding the first-finger (left hand) position on the 3rd string (G), place the tip of the second finger (left hand) on the 1st string (E) close to the 2nd fret and play the 1st string with the right hand, using the alternating **Rest Stroke** as before.

3. Holding the 1st and 2nd fingers (left hand) in position on their strings (G and E), place the 3rd finger (left hand) on the 2nd string (B) close to the 3rd fret and proceed as above, playing the 2nd string with the right hand. Use the alternating **Rest Stroke** (right hand) again to verify a clear, ringing tone.

4. Once you have obtained a clear, ringing tone from each of the 3 strings individually, you are ready to play your first chord (D-major). Here's how.

## The Right-Hand Basic Strum (Brush Stroke)

With the right forearm resting lightly on the lower sideboard, place the right thumb obliquely on top of the 3rd string (G), over the sound hole. The other 4 fingers should be drawn slightly inwards without making a fist. Keeping all the three left-hand fingers in the chord position indicated above, pass the right thumb evenly over the three strings G, B and E to make the three strings sound together to produce the chord of D-major. This is the **Basic Strum** or **Brush Stroke**, the most commonly used form of guitar accompaniment.

Turn now to the song "Row Your Boat" (page 87). Notice that it is in $\frac{6}{8}$ time. That means two beats per measure, so practise slowly strumming the D-major chord in 2s as follows:

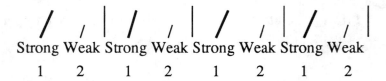

The first strum in each measure should be stronger or louder than the second one.

Now sing "Row Your Boat" to your own guitar accompaniment.

The steps indicated above for finding and verifying chord tones should be followed for each new chord learned. Soon, the process will become automatic.

Consult the list of one-chord songs on page 361. Using the D-major chord you can now accompany

"Are You Sleeping," "Charlie Over the Ocean," "Old MacDonald," "Shortnin' Bread," "Swing Low Sweet Chariot," and many others that are written in major keys.

Now let us learn a minor chord so that you can also accompany one-chord songs in minor keys.

**A-minor chord**

X 0 2 3 1 0

Proceed as for the D-major chord — find and verify each note as indicated on the chord chart for the A-minor chord.

Turn to the "Praetorius Round" (page 149). Here is a song in a minor key that can be accompanied by one chord. This time the meter is $\frac{3}{4}$ so the strumming pattern will be different.

| / | / | / | / | / | / | / | / | / | / | / | / |
|---|---|---|---|---|---|---|---|---|---|---|---|
| Strong | weak | weak | Strong | Weak | Weak | Strong | Weak | Weak | Strong | Weak | Weak |
| 1 | 2 | 3 | 1 | 2 | 3 | 1 | 2 | 3 | 1 | 2 | 3 |

Accenting the first strum in each measure, sing and accompany "Praetorius Round" using the **Brush Stroke**. Notice that the downward stroke of the right thumb begins on the 5th string.

## Two-Chord Songs

Now that you can accompany one-chord songs in major and minor keys, you will look at some new chords and prepare to accompany two-chord songs.

The $A^7$ chord along with the D-major chord will enable you to accompany many two-chord songs:

$A^7$

X 0 1 0 2 0

The $A^7$ chord is very easy to play, requiring only two finger placements in the left hand. Find and verify these two notes. Play them together, using the Brush Stroke with the right-hand thumb, beginning on the 5th string. Any of the following songs can be accompanied using the two chords D and $A^7$.

Start with "This Old Man." The strumming pattern will be:

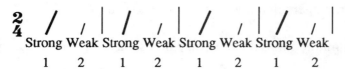

## This Old Man

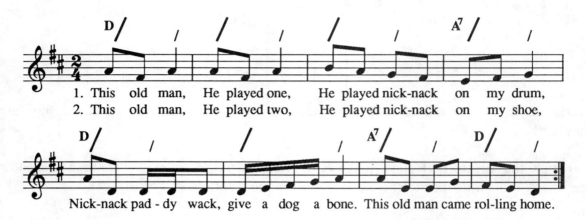

The following four songs can also be accompanied using the chords D and A⁷. Start out with the D chord and let your ears tell you when to change to A⁷ and then back to D as you sing along.

## Go Tell Aunt Rhody

## Skip to My Lou

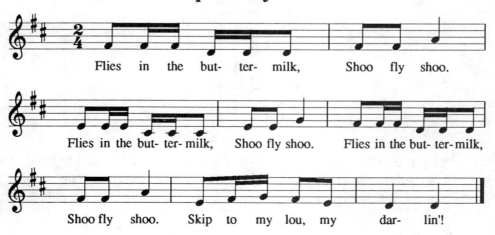

# Whole World in His Hands

"The Sloop John B." requires a third chord, G-major. Can you tell when it should be used?

### G-Major Chord

# The Sloop John B.

**Calypso Song**

For additional verses see page 157.

## New Strumming Styles

**The Bass Strum**

A variation of the Brush Stroke is the Bass Strum. Instead of brushing all the strings together with the right hand thumb, try the following steps:

1. Place the thumb on the bass string (in the D chord, that means the open 4th string — D). Using the **Rest Stroke** slide the thumb off the D string letting it come to rest on the G string.

2. Then use the **Brush Stroke** to play the other 3 strings (G, B and E) simultaneously.

In the A$^7$ chord, the bass is the open 5th string (A).

In the G and G$^7$ chords*, the bass will be the 6th string (E) with the left hand fingers in the chord position.

In the C chord*, the bass will be the 5th string (A) with the left-hand fingers in the chord position.

In the D$^7$ chord*, the bass will be the same as for the D chord — the open 4th string (D).

A good rule of thumb for remembering the bass string is: "the bass string will be the one sounding the lowest note of the chord."

**The Basic Finger Style**

This is a variation of the Bass Strum. Use the right hand thumb as in the Bass Strum to sound the bass note in Rest Stroke style. The first three fingers (i, m, a) will be used to sound the 3rd, 2nd and 1st strings of the guitar respectively. For all chords it is these three strings that will be sounded by i, m and a. Here's the technique:

1. Before sounding the bass note, place the right thumb on the bass string as indicated in the figure below. Place the tips of fingers i, m, a beneath the 3rd, 2nd and 1st strings respectively as illustrated.

2. Sound the bass note first using the Rest Stroke, then—

3. Pluck the other three strings **simultaneously** drawing the fingers upwards toward the palm of the hand (do not close the fist, however).

The illustration on the following page may help in visualizing the technique:

---

* For the fingerings of these new chords, see the Guitar Chord Chart on pages 366-367.

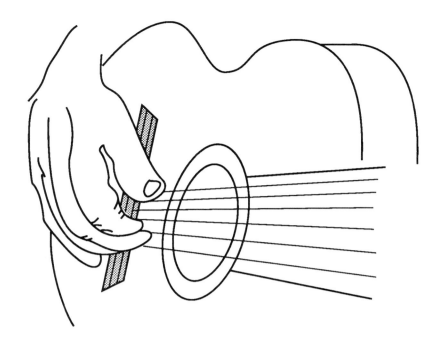

A musical illustration may also be helpful:

## Basic Finger Style with Alternating Bass

A variation of Basic Finger Style, this technique uses the bass note and an interval of a Perfect Fifth above it. In the Key of D, the Perfect Fifth would be A. The bass notes are alternated with the plucking of the three upper strings as follows:

These accompaniment styles are suitable for songs in 2/4 and 4/4 meters.

## More New Chords

Sometimes major and minor chords are combined, especially in accompanying songs in minor keys. Here are some useful chords:

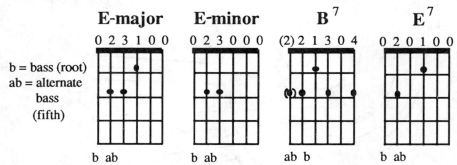

b = bass (root)
ab = alternate bass (fifth)

Combine Em (E-minor) and B⁷ to accompany "Joshua Fit the Battle" (page 261).

Combine Em and D-major to accompany "Drunken Sailor" (page 278).

## Playing Melodies

**Notes on Strings 1 (E) and 2 (B)**

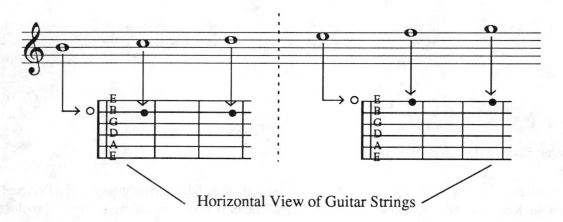

Horizontal View of Guitar Strings

Exercise a, String 1 (E)

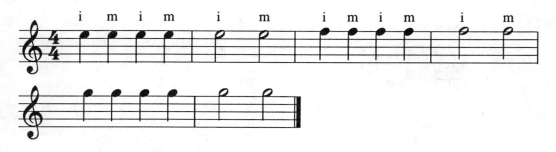

Exercise b, String 1 (E)

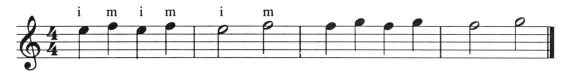

Exercise c, String 2 (B)

Exercise d, Combining strings 1 and 2

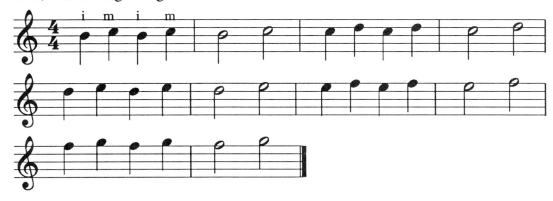

For all of the above exercises use the alternating Rest Stroke (i, m). This style of melody playing is also called **Apoyando Style**.

Exercise e, "Ode to Joy" (Beethoven)

Use the chords C and G$^7$ (page 366) to accompany "Ode to Joy" with the Basic Finger Style accompaniment.

# Notes on String 3 (G)

## Combining Melody and Accompaniment in Ensemble Playing

Turn to the song "Skip to My Lou" (page 269). Find a partner or form two small groups.

      Group 1 plays the melody and
      Group 2 plays the chords (choose your own style of accompaniment).

You will need to use the chords G and D⁷. Begin with G and let your ears tell you where to change the chord.

## More Accompaniment Styles

    Another variation of the Basic Finger style is the **arpeggio**. An arpeggio is formed by playing the notes of a chord in sequence. Two basic variations of arpeggio accompaniment named after the finger picking patterns employed in each case are **pima** and **pimami**.

## Pima

The pima pattern is appropriate for songs in quadruple (4-count) time, for example:

Notice that the bass note in each case equals the durational value of all the notes in each group of four. That is because the **Rest Stroke** with the thumb produces a note of longer duration than each of the eighth notes (♪) which are picked lightly one after another. This technique of picking the notes in the arpeggio is called **El Aire** — a short staccato effect quite different from the smooth legato produced by the **Rest Stroke** (Apoyando).

The song "Kumbaya" uses three chords — D, G and A⁷. Try playing these chords in pima style. The sequence will be:

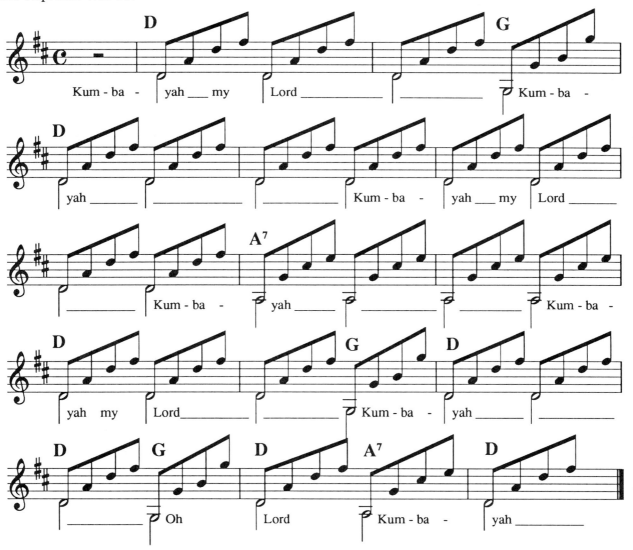

-259-

Practise playing the accompaniment while a partner or a group sings the song. Then switch and sing to your partner's or groups accompaniment.

**Pimami**

This style of accompaniment is a variation of pima and is suitable for accompanying songs in triple (3-count) meter. The pattern looks like this:

## Where, Oh Where Has my Little Dog Gone?

The song "Where Has my Little Dog Gone" (above) can be accompanied using the two chords D and A⁷ in pimami as indicated above. Other songs that can be accompanied in the same style are "Where the Coho Flash Silver" (page 170), "Old Smokey" (page 144) and "The Streets of Laredo" (pages 295-296).

There are many other variations of the various accompaniment styles illustrated above, but these are the most basic forms for the beginning guitarist to learn. You are also encouraged to experiment with your own variations. The guitar is an instrument that lends itself admirably to the development of a personal style of playing.

As you gain more experience, you will need more chords and combinations of chords to accommodate your accompaniments. You will find some of the most common chord combinations you will need for playing in various keys on pages 366 and 367.

# Joshua Fit The Battle

# UKULELE

— by Bonnie Butchart Smith

This section is provided to help student teachers develop skills on the ukulele to support your teaching of music. The goals are:

1. To begin to learn to read music:
    - in order to determine the starting pitch of a song for oneself and one's students
    - in order to use the ukulele to assist with the beginning stages of melodic ear training

2. to learn to strum chords rhythmically on the ukulele:
    - in order to accompany yourself and your class while singing
    - in order to use the ukulele to assist with harmonic ear training in its early stages

## The Open Strings

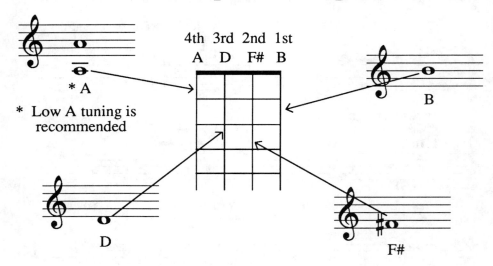

## OPEN STRING MELODIES

# THE LEFT HAND

A DIAGRAM of a Ukulele looks like this:

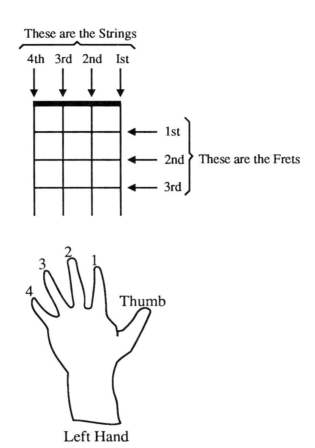

# THE FRETBOARD

The letters on these fretboards symbolize the names of the pitches which they represent. The top of the diagram corresponds to the top of the fretboard. The pitches in between the lettered pitches can be sharps or flats. For instance the pitch that is notated by the ☆ can be called A# or B♭.

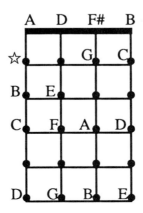

**Preliminary exercises on the fretboard for finger dexterity and placement:**

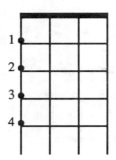

- On the fourth string (a) place the first finger on the first fret and pick that note four times (B♭).
- Add another finger so that you have two fingers side by side and pick the resulting note (B) four times.
- Add another finger — three fingers down — the note C. Pick C four times.
- Add the baby finger — all fingers down — the note C#. Pick C# four times.
- Smoothly, without stopping see if you can pick the notes four times each in reverse order, starting with all of the fingers down, removing one finger at a time, picking each note four times and ending with an open A string.
- Repeat this exercise on each of the other strings. Work to play the entire exercise smoothly without a break.

## THREE NOTE EXERCISES ON THE F# AND B STRINGS

# BEGINNING TO WORK WITH THE UKULELE
# KEY OF D MAJOR

Begin working with the ukulele using familiar two chord songs that one can try to figure out by ear.

# This Old Man

1. First you need to be certain that you can sing the tune in the key of D. Using knowledge from the reading exercises at the top of the page, try to pick the melody for "This Old Man." Do this several times singing along with it.

2. Sing the entire song beginning on the notes that you picked in the first step. Do this unaccompanied.

3. Learn to strum the D chord and the $A^7$ chord. Strum each chord by itself for a long time concentrating on how you are holding the ukulele. You are strumming where the neck and the body of the instrument meet. When you strum down towards the floor you are strumming with the nail of the index finger of the right hand. The thumb of your left hand is behind the second fret of the ukulele and is not visible from the front.

   When a chord is strummed, several notes are played at the same time. The hand moves both down across the strings and then back up again.

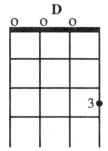  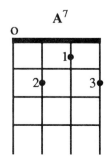

4. Making certain to start in the right key, sing the song without accompaniment once again.

5. The next step is to select the correct starting pitch for the song. Begin strumming on the D chord.

When musicians strum the D chord, the note that they hear with the inner hearing is the tonal center (root of the chord) — in this case the note "D." Many songs do not start on this note — the song "This Old Man" is just one example. Essentially pitches wander both above and below this tonal center and often at the end of the song resolve back to it.

When a song does not start on the tonal center (root note), musical tension that demands resolution is immediately created. For this reason, an inexperienced musician should begin by strumming the D chord; hum, sing and hear the note D then pick the starting pitch of the song (the note A for "This Old Man") and recognize that, in this case, it is higher than the root note of the chord.

It is important to realize that the various notes we sing in a simple folk song can usually be found as one the members of the chord we are currently strumming. The reason we change chords is that the voice has moved to a note no longer found within the old chord. To put it another way, when we sing a note not found in the chord it is generally considered dissonant. The reason there are three chords used to accompany most songs is that all of the notes of the scale are harmonized by one or another of the three chords.

For example, the D scale can be harmonized with the chords built on the I chord, the IV chord and the $V^7$ chord— that is the chords with the roots on the first, fourth and fifth notes of the scale — the D chord, the G chord and the $A^7$ chord.

### D SCALE WITH HARMONIZATIONS

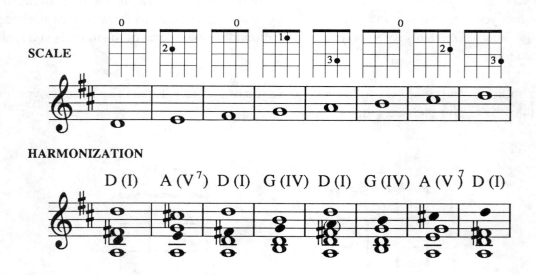

Now back to "This Old Man." Again strum the D chord; sing the "D" note; now pick the "A" and the "F#" notes of the opening measure.

-266-

Strum four D chords; four A⁷ chords; four D chords and begin to sing "This Old Man" while strumming the D chord the fifth time. Keep playing the D chord and singing the melody until your ear tells you that it no longer fits; at this point switch to the A⁷ chord and remain on that until it is no longer appropriate; at this point switch back to the D chord.

6. Continue in like manner until the entire song is harmonized.

7. Once you are comfortable singing and strumming "This Old Man" in the key of D, try the same process for "Shortnin' Bread." (The first note of the melody is your open string "D".)

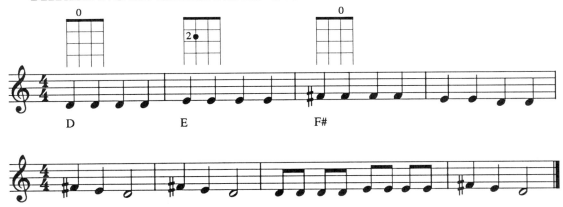

"Aunt Rhody" is another two chord song in the key of D. You can find the new picking notes that you need from the exercise above.

# FOUR NOTE EXERCISE ON THE B STRING

## TWO CHORD SONGS IN THE KEY OF G MAJOR

Practice strumming the new chord G.

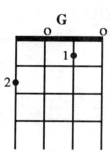

Practice switching back from the G chord to the $D^7$ chord and back again.

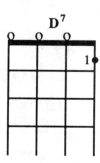

Follow the same procedure you used for "This Old Man" to figure out the chord changes for the following songs. You will use the information from the above reading exercises to get your starting pitches for singing and when you begin strumming you will begin on the G chord.

# Skip To My Lou

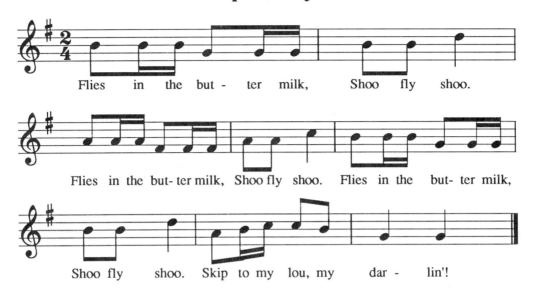

# Polly Wolly Doodle

# This Old Man

Now you have five songs that you can sing with your students. You can use these same songs to play melodic ear training mystery games with the children in two ways:

1. Pick a section of one of the songs and ask the children to tell you the name of the song.

2. Have a student select one of these songs for the class to sing. You pick the opening phrase of that song or a different song and ask the children if you got it right.

You may also begin working with children on harmonic ear training using your two chord songs. Tell children that you need THEIR help to know when to change chords; that you are going to stay on one chord and will only change when they tell you it's time to change by standing up. They signal the next chord change by sitting down, etc.

> **CAUTION:** This activity is only appropriate if both the ukulele and the teacher's singing are securely in tune. This activity should move very quickly and be done only once with one song in a single class period. This skill is not mastered in one class but in repetition over time.

## EXPANDING CHORDAL KNOWLEDGE

If you play three chords (the I, IV and $V^7$) in several keys on the ukulele, you will be able to accompany children for singing most campfire songs and most of the songs found in music series in the public schools.

Begin learning to strum several three chord songs in the key of D; then add songs in the key of A; follow this with the key of G; and finally in the key of C.

The key signatures and the tablature for the I, IV and $V^7$ chords in each of these keys are presented on the next page.

### I  IV  V⁷

**Chords in the Key of D**

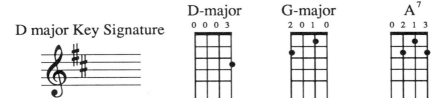

**Chords in the Key of A**

**Chords in the Key of G**

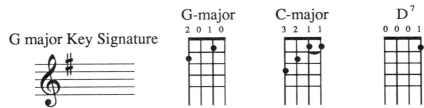

When you learn a PARTICULAR three chord song by ear, please keep the following information in mind:

1. Do I know the melody of the song I am planning to sing and strum?

2. In what key is the melody written?  Do I know how to strum the I, IV and V⁷ chords in that key?

3. Am I able to pick the starting pitches of the melody in the appropriate key according to the key signature?  (I want to be singing and strumming in the same key.)

At this point you may begin to learn to sing and strum the three chord song that you have selected. Please remember to start on the (I) chord, and be aware that when it is time to change chords, you will have two choices. You may need to experiment at each of the changes to determine which of the available chords is the better choice.

## THREE CHORD SONGS IN THE KEY OF D

## Crawdad Song

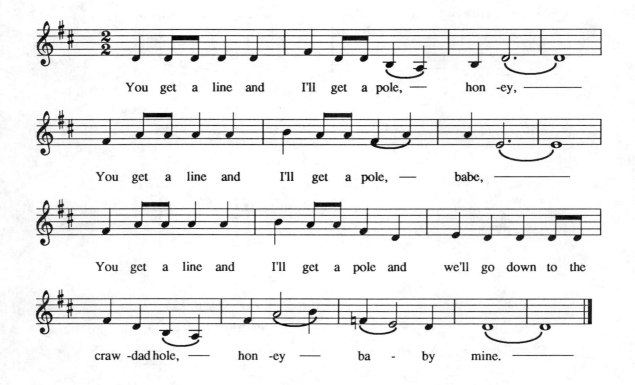

## Old Smokey

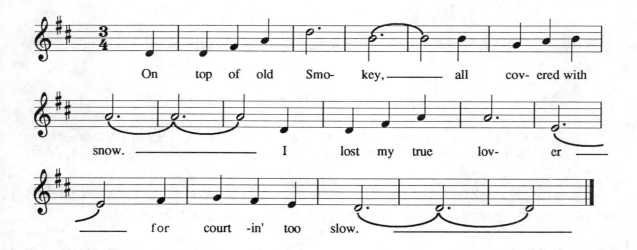

# THREE CHORD SONGS IN THE KEY OF A

NOTE: To pick the melody note C# you use your second finger on the first or "B" string.

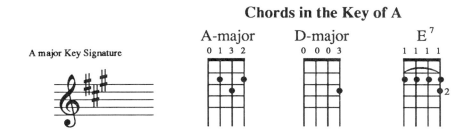

# Five Hundred Miles

# This Train

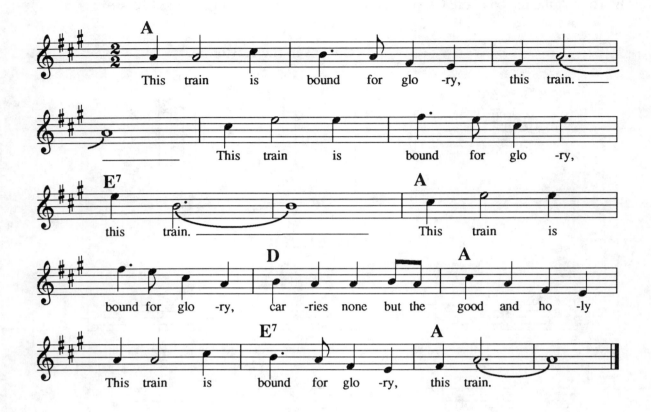

## USING YOUR UKULELE TO ASSIST IN ADDITIONAL EAR TRAINING WORK WITH YOUR CLASS

**Major and Minor Tonalities**

Sing a pair of two chord songs ("This Old Man" and "Drunken Sailor" for example). Ask students to identify whether or not they are both major, both minor, or whether there is one of each and which is which.
Later students will be able to identify the tonality of single songs and after that for single chords strummed by the teacher.
   (NOTE: Refer to page 277 for minor chords).

**Tonic and Non-Tonic** (NOTE: For this exercise you need to be able to pick the final two measures of any of the songs we have done in major keys — "This Old Man" or "Crawdad" for example. Use only one song per day for this exercise.)

Strum the $A^7$ and D chords on the ukulele several times. Then have students sing the last two measures of the song "This Old Man" as you strum the appropriate chords (*This old man came rolling home*).

Guide students to discover that the tonic (home note/resting note) occurs only in the last measure. Pick the last two measures of This Old Man several times – sometimes the last note incorrectly or the last two or three notes incorrectly. Have students stand on the phrase endings that do not end on the tonic and sit on the phrase endings that do end on the tonic (the song comes to a rest so students may rest by sitting).

Encourage students to help you accompany the class on the autoharp or bells reading chord names from songs on sheets or in their music books. Children will hear your changes on the ukulele and that will help them with their own changes.

## THREE CHORD SONGS IN THE KEY OF G

The three chords in the key of G are: G, C and $D^7$.

## Donkey Riding

# Jingle Bells

## THREE CHORD SONGS IN THE KEY OF C

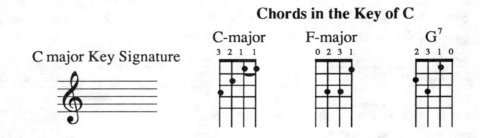

## Michael, Row the Boat Ashore

# For He's A Jolly Good Fellow

## Minor Chords That You may Need!

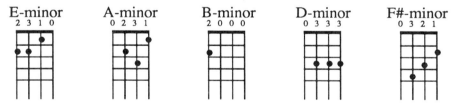

# Canoe Song

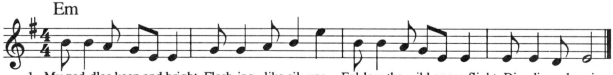

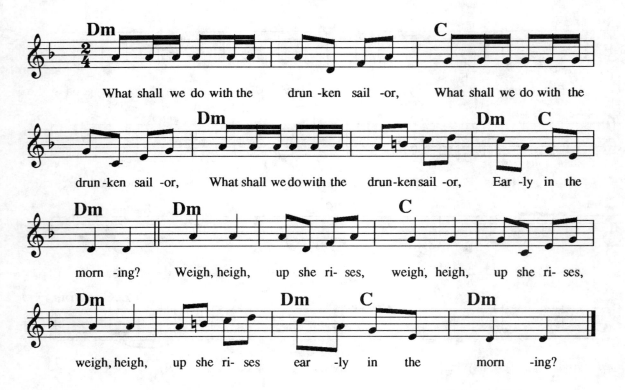

## PERFORMING AT THE SCHOOL ASSEMBLY:

Classroom songs which you have learned to sing with ukulele accompaniment are easily adaptable to performance situations by adding classroom percussion instruments or novelty breaks. Three examples in the key of D are included here.

# Mama Don't 'Low

Ma-ma don't 'low no jazz-y sing-in' 'round here,

Ma-ma don't 'low no jazz-y sing-in' 'round here,

I don't care what ma-ma don't 'low, gon-na

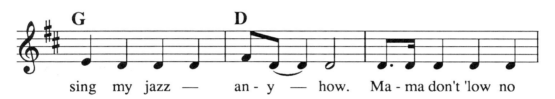
sing my jazz — an-y — how. Ma-ma don't 'low no

jazz-y sing-in' 'round here.

2nd Verse. Mama don't 'low no bell playin' 'round here.
3rd Verse. Mama don't 'low no noise makin' 'round here.

## Novelty Breaks

# Summer Song

**Lyrics by Lorna McPhee**  **Music by J. Chalmers Doane**

Used by permission

2. Oh, when you see the shining flash of a cardinal,
   Let your spirit fly with it;
   And all the summer long
   You'll have a summer song
   As a way to welcome each day.

Arrangement: Add Latin percussion instruments to provide a rhythmic accompaniment.

As an introduction, build up the Latin layer one instrument at a time beginning with the maracas for two measures, add claves for two measures, add triangle for two measures (or cowbell), and strumming for two measures, and only then begin to sing along.

End the piece with a "cha–cha–cha" on the final chord with all of the Latin instruments.

# New York Strum

**Words by Lorna McPhee**  **Music by J. Chalmers Doane**

3. Come on now it's easy and it's fun
   You feel a whole lot better when you're done
   It's something neat that anyone of you
   Can learn if you're really tryin' to
   There you go – you've got the New York strum.

Used by permission

## WHERE TO GO FROM HERE

Ask your teacher to explain the concept of transposition and how you can adapt songs you find in the keys of B flat, E flat and F so that you might use them with your ukulele to accompany class singing.

If you wish to expand your ukulele skills so that you are able to teach yourself new songs by picking the notated melodies in any key, and, strum comfortably in all keys to accompany classroom singing, you should take either an additional university course or provincial workshops available in Doane ukulele. This would also be necessary if you wish to teach ukulele to intermediate grade students as your classroom music program (see the video *Fleabag Blues: An Introduction to Doane Ukulele* ).

In the meantime you have developed musical skills on the ukulele which will be very useful to you in school classrooms.

# Piano

This section is provided to help you develop skills on the piano keyboard to support your teaching of music. As a general principal the music should be sung and played first following the modeling of the teacher, then after some fluency is attained, the music scores as presented here can be followed. Music reading skills are learned in a gradual, developmental way. You should be exposed to a complete musical score soon after learning to perform it and should not be concerned if you do not at first understand every written symbol on the page. For example, the key signature and time signature of Row, Row, Row Your Boat will be taught later. In the beginning stages, your eyes should follow the words and the placement of the note D in both clefs.

Many students are most familiar with the treble clef (or G clef) through playing recorder and other classroom instruments. One advantage in developing piano skills is that a full range of pitches is learned, including the bass clef (also called the F clef). This clef ( 𝄢 ) encompasses the pitch range normally associated with men's voices and the pianist's left hand. It is found on the keyboard to the left of middle-C.

The clef sign itself circles around the line which is designated F just below middle-C. The note D (first bass note in "Row, Row Your Boat" on the next page) is another easy one to remember because it is on the middle line and D is the middle of the word mi**dd**le.

Names of the lines and spaces in the bass clef should be learned when the note they represent is introduced and used in a song (eg. p. 285, "Clap, Clap #3" for the notes A and F#). For reference purposes the names of the F clef lines and spaces are as follows:

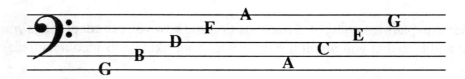

Sing the round in D, then play these accompaniments on the beats, with left hand and right hand alternating. Hands should be in the following positions. (Remember that the thumb is called finger number 1.)

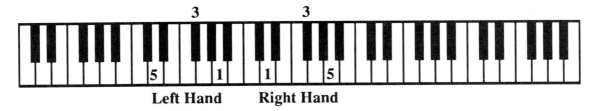

# Row, Row Row Your Boat #1

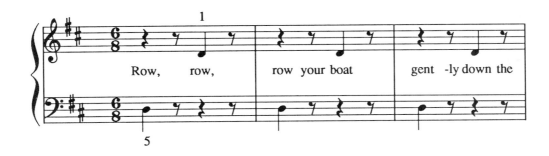

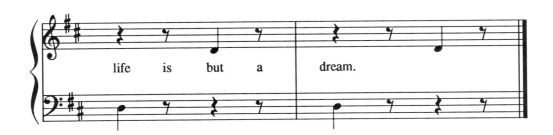

# Row, Row, Row Your Boat #2

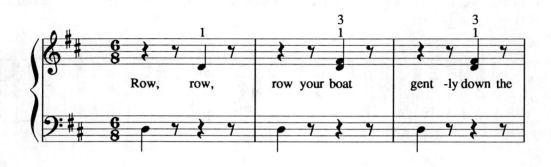

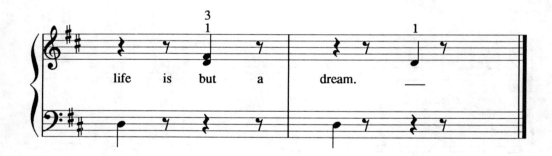

## Clap, Clap #1

For illustrating pulse and pattern (beat and rhythm pattern) as well as developing coordination of the two hands

## Clap, Clap #2

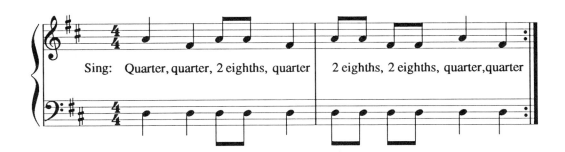

## Clap, Clap #3

## Clap, Clap #4

# More Clap, Clap Accompaniments

It is even easier to play on the black keys (sharps and flats) because they are raised above the white keys and are grouped in 2s and 3s. Try the following with these hand positions:

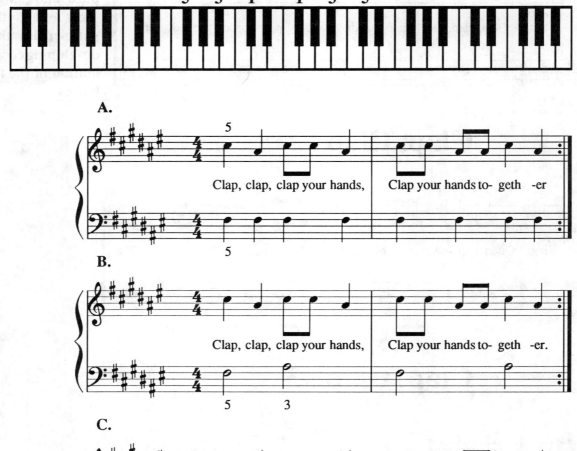

**Now slide every finger down to the nearest key on the left and play again in the key of F.**

# Clap, Clap Variations

**Try transposing variations E through H to the key of F#; then to the key of F.**

-287-

The pentatonic (5 note) scale is convenient for the piano because its five tones can correspond to the five black notes of the keyboard. Play the following on black notes (key of F#), and in the key of F (moving every finger down to the nearest white key).

## Shortnin' Bread #1

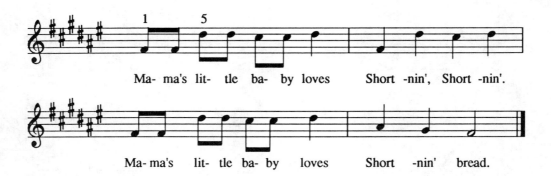

## Shortnin' Bread #2

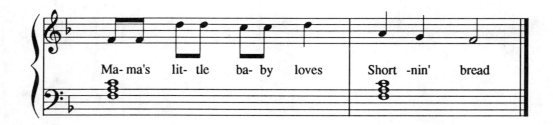

Now transpose number 2 up to the key of F# (every finger up to the right).

## Left Hand Variations

The following two pages will reinforce the positions of the D chord on the keyboard and the printed page, as well as developing some independence and coordination between the left and right hands.

## Mouse, Mousie

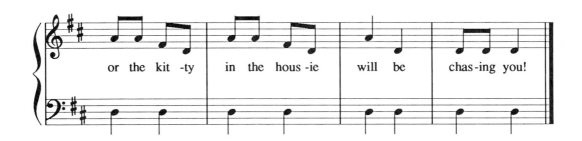

## Old Woman

# Whistle Daughter

The added 2nd and 4th fingers provide a smoother melodic line, filling in the melodic skips between 1st, 3rd and 5th fingers. These notes, usually on weak beats, do not affect the underlying harmony (chord) and are called **passing tones.**

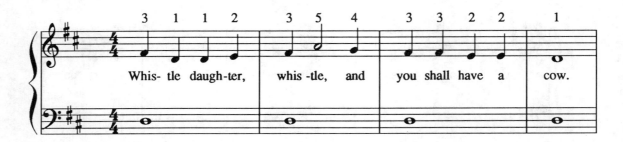

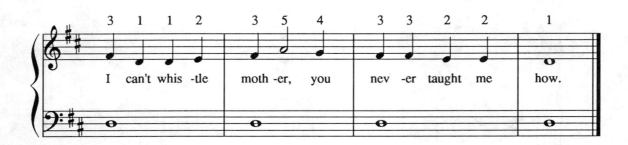

## Whistle Daughter Accompaniment

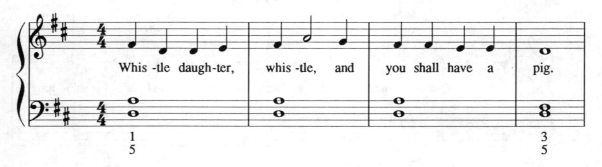

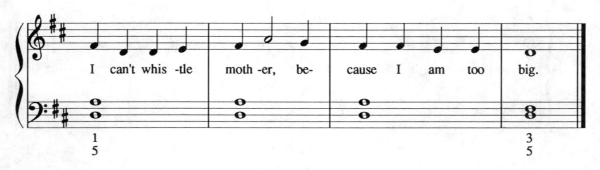

# He's Got the Whole World in His Hands

The hand position for the new chord (V$^7$) in the key of D major is the following:

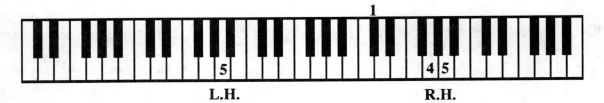

If the V$^7$ chord is played in the left hand, the fingering is **5-2-1**.

# He's Got the Whole World in His Hands
## Accompaniment Variations

# Alouette

Hand positions for the I and $V_7$ chords in the key of G are:

## I Chord

## $V_7$ Chord

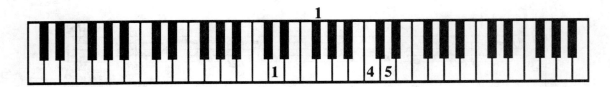

# This Old Man

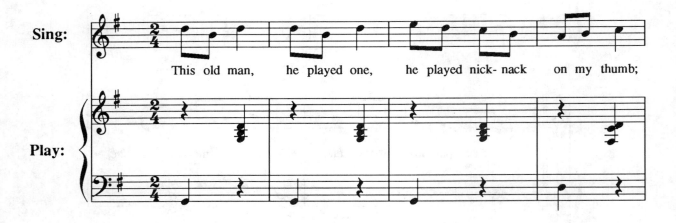

This old man, he played one, he played nick-nack on my thumb;

nick-nack pad-dy whack, give a dog a bone, this old man came rol-ling home.

# Tom Dooley

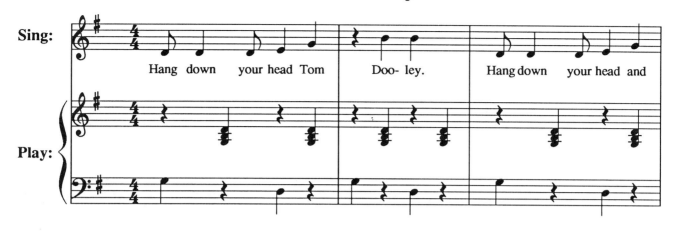
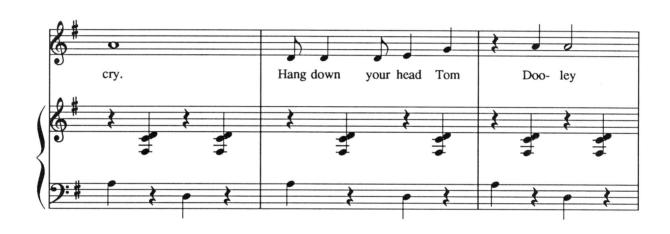
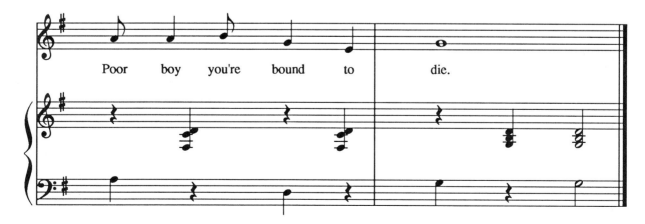

Use the same accompaniment pattern for "Skip to My Lou" and "Polly Wolly Doodle" (page 269).

# Streets of Laredo

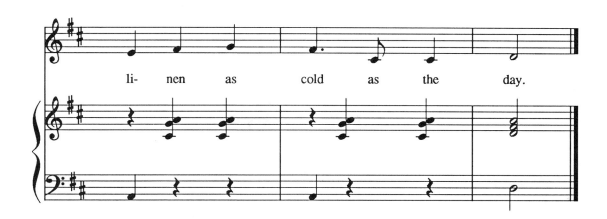

2. "I see by your outfit that you are a cowboy."
   These words he did say as I boldly walked by.
   "Come sit down beside me, and hear my sad story,
   I'm shot in the breast, and I know I must die."

3. "Get six jolly cowboys to carry my coffin,
   Get six purty maidens to sing me a song;
   Take me to the valley, and lay the sod o'er me,
   For I'm a young cowboy and know I've done wrong."

4. "O, beat the drum slowly and play the fife lowly,
   And play the dead march as you bear me along;
   Put bunches of roses all over my coffin,
   Put roses to deaden the sods as they fall."

**Use the same accompaniment pattern for "Where, Oh Where Has My Little Dog Gone?" (page 260).**

# Down She Sat #1

# Down She Sat #2

2nd verse:  Bread they baked an oven full,
Aye, aye oven full;
Down she sat and ate it all,
Aye, aye ate it all.

3rd verse:  She could never get her fill,
Aye, aye get her fill;
There she sits, she's eating still,
Aye, aye eating still.

# Hop Old Squirrel

# Run Old Squirrel

The new chord (IV) hand position in the key of D is as follows:

# Kookaburra

Australian Round

Sing: Koo-ka-bur-ra sits in the old gum tree

mer-ry, mer-ry king of the bush is he. Laugh koo-ka-bur-ra,

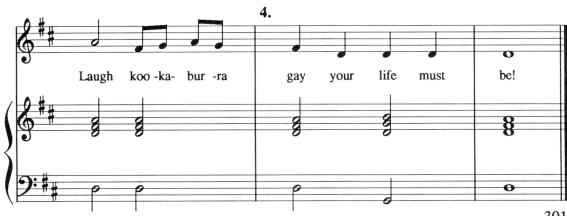

Laugh koo-ka-bur-ra gay your life must be!

-301-

# Kookaburra Accompaniment Variations

A.

B.

C.

# Five Hundred Miles Accompaniment

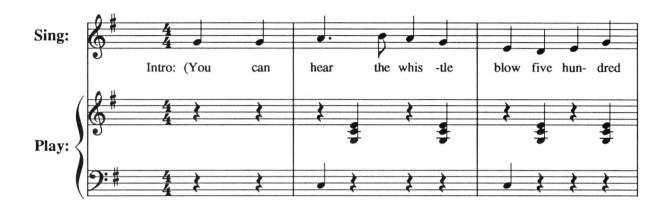
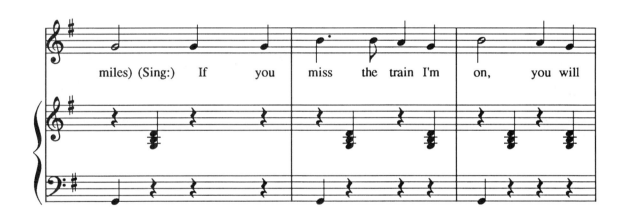
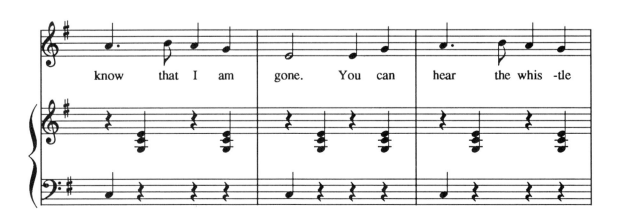

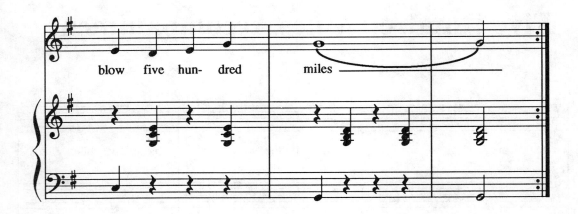

The IV chord hand position in the key of G is as follows:

# Little Brown Jug

-305-

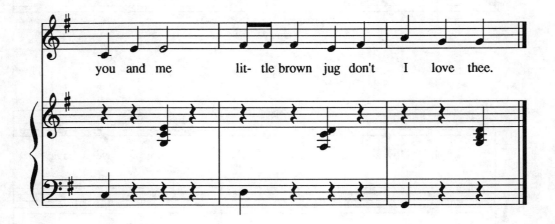

**Use the same accompaniment pattern for "The Sloop John B." (page 157).**

# Old Smokey

When the chords are played down an octave from previous pieces the sound is more mellow.

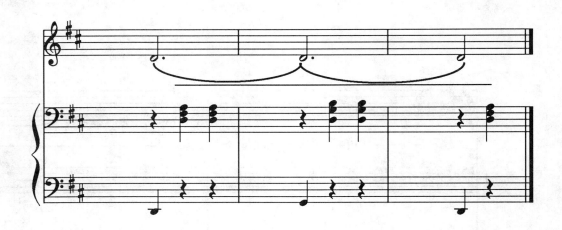

2nd verse: For courtin's a pleasure
And parting is grief
But a false-hearted lover
Is worse than a thief.

3rd verse: For a thief, he will rob you,
And take what you have
But a false-hearted lover
Will send you to your grave.

# Can't You Dance the Polka?

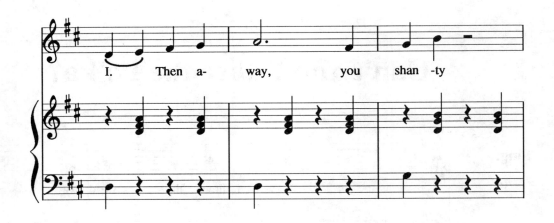

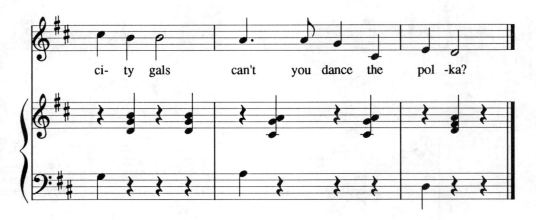

2: To Tiffany's I took her
   I did not mind expense.
   I bought her golden earrings
   They cost me fifty cents.
   Then away, etc.

**Use the same accompaniment pattern for "Tzena" (page 168).**

This piece has been played by rote by generations of "non-pianists." Play it first, then follow the score to associate the notation with the sounds indicated. Note the different position of the chords.

## I Love Coffee

-311-

# Clementine Accompaniment

The following melodies ("500 Miles," "Draw a Bucket of Water," "Sally Go 'Round the Sun" and "Ol' Texas") are pentatonic and therefore can be played entirely on the black keys.

# Five Hundred Miles

# Draw a Bucket of Water

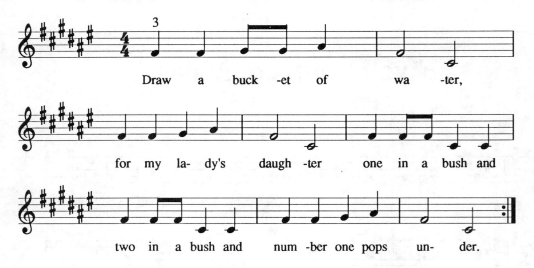

# Sally Go 'Round the Sun

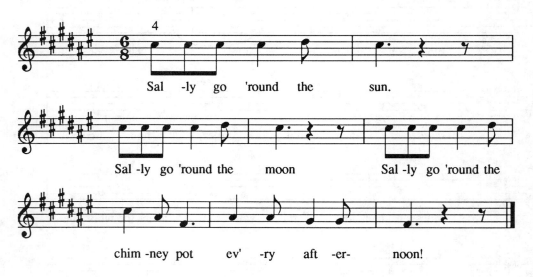

# Ol' Texas

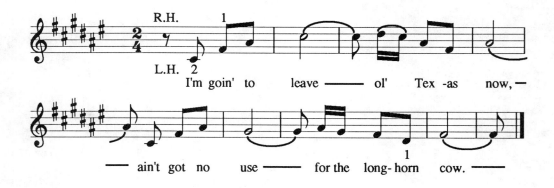

This pentatonic tune is played on white keys. In a piano class, some students may play the ostinati while others play the whole melody. In the general classroom, the melody may be sung while class members play and/or sing the ostinati either singly or in combination.

## Great Big House

## Great Big House: Ostinati

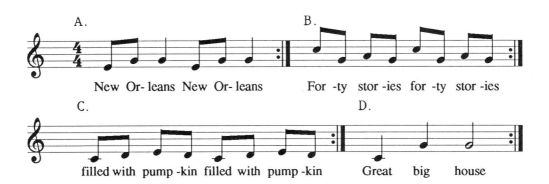

This piece can be accompanied by the three basic chords — I, IV, $V^7$. Work out a chordal accompaniment using the "ear" procedures used in "Old Smokey" (page 144). The melody again is pentatonic.

# Auld Lang Syne

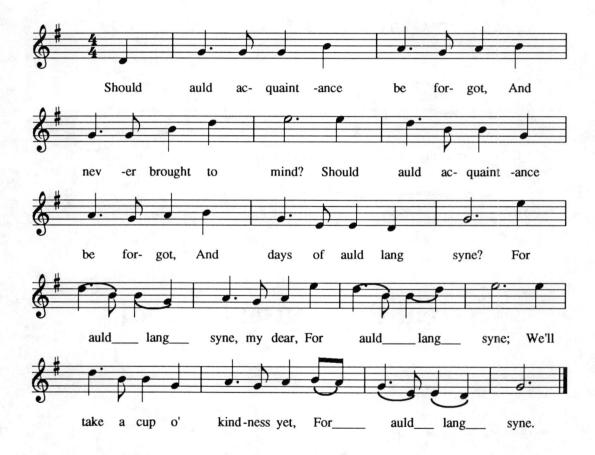

# UNDERSTANDING MUSIC

# The Materials of Music

This section presents a detailed analysis of **Music Concepts**—the "stuff" from which music is built. It is important to understand that concepts are organized in a hierarchy—from the simple to the more complex, but that no grade or age levels are indicated as being particularly appropriate to the introduction or development of certain concepts, as this bears very much upon the previous experience and capabilities of individual students. Teachers must be aware, however, of the fact that it is necessary for students to have a firm grasp of the more elementary concepts before they can be expected to understand and use the more complex. In addition, the following organization is not meant to imply that rhythmic elements should be considered first, followed by melodic elements, and so on. The understanding of musical concepts must take the form of a cyclical pattern which is best illustrated in the publications of the Manhattanville Music Curriculum Project (MMCP) one "cycle" of which is illustrated on the page following. As this model suggests, each conceptual area is considered in turn with each cycle building upon previous learnings.

Composers use the "stuff" of music in expressive ways which are encountered by the listener. The concepts discussed in "The Materials of Music" do not constitute the experience of music but, rather, are generalizations which allow people to discuss and enrich their musical perception.

The purpose for organizing musical learnings in this manner is not to fragment the experience of music by breaking it up into small chunks which can be labelled, but rather to provide a framework within which those elements which comprise the vocabulary of music can be identified and related to each other. It is therefore important to examine the expressive meaning of the particular application of a concept in a selection. For example, it is not enough to be able to identify the tempo of a piece as *slow*; it is necessary to consider **why** the slow tempo is appropriate and to make this consideration a musical, not a referential one. It is a good idea for the teacher and the students to ask such questions as: "Would the melodic contour be as effective at a faster tempo?" and "Would the feeling of tension and release be as strong at a faster or slower tempo?"

The following pages will present examples of materials drawn, wherever possible, from this manual and from various classroom music series, each illustrating a particular musical concept. Examples have been taken from various grade levels, the more complex concepts obviously being more appropriate to higher grades. The classified index found in the Appendix A will direct you to other appropriate materials to introduce or reinforce each concept, both from this volume and from popular music series textbooks. As you examine each example, attempt to identify other musical elements which could be reinforced using the same selection.

# MANHATTANVILLE MUSIC CURRICULUM PROJECT (MMCP)

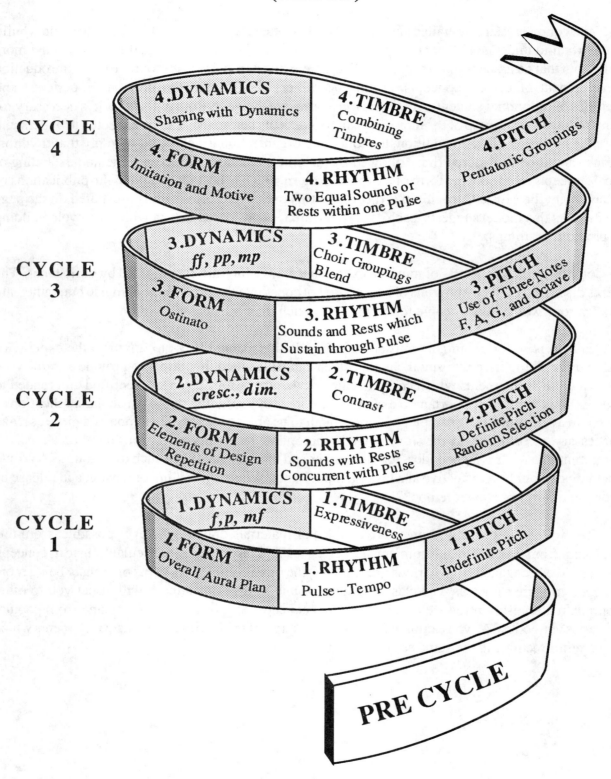

Ronald B. Thomas. *MMCP Final Report*, Part I, Abstract (Washington: United States Office of Education, ED 045 865, August, 1970). pp. 39-49.

# 1.0 CONCEPTS OF RHYTHM

- Rhythm in music must be experienced and felt.
- Physical movement is one of the most direct tools for teaching rhythm.
- The use of rhythm instruments to aid in teaching rhythm is encouraged.

### 1.1 Steady Beat or Pulse

1.1.1 Definition: Steady beat or pulse is the underlying beat of a piece of music which goes on and on underneath the singing or playing which are superimposed upon it. The steady beat may be fast or slow, and may get faster or slower (see Section 2.1, page 329) but it remains a regular pulse. The steady beat is sometimes called the **tactus**; it is one of the major elements which is outlined when you conduct.

1.1.2 Concept Statement: **Music may have a steady beat.**

1.1.3 The following illustration from "Hey, Hey, Look at Me" (page 74) shows the relations between steady beat (often indicated by the "heartbeat" symbol ♥ ) and the melodic rhythm in the melody of the first phrase:

### 1.2 Accent

1.2.1 Definition: Accented beats are "heavier" or stressed beats. They are normally indicated by such signs as > or ^. Accented beats recurring in regular patterns reveal **meter** (see Section 1.3, below).

1.2.2 Concept Statements: **Music may have accents (> or ^).**
**Music may have regular accents.**

1.2.3 Observe how accents may be used to add extra emphasis to certain words in "Donkey Riding" (page 106).

### 1.3 Meter

1.3.1 Definition: Regular accents (see Section 1.2, above) normally produce **meter**. Meter is the measuring of beats into groups of 2, 3, 4, 6, and so on. Music where accents group in sets of two (i.e. strong-weak, strong-weak) is said to

-321-

"swing in twos" producing **duple meter**. Music where accents group in sets of three (i.e. strong-weak-weak, strong-weak-weak) is said to "swing in threes" producing **triple meter**. In music notation, meter is identified through the use of a **meter signature** or **time signature**, as it is often called. Thus duple meter may be indicated by any of the following meter signatures:

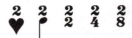

where the top digit represents the number of beats per measure, and the bottom digit (or icon) represents the beat note (the type of note which receives one beat).

**Triple meter** may be indicated by:

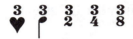

**Quadruple meter** (swinging in fours, strong-weak-medium-weak) may be indicated by:

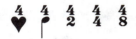

**NOTE:** See also Sections 1.6 (compound meter); 1.8 (irregular meters) and 1.9 (shifting meters) below.

1.3.2 Barlines "|" divide music into **measures** (sometimes called **bars**) according to the meter signature, with the first (strongest) beat of the meter appearing at the beginning of the measure. In duple meter there will be 2 beats in each measure, triple meter will contain 3, and quadruple meter will contain 4 beats.

1.3.3 Quadruple meter ($\frac{4}{4}$) is sometimes indicated by the symbol **C** (meaning "common time"), and duple meter ($\frac{2}{2}$) is sometimes indicated by the symbol ₵ (meaning "cut time" or *alla breve*).

1.3.4 Concept statements: **Music may have meter.**
**Beats may be grouped in sets.**

1.3.5 The following examples show duple, triple and quadruple meter. Notice how the composition of measures (the number of beats) differs in each example, according to the meter signature.

1.3.5.1 "Are You Sleeping" (page 97):

1.3.5.2 "Old Smokey" (page 144)

1.3.5.3 "Dona Dona" (*Music Builders VI*)

1.3.5.4 "Great Big House" (page 121)

1.3.5.5 "If You're Happy" (page 78)

## 1.4 Duration

1.4.1 Definition: Duration deals with long and short sounds in melodic or rhythmic patterns. If you tap a steady beat while singing a song, you will find that some words (sounds) are held for one beat, while others are held for two beats, or three beats, and that sometimes you sing two or more notes while tapping one beat. Periods of silence (called **rests**) also form significant aspects of duration. Each durational value has a specific symbol and this symbol relates mathematically to the values indicated in the lower symbol of the meter signature (indicating the type of note symbol which receives one beat).

In simple meter signatures with **4** as the lower numeral, the durational values are as follows:

one beat    = ♩ = quarter note
two beats   = ♪ = half note
three beats = ♩. = dotted half note*
four beats  = o = whole note

*The dot increases the value of the note symbol by one-half.

If the lower numeral of the meter signature is **8**, then the durational values of the symbols would be as follows:

one beat    = ♪ = eighth note
two beats   = ♩ = quarter note
three beats = ♩. = dotted quarter note
four beats  = ♪ = half note

If the lower numeral of the meter signature is **2**, then the durational values of the symbols would be as follows:

one beat    = ♩ = half note
two beats   = o = whole note
three beats = o· = dotted whole note
four beats  = ⊨ = double whole note (breve)

Older children should also be aware that, in addition to multiples of the beat, there may also be divisions of the beat. With the quarter note as the beat note (lower numeral **4**) these divisions would appear as:

one-half beat    = ♪ = eighth note
one-quarter beat = ♬ = sixteenth note

1.4.2 All of the above durations have corresponding symbols for periods of rest:

— ▬ 𝄽 𝄾 𝄿
Whole Half Quarter Eighth Sixteenth

## 1.5 Even and Uneven Patterns

1.5.1 Definition: The steady beat may be divided into **even** or **uneven** groups of notes. For example, if the quarter note ( ♩ ) is the beat note, it may be divided into two **even** eighth notes ( ♫ ) or a group of **uneven** dotted eighth and sixteenth notes ( ♩. ♪ ). Make sure that uneven groups are sung as:

ti-(ri-ti)-ri
tim - ri

(division by fours) and not as:

tri-(o)-la

(division by threes).

1.5.2 Concept Statements: **Music may have equal division of the beat.**
**Music may have unequal division of the beat.**
**Music may have equal and unequal division of the beat.**

1.5.3 The song "Kookaburra" (page 138) shows equal divisions of the beat:

1.5.4 The song "Loo-Lah" (page 140) shows unequal divisions of the beat.

## 1.6 Compound Meter

1.6.1 Definition: Meter signatures are organized or grouped into **simple meters** such as $\frac{2}{4}, \frac{3}{8}, \frac{4}{4}$, and so on (see section 1.3, above) and **compound meters** such as $\frac{6}{8}, \frac{9}{4}, \frac{12}{8}$, and so on. In simple meters the basic note value normally divides by twos:

$\quad \♩ = \♫ = \text{\textnormal{♬♬}}$

while in **compound meters** the beat note (which is always a dotted note) divides by threes and then by twos:

$\quad \♩. = \text{\textnormal{♫♫♫}} = \text{\textnormal{♬♬♬}}$

> There are two methods of "counting" in compound meters.
>
> (a) In fast tempos, the primary beat ( ♩. ) is used as in:
>
>
>
> (b) In slow tempos, the tertiary (3-pulse) beat is used as in:
>
> 6/8  ♪ ♪ ♪  ♪ ♪ ♪
>      1 2 3  4 5 6

1.6.2 The song "Eency Weency Spider" (page 70) is written in a compound meter. Try to determine if the song would be counted using the dotted note as the beat note (i.e. 1-2), or using the tertiary division of the primary beat as the beat note (i.e. 1-2-3-4-5-6).

Een - cy ween - cy    spi - der went    up    the   wa - ter    spout

Notice that compound meters give a lilting or "skipping" feel to a piece of music. Skipping games are almost always in compound meters.

## 1.7 Syncopation

1.7.1 Definition: Briefly described, syncopation in music occurs when:
(a) a strong beat is absent where it is normally expected;
(b) a strong beat is present where it is not normally expected; or
(c) a combination of the two (i.e. an accented weak beat followed by an unaccented strong beat).

Below are examples of the three types. Notice that type (c) often makes use of a **tie** ( ⌣ ).

**1.7.2 Concept Statement: Music may have syncopations as rhythmic devices.**

1.7.3 The song "Who Built the Ark" (page 173) uses the syncopation as a rhythmic device:

## 1.8 Irregular Meters

1.8.1 Definition: Irregular meters normally consist of two or more alternating simple meters. The two most common irregular meters consist of 5 and 7 beats per measure. 5-beat meters consist of combinations of duple and triple meters while 7-beat meters consist of combinations of duple and triple or triple and quadruple meters, as the following examples suggest:

2.8.2 Irregular meters are not often found in elementary music materials, but isolated examples can be found.

(a) "The Tambourine," a Spanish folk song.

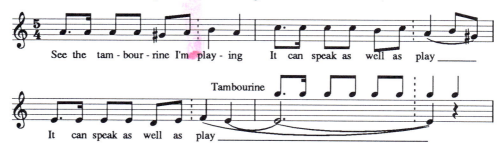

(b) "Man Must be Free," music by David L. Plank, words by Carroll Rinehart.

Free, free as birds in the sky, you and I, like leaves soft-ly flut-ter-ing by.

### 1.9 Shifting Meters

1.9.1 Definition: Shifting meter is much related to the irregular meters above, in that it consists of a change in the metrical pattern from time to time, but not with the regularity of irregular metrical patterns. You will notice several changes of meter signature within the song (although sometimes all signatures are grouped together at the beginning of the song, and you must "sort them out" as you go along). When meter shifts within a piece of music it can add interesting contrasts and expressiveness. The meter changes, however, should be done smoothly and with feeling.

1.9.2 Songs with shifting meters are seldom found in elementary music materials, but the song "Shenandoah" from *The Spectrum of Music* for grade 6 is a typical example:

Oh, Shen-an-doah, I long to see you, And hear your roll-ing.....

### 1.10 Polyrhythm

1.10.1 Definition: The simultaneous use of different or contrasting rhythms within a piece of music creates polyrhythmic structures. A good example of polyrhythm occurs when you have one group of students clap or tap in quadruple meter while another group claps or taps in triple meter, as the following example suggests:

1.10.2 Polyrhythmic structures are created when you sing Partner Songs which are in two different meters. The following example from *Search for a New Sound* (Grade 8) is a typical example:

### 1.12 Unmetrical Rhythm

1.12.1 Definition: Songs without a meter which divides them neatly into measures of 2, 3, 4, 5 or 6 beats are rare today, but there was a time (principally between 600 and 1000 A.D.) when most music was unmetered. Until as recently as 1963 this type of music, called **plainchant** was still in use in many modern churches. Plainchant is characterized by a free-flowing rhythm which often takes on the speech rhythm of the text for its rhythmical organization. Some works by modern composers, in a free-form style, use some of the rhythmic characteristics of this ancient style.

1.12.2 The following is an example of a plainchant which is still used during the Christmas season in many Christian churches:

## 2.0 CONCEPTS OF TEMPO

### 2.1 Fast and Slow Tempo

2.1.1 Definition: **Tempo** is the speed of the underlying beat of a piece of music. It may range from very fast to very slow, the relative speed often being indicated by such Italian terms as ***largo*** (very slow), ***moderato*** (at a moderate speed), ***allegro*** (fast), or ***presto*** (very fast), or by metronome indications such as:

**M. M.** ♩ = **60**

indicating that the pulse of the quarter note is one every second (or sixty quarter notes in one minute).

2.1.2 Concept Statement: **Tempo in music may be fast or slow.**

2.1.3 The mood or "feel" of a piece of music often dictates the tempo which best expresses the inner meanings of the melody and text. The song "Old Texas" (page 145) demands a tempo which is fairly slow:

while the character of the song "When the Saints" (page 169) demands a faster tempo in order to achieve the effect which the composer desires.

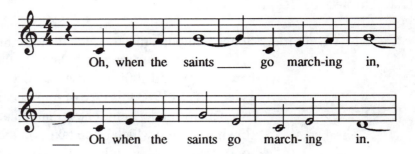

## 2.2 Getting Faster – Getting Slower

2.2.1 Definition: This concept deals with the increase or decrease in speed or tempo of a piece of music. Formal designations of this concept include the Italian terms *accelerando* (getting faster) and *ritardando, rallentando* or *ritenuto* (getting slower). These terms are often abbreviated as *accel., rall.* or *rit.* The change in tempo is a gradual one.

2.2.2 Concept Statements: **Tempo in music can get faster.**
**Tempo in music can get slower.**

1.2.3 The particular mood of a piece of music often dictates the use of "getting faster" or "getting slower." In the song "J'entends le moulin" (page 133), for example, if we imagine that the wind is blowing stronger as the mill wheel turns, we could use an *accelerando* to indicate this fact.

*Ritardandi* are more often used toward the end of a piece of music, in order to give a sense of finality or "ending" to the selection. A good example of this use would be at the end of "The Huron Carol" (page 129).

# 3.0 Concepts of Dynamics

3.1 Definition: Dynamics refers to the volume of sound which is employed on specific tones or groups of tones. It is a very important element in music and adds a significant dimension of expressiveness. In some songs the dynamic level for performance is not stated and must be determined by the musician from the basic mood or character of the music. Other pieces simply employ the terms **loud** or **soft** to indicate the approximate dynamic level. The traditional method of indicating the dynamic level, however, is through the use of such Italian terms and abbreviations as the following:

| Musical Sign | Italian Term | Meaning |
|---|---|---|
| *pp* | *pianissimo* | very soft |
| *p* | *piano* | soft |
| *mp* | *mezzo-piano* | moderately soft |
| *mf* | *mezzo-forte* | moderately loud |
| *f* | *forte* | loud |
| *ff* | *fortissimo* | very loud |

Infrequently found, but possible, dynamic markings include:

| *ppp* | very, very soft |
|---|---|
| *fff* | very very loud |

Another characteristic of dynamics in music involves either a gradual increase in volume from soft to loud, called a ***crescendo***, or a gradual decrease in volume from loud to soft, called a ***decrescendo*** or ***diminuendo***. The musical signs and terms for these characteristics are as follows:

| **cresc.** | <  | crescendo | gradually louder |
|---|---|---|---|
| **dim** |  > | diminuendo | gradually softer |
| **decresc.** |  | decrescendo | gradually softer |

Some special effects of musical dynamics include the ***sforzando* or *sforzato*** (abbreviated *sfz*) which involves a sudden strong accent on a note or chord (see Section 1.2, above), and the *forte-piano* (abbreviated *fp*) which involves beginning the tone at a *forte* (or loud) level and immediately softening it to a *piano* (or soft) level.

## 3.2 Loud and Soft

3.2.1 Concept statements: **Music may be loud.**
**Music may be soft.**

3.2.2 In the song "Who Built the Ark" (page 173) notice how the noted dynamics add to the musical interest:

Who built the Ark? No - ah, No - ah

3.2.3 The spooky character of the song "The Ghost of John" (page 116) can be increased by singing the song softly.

Have you seen the ghost of John? Long white bones and the

3.2.4 In the song "Hurling Down the Pine" (page 128) both the words and melody dictate that the dynamic level should be loud.

Come all you jol - ly fel - lows

## 3.3 Getting Louder, Getting Softer

3.3.1 Concept statements: **Music can get gradually louder.**
**Music can get gradually softer.**

3.3.2 Both the words and music at the end of "The Huron Carol" (page 129) indicate that a gentle rise and fall in the dynamic level would add to the expressiveness of this song.

In ex cel - sis glo - ri a."

3.3.3 A gentle increase in volume on the long tone *leave* in the song "Old Texas" (page 145) will give a sense of forward movement in this measure.

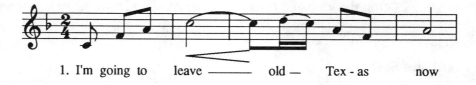
1. I'm going to leave old Tex - as now

3.3.4 A gentle decrease in the volume level at the end of a song gives a sense of finality. Try this technique for the song "Bluebird" (page 64).

Oh, John-ny aren't you tir - ed?

3.3.5 The shaping of musical phrases to give expression is a characteristic of getting louder and getting softer that is implicit but unstated in many songs which we sing.

# 4.0 Concepts of Melody

## 4.1 High and Low Pitches

4.1.1 Definition: The first melodic concept that children must perceive and understand is that pitches in a song may be described as higher or lower. Some tones in a song are **higher** while others are **lower** in pitch.

4.1.2 Concept Statements: **Melodies have higher and lower pitches.**

4.1.3 The song "Clap Your Hands" (page 69) consists of only two pitches (**C** and **A**). By drawing levels on the chalkboard and/or tracing the sounds in the air, the concept of high/low can be easily established.

Clap, clap, clap your hands, Clap your hands to - geth - er.

## 4.2 Melodic Contour

4.2.1 Up and Down

4.2.1.1 Definition: Students must be able to tell when melodic patterns go **up** (rise in pitch) or when they do **down** (fall in pitch) or when they **stay the same** (maintain the same pitch).

4.2.1.2 Concept Statement: **Melodies may move upward and downward.**

4.2.1.3 The song "Barnacle Bill" (page 58) illustrates the downward moving melodic line at the end of the song.

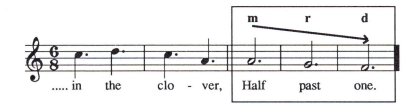

..... in the clo - ver, Half past one.

4.2.1.4 The song "Fish and Chips" (page 113) illustrates the upward moving melodic line at the beginning of the song.

4.2.1.5 The song "Barnacle Bill" (page 58) also illustrate pitches which remain the same.

4.2.2 Step–Leap–Repeated Pitches

4.2.2.1 Definition: This concept is related to **up and down**, above, but is more sophisticated in that students are expected to discriminate the distance of movement as being by **step** (i.e. half-step, whole-step) or by **leap** (i.e. intervals larger than a whole-step). Notes that move by step appear on consecutive lines or spaces in the staff:

while notes that move by leap appear with lines and/or spaces between the notes:

Musical distances are measured by units called **intervals** and each interval has a specific name. Thus the interval **C** to **E** is known as a **third** (you count **C** as 1, the intervening **D** as 2, and the **E** as 3 to arrive at this measure of musical distance). **C** to **F** is a **fourth**, **C** to **G** is a **fifth**, and so on.

The smallest unit of musical distance, the **step**, may be either a **half-step** (sometimes called a **semitone**) or a **whole-step** (sometimes called a **tone** or **whole tone**). For further information on the use of half-steps and whole-steps, see the sections on SCALES, below.

The distance of a **step** is also an interval, a **second** (regardless of whether it is a half-step or whole-step). Notes that appear on the same pitch may also be *theoretically* measured in the same manner, and are called a **unison** or **prime**. The following example shows musical distances called **intervals**:

The following table shows the solfège equivalents of the common intervals with **C** as **doh**.

| | | |
|---|---|---|
| Unison | doh-doh | c-c |
| Second | doh-re | c-d |
| Third | doh-mi | c-e |
| Fourth | doh-fa | c-f |
| Fifth | doh-sol | c-g |
| Sixth | doh-la | c-a |
| Seventh | doh-ti | c-b |
| Octave | doh-doh' | c-c' |

Intervals also have names which describe their **quality** (i.e. major, minor, perfect, diminished and augmented). Any good music theory textbook will describe these designations. The most common of these quality designations and their *solfège* equivalents are listed in the figure below, with C as doh.

major 3rd  minor 3rd  perfect 4th  perfect 5th  perfect 8ve
doh-mi     mi-sol     doh-fa       doh-sol      doh-doh'

4.2.2.2 Concept Statement: **Music may have steps, leaps and repeated pitches.**

4.2.2.3 The song "Barnyard Song" (page 59) contains examples of steps, leaps and repeated pitches:

fidd - dle - i - dee  /  his - sy, his - sy  /  quack, quack.

## 4.3 Chromatic Scale Patterns

NOTE: In the following sections, these symbols will be used to show the size of intervals between scale steps:

half step = ∨

whole step = ⊔

one and one-half steps = ⌴╱

4.3.1 Definition: The root of the word **chromatic** is *chroma*, meaning "colour." The chromatic scale is so called because it contains all the tone (or "colours") in the musical palette.

Scales are made up of arrangements of pitches, some of which are a half step apart while others are a whole step apart. The **chromatic scale** consists of half-steps (or semitones) only, with some pitches raised by a half step when going up (ascending) the scale through the use of a **sharp** (#) and lowered by a half step when coming down (descending) through the use of a **flat** (♭).

> A sharp # raises a note by a half tone.
> A flat ♭ lowers a note by a half tone.

A chromatic scale, ascending and descending, from **middle C** and the **C** one octave above looks like this:

Notice that no sharps or flats are used between **E-F** and between **B-C**. These intervals are known as **natural half-steps** or **natural semitones** and therefore do not need alterations through the use of sharps or flats. This is an important phenomenon to bear in mind when constructing scales of various types.

Few simple children's songs employ chromatic scale passages to any significant degree.

### 4.4 Whole-Tone Scale Patterns

4.4.1 Definition: As the name suggests, whole-tone scale patterns employ only whole steps in the construction of the scale.

Many pieces by the French Impressionist composers, such as Claude Debussy and Maurice Ravel are built upon whole-tone scale patterns. Listen especially to Debussy's Prelude for Piano entitled "Voiles" (Sails).

Almost no simple children's songs use the whole-tone scale.

### 4.5 Major Scale Patterns

4.5.1 Definition: Many simple children's songs are based upon an arrangement of whole- and half-steps known as the **major scale**. The first or **home** tone of the major scale gives the scale its name, thus the **C major scale** begins on **C**, the **D major scale** begins on **D**, and so on. In *solfège*, the home tone of the major scale is **doh**. Regardless of the home tone, all major scales employ the same pattern of whole- and half-steps:

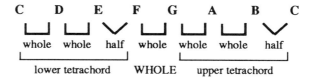

Some people remember the major scale pattern by observing that the scale is composed of two **tetrachords** (i.e., 4-tone sequences) with the pattern **whole-whole-half**, with the two tetrachords separated by a whole tone.

Using this pattern, the **C major scale** may be constructed as follows:

Remember that the intervals between **E-F** and **B-C** are natural half tones.

The **D major scale** requires that the notes **F** and **C** be raised through the use of a **sharp** (#) to maintain the major scale pattern.

Only one instance of each letter name is used in scales, therefore we use $F^\#$ (not $G^\flat$) and $C^\#$ (not $D^\flat$). Using this rule to construct the **F major scale** we find that we must employ a $B^\flat$ (not an $A^\#$) for the fourth note in order to maintain the major scale pattern.

Play or sing these scales until you have the major scale pattern firmly in your ear. Then when you construct other scales, your ear can help you tell if you have made an error.

4.5.2 Concept Statement: **Music may consist of major scale patterns.**

4.5.3 The Christmas Carol "Joy to the World" employs the descending major scale pattern as its opening phrase:

-337-

4.5.4 Examine the song "Elevator" (page 72). This song employs only the major scale pattern.

4.5.5 In most songs, the sharps or flats which are necessary to indicate the scale upon which the song is constructed are grouped at the beginning of the song in a **key signature**. A knowledge of these key signatures will help you easily determine the home tone or **doh**, and will also help you in determining chord patterns to harmonize songs.

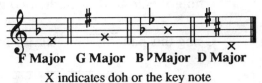

X indicates doh or the key note

## 4.6 Minor Scale Patterns

4.6.1 Definition: Like major scales, minor scales, of which there are three common types, employ specific patterns of tones and semitones in their construction.

(a) The **natural** or **Aeolian minor** employs the following pattern:

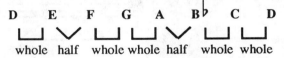

This minor scale is most commonly found in simple children's songs and folk songs.

(b) The **harmonic minor scale** (used principally in songs where the emphasis is on the chordal or harmonic structure) retains the half-step (leading tone) found in the major scale between notes 7 and 8 by raising the seventh tone by a half-step. This creates an interval which is very difficult to sing between steps 6 and 7 (an augmented second).

(c) The **melodic minor scale** raises both steps 6 and 7 in order to overcome the difficult interval between steps 6 and 7 of the harmonic minor scale. This scale is used to create melodies which are supported harmonically by chords derived from the harmonic minor scale.

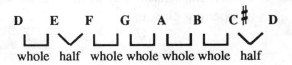

The above form is used when melodic patterns are **ascending** and the **natural** (or **Aeolian**) form is used when melodic patterns are **descending**.

Using the home tone **D** (*solfège* **la**) the three forms of the **D minor scale** would appear as follows:

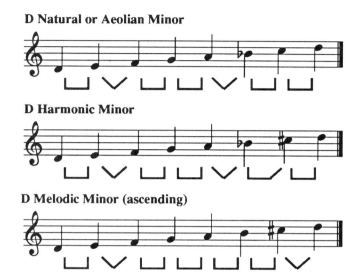

### 4.7 Pentatonic Scale Patterns

4.7.1 Definition: Many simple tunes and folk songs are built upon a special type of scale known as the pentatonic scale (penta means five) or five-tone scale. To build a pentatonic scale beginning on G, use the following pattern. One of the intervals is a whole tone and one-half.

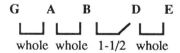

4.7.2 Concept Statement: **Melodies may use the notes of the pentatonic scale.**

4.7.3 The song "Tom Dooley" (page 165) is built upon the G pentatonic scale. Notice that the tones C (4th degree) and F# (7th degree) of the G major scale are not used in the song.

4.7.4 In order to get the sound of the pentatonic scale "in your ear," try improvising some song on the black keys of the piano. Here are some suggestions:

        Amazing Grace (begin on C#)

        Auld Lang Syne (begin on C#)

        Old MacDonald Had a Farm (begin on F#)

## 4.8 Twelve-Tone Scale Patterns

4.8.1 Definition: Many modern composers use all the tones within the octave as a basis for their music. The twelve tones are not arranged in a strict ascending or descending order (as they would be in the chromatic scale, see Section 4.3, above) but are ordered in a specific manner devised by the composer, and called a **tone row**.

Each of the twelve tones in a tone row is considered to be equally important, thus there is no home tone or key note. Music based upon a tone row is called **atonal** (i.e., not conforming to any tonality or system of keys).

An example of a tone row is shown below. Construct this tone row using bells and play the row from left to right (called the **original** row) and then from right to left (called the **retrograde** row).

Original ———>          <——— Retrograde

Groupings of any three consecutive tones shown above may be used to build chords. Play these chords to see how they differ in quality from chords built upon the tonal (i.e., major-minor) system, as opposed to the atonal system.

4.8.2 Almost no simple children's songs use atonal or twelve-tone scales. The song "My End is My Beginning" (with thanks to Guillaume de Machaut) was specifically devised to show children how tone rows operate. The tone row used is that from the example above. Notice that the tone row is first presented in its original form, and then in its retrograde (reverse) form to complete the song.

## 4.9 Modal Scale Patterns

4.9.1 Definition: Some songs (especially folk songs) are built upon a special type of scale called a **mode**. These modes were first used by the Greeks in the composition of their music and were later adopted (with some changes) by the early Christian Church in the development of Gregorian Chant (see Section 1.12, above, for an example). Four of these modes, the Ionian, Aeolian, Dorian and Mixolydian, appear in some music we sing today, the first two being found far more frequently than the latter pair.

(a) **Ionian Mode**: This was only a *theoretical* mode in medieval music theory, and was never used in actual practice. We know this mode today as our **major scale** (see Section 4.5, above).

*Major mode*

```
C    D    E    F    G    A    B    C
└┘  └┘   ∨   └┘  └┘  └┘   ∨
whole whole half whole whole whole half
```

(b) **Aeolian Mode**: This mode has survived as our **natural minor scale** (see Section 4.6, above).

*Natural minor scale*

```
D    E    F    G    A    B♭   C    D
└┘   ∨   └┘  └┘   ∨   └┘  └┘
whole half whole whole half whole whole
```

(c) **Dorian Mode**: This mode appears far less frequently in modern music than the other two. It may be recognized as what appears to be a D minor scale with with no B♭ in the key signature.

```
D    E    F    G    A    B    C    D
└┘   ∨   └┘  └┘  └┘   ∨   └┘
whole half whole whole whole half whole
```

(d) **Mixolydian Mode**: This mode may be recognized by its flatted 7th degree (i.e. as a G major scale without the F#, or as a D major scale without the C#).

```
G    A    B    C    D    E    F    G
└┘  └┘   ∨   └┘  └┘   ∨   └┘

D    E    F#   G    A    B    C    D
└┘  └┘   ∨   └┘  └┘   ∨   └┘
whole whole half whole whole half whole
```

4.9.2 The song "Scarborough Fair" is written in the Dorian Mode. Notice that the song appears to be in D minor, but has no B♭ in the key signature.

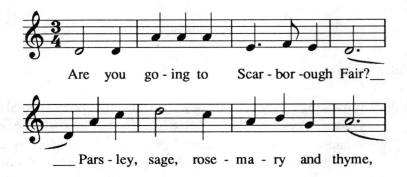

4.9.3 The song "The Ol' Grey Goose" is written in the Mixolydian Mode. Notice that it appears to be in the key of D Major, but lacks a $C^{\#}$ in the key signature.

# 5.0 Concepts of Texture

## 5.1 Density of Sound

5.1.1 Definition: Texture in music is perceived as a consequence of the density of sound.

5.1.2 Sound may be described as thicker or thinner. The aural effect is created by a number of possible manipulations; the number of instruments playing, the particular timbre of the sound source, the manner of producing the sounds, the complexity of the harmony the density of the melodic rhythm, and the register. For example, the sound of a tuba is more dense than that of a flute; the sound of a tone cluster in the lower register of a piano is thicker than that of a single tone in a high register.

5.1.3 Concept Statements: **Texture in music is the density of the sound.**
**Texture in music sounds thicker or thinner.**

## 5.2 Horizontal and Vertical Arrangements

5.2.1 Texture in music is created through the horizontal and vertical arrangements of melody and harmony. Texture in this context is described as: **monophonic**, **polyphonic**, **homophonic**, or mixed.

5.2.1.1 Monophonic texture occurs when a single melody is sung or played solo or in unison. A graphic symbol for monophonic texture is:

5.2.1.2 Polyphonic texture occurs when two or more melodies interweave. A graphic symbol of polyphonic texture is:

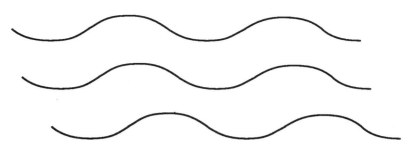

- A melody performed as a round is an example of a polyphonic texture (see "The Ghost of John," page 116).

- Partner songs, in which two or more melodies can be sung or played together, produce a polyphonic texture (see "Fish and Chips," page 113).

5.21.3 Homophonic texture is a result of a single melody supported by chords. Music with this texture occurs when a melody such as "This Train" (page 274) is accompanied by chords on the piano, ukulele, guitar or other chord instrument.

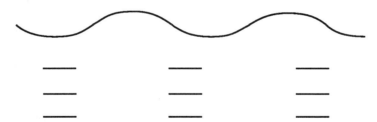

5.21.4 Music which has both homophonic and polyphonic textures has a **mixed** texture.

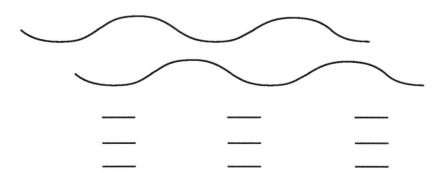

5.21.5 Concept Statement: **Texture in music may be monophonic, polyphonic, homophonic or mixed.**

# 6.0 Concepts of Harmony

## 6.1 Vertical Combinations of Two or More Pitches, through:

### 6.1.1 Drone:
A single tone or group of tones which may be repeated several times as an accompaniment to a tune. All one-chord songs and some two-chord songs may include a drone or drones as an accompaniment part.

#### 6.1.1.1 The selection "Canoe Song" (page 102) is a one chord song.

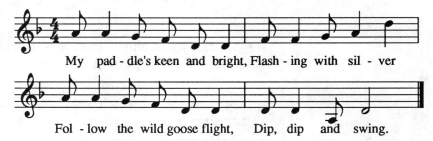

In this example, the key or **tonality** is that of **d minor** (the example on page 102 is in the key of e minor). The keynote (or **la**) of this key may be used to accompany the song, using such patterns as the following:

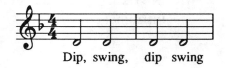

This pitch is the bottom tone or **root** of the **chord** of d minor (see Section 6.2.3, below). Other notes in this chord, either singly or in combination, may also be used to accompany the tune. The **bottom two** notes of the d minor chord are **D** and **F**, and these two notes may also form a drone:

In fact, all three notes of the d minor chord (**D**, **F** and **A**) may form a drone:

The last phrase of "Canoe Song" (or any other phrase, for that matter) may be used as a **chant** (see Section 6.1.2, below) to further enrich the harmony of the song.

6.1.1.2 Concept Statement: **Harmony can be created through the use of drones.**

6.1.1.3 Other one-chord songs which you may want to experiment with include:

    (a) Are you Sleeping (page 97, avoid chord changes on weak beats)
    (b) Row Your Boat (page 87)
    (c) The Farmer in the Dell
    (d) Three Blind Mice
    (e) Swing Low, Sweet Chariot
    (f) Taps
    (g) Little Tommy Tinker
    (h) Zum Gali Gali

6.1.2 Ostinato: This is a short melodic fragment (sometimes as limited as two tones) or a rhythmic pattern which is repeated throughout a song. Almost any single phrase of a round (or even a portion of a phrase) may be used as a ostinato (pl: **ostinati**).

6.1.2.1 Concept Statement: **Harmony can be created through the use of ostinato.**

6.1.2.2 The last phrase ("Dip, dip and swing") from "Canoe Song" (above) could be used as a ostinato. Try using the last phrase of "Are you Sleeping" (page 97) as an ostinato to accompany this song.

6.1.2.3 The ostinato of "Zum Gali Gali" can serve as both a melody in its own right, in addition to serving in the role of accompaniment.

## Zum Gali Gali

6.1.3 Descant: **Descant** is a second melody (often called a **countermelody**) which is sounded simultaneously with and is of equal importance to the main melody or theme of a song. Descants are traditionally higher in pitch than the main melody, but sometimes dip lower than the tune for a few tones. Descants are usually easier to learn than a standard "second part" since they have an intrinsic melodic character of their own.

6.1.3.1 Concept Statement: **Harmony can be created through the use of descant.**

6.1.3.2 The song "My Darling Clementine" is found below with a descant written by B. Beagle. This is a good example of how a descant can enrich a melody.

6.2 Combining Three or More Pitches to make chords, as in:

6.2.1 Rounds and Canons: In practice, the terms **round** and **canon** mean the same thing, i.e. the same melody is sung by different groups of voices, with each group beginning to sing at a different time. The overlapping of the different parts thus creates **chords** (see Section 6.2.3, below). Most rounds are one-chord songs.

6.2.1.1 Concept Statement: **Harmony can be created through the use of rounds.**

6.2.1.2 The song "Are You Sleeping" (page 97) is a round. The tonality of the song is **F Major** and thus the chord produced when the selection is sung as a round is the **F Major chord.**

6.2.1.3 Rounds and canons can be very complex, and are fun to sing even for older children. The Hungarian round "Come and Sing Together" is "at the half measure," i.e. the second voice begins when the first voice reaches beat three of measure one. While the round is indicated as being for two parts, as many as six or eight may be employed. The more parts you add, the more complex the resulting chords become.

6.2.2 Quodlibets and Partner Songs: The use of partner songs (the technical term is **quodlibet**) for the development of independence in part singing can provide a lot of enjoyment for students while helping them to maintain a "second part." Partner songs are normally well-known tunes within which the harmonic sequence (or succession of chords) is identical. Thus the two songs can be sung together with considerable harmonic effect.

6.2.2.1 Concept Statement: **Harmony can be created through the use of partner songs.**

6.2.2.2 Try the following combinations of songs to see how this phenomenon works:

(a) "Cielito Lindo" and "My Bonnie Lies Over the Ocean" (only the refrains may be used together);

(b) "Home on the Range" and "My Home's in Montana;" and

(c) "Go Down Moses" and "Joshua Fit the Battle of Jericho."

6.2.3 Major and Minor Chords: Chords are the building blocks of the harmonic structure of music, and can greatly enrich the texture of music. The simplest of all chords is the **triad** which is, as its name suggests, composed of three tones, a bottom or key tone called the **root**, and normally an interval of a **third** and a **fifth** above the root (see Section 4.2.2.1 with respect to intervals). Chords are most easily derived from scales (see Section 4.5 and 4.6 on the major and minor scales). Beginning with the C Major scale, we may construct a **C Major chord** by beginning with the root as **C**, then adding an intervals of a third above the root (**E**) and then an interval of a fifth above the root (**G**):

In the key of C Major this chord is given the designation **I** since it is built upon the first degree (or **1**) of the scale.

In a similar manner, we can build a chord on the fourth degree of the C Major scale using the tones **F**, **A** and **C** (an **F Major chord**), and use the designation **IV** to indicate its position in the scale of C Major. Notice that you must "think" temporarily in the scale of F Major as you construct this chord.

Another useful chord is that build upon the fifth degree of the scale. In the scale of C Major this chord uses the tones **G**, **B** and **D**, has the name **G Major**, and the position designation **V**. Notice that you must "think" temporarily in the scale of G Major as you construct this chord.

As you begin to construct chords in other keys you will notice that the C Major, F Major and G Major chords will have the same names, but different position designations in other scales. Thus the C Major Chord has the designation I in the scale of C Major, V in the scale of F Major and IV in the scale of G Major; The F major triad has the designation I in the scale of F Major and IV in the scale of C Major, but is not found as a regular or primary triad in the scale of G Major, since G Major contains an F# which is not found in the triad; the G Major triad is I in G Major and V in C Major, but is not normally found in F Major since the chord contains no B♭.

The following example shows the three primary triads designated **I**, **IV** and **V** in the keys of **C Major**, **F Major** and **G Major**. You should construct these triads in many keys to get familiar with how they look, and play them on piano, uke or guitar to hear how they sound.

You should be aware that when you play these chords on uke or guitar (and sometimes on the piano) they do not necessarily sound with the notes in the above positions. Triads may be played in **root position** or in one of two **inversions**, where one or more of the tones are displaced by an octave. Inversions are desirable in order to let the chords "fit nicely under the hand" and to allow ease of movement from one chord to another, especially when the chords changes come quickly. The following example shows the root position and **first** and **second inversions** of the C Major triad. Other triads operate in a similar manner.

When you examine some of the songs in this manual which have chords symbols added, you will notice that the chord on the fifth degree (chord V) often has the numeral "7" added to its name as in $V^7$. This numeral indicates the use of a special form of the V chord which, in addition to the root, third and fifth, has an added note which is an interval of a seventh above the root, hence the "7" designation. The construction of seventh chords can be confusing, since the added 7th is a **minor 7th**, not a major 7th above the root. To construct the $V^7$ chord (i.e. $G^7$) in the scale of C Major, use the intervals of a third and a fifth above the root while "thinking" temporarily in the key of G Major (the root note of the chord), but when you add the seventh remember that you are placing the chord in C Major (which has no F#), not in the key of G Major (which contains an F#). If this "double think" seems too difficult for you, simply remember that a minor 7th is a semitone or half-tone smaller than a major seventh, and lower the F# to an F♮. The example below shows $V^7$ chords in the keys of C Major, F Major and G Major. You should construct these chords in several other keys. Notice that the $V^7$ chord has a root position and three inversion because it consists of four tones. In $V^7$ chords the fifth above the root is sometimes omitted in order to make the chord easier to play.

\* Displaced by an octave for clarity in reading

You will find that the chords of I, IV and $V^7$ are the most common chords which you will use in accompanying simple children's songs and folk songs, but chords may be constructed on any degree of any scale. If you follow the procedures outlined above, you should be able to construct most chords you will use. If in doubt, consult any of the common music theory textbooks for assistance.

You will soon notice that the use of these three common chords often follows a fairly regular pattern. Songs will often begin with the **I** chord, move through the **IV** chord, then to the **V⁷** chord and back to the **I** chord. This pattern is logical when you examine the tones in each chord and their resulting quality within a key or tonality. The I chord contains the home or key tone (the tone C in the key of C Major) as its root tone, thus it is logical that this home chord would be found at the beginning and/or ending of a piece of music, where a feeling or quality of rest or repose is necessary. The IV chord also contains the key note, but not at the root of the chord, while the other two tones are completely unrelated to the I chord, and the resulting quality of this chord is one of movement (i.e., it wants to "move" to some other chord). The V chord does not contain the key note and its "sister" chord, V⁷, also contains the 7th degree of the scale, the so-called "leading tone" which is a semitone removed from the key note and has a considerable tendency to resolve to the keynote. Thus the V chord has a quality of some movement or activity, while the V⁷ chord has the potential for even greater movement or activity. The logical place for the V⁷ chord to move is to "home" or I, thus the chord sequence **I-IV-V⁷-I** is one of the strongest chord progressions in music.

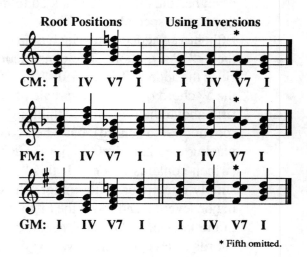

\* Fifth omitted.

Examine some of the selections in this manual, and discover how many use the I-IV-V⁷-I pattern. Other simple chord patterns include **I-IV-I** and **I-V⁷-I**. Find out how many songs use these patterns. Discover other common chord patterns by examining music from other sources or experimenting with piano, uke or guitar.

Minor chords are constructed in a similar manner to that described above. In major chords the bottom third is a **major third** (4 semitones) while in minor chords the bottom third is a **minor third** (3 semitones). In both chords the second tone is an interval of a **perfect fifth** (hence the name, since it applies to both major and minor). The following example gives some common minor chords:

c minor   a minor   f minor   e minor

Like major chords, minor chords may be found in inversions. Unlike major chords, the position designations of minor chords are often given in lower case Roman numerals (such as **i, ii, vi**, and so on).

Minor chords are sometimes used to harmonize melodies in major keys, and they give considerable colour to the texture of the harmony. If you construct chords on the second, third and sixth degrees of a major scale you will find that these are minor chords. In the scale of C these chords are **d minor** (ii), **e minor** (iii) and **a minor** (vi):

ii   iii   vi
d minor   e minor   a minor

In harmonizing melodies "by ear," if you substitute the chord ii for the chord IV occasionally you can get some very interesting effects. Similarly, if you substitute the chord vi for the chord I (except at the beginning or end of a melody) interesting harmonic variations can be realized.

In harmonizing melodies in minor keys, the pattern **i-iv-V⁷-i**, which is similar to the chord pattern given for major melodies, above, is often employed. Other common chord patterns are **i-iv-i** and **i-V⁷-i**. Notice that the V⁷ chord is a **major** seventh chord in both cases (a major chord with an added minor seventh).

6.2.3.1 Concept Statement: **Chords can be major or minor.**

6.2.3.1 The singing or playing of patterns of block chords as an accompaniment to a tune will help to give students a sense of harmonic security before the beginning of their study of part songs. Begin by having the class sing or play only the roots of chords in simple 2-chord and 3-chord songs, then move on to 2-note chords (use the root and the third of each chord) and then to full 3-note chords. (See especially the use of single chords to accompany "Canoe Song" in Section 6.1.1, above)

6.2.3.2 The song "Kookaburra" (page 138) employs the chord pattern I-IV-I as its basis. Students can use the following chord sequence to accompany the song throughout:

Sing, sing, sing.

Begin by having students sing only the bottom tone (D), then add the second note of each chord (F#-G-F#) and then, when they are comfortable with this, add the third note of both triads. Notice that the IV chord is in second inversion.

6.2.3.3 Find other songs in this manual which can be accompanied by simple chord patterns, and consult the list of one-, two-, and three-chord songs in the appendix for more examples.

6.2.3.4 This introduction to major and minor chords has included only basic information. You are advised to consult one of the several theory textbooks which are available if you wish to know more about chords.

6.2.4 Songs in Two, Three and Four Parts: When they understand the basic concepts of harmony and have gained the skill to become independent in singing or playing a harmony part, students enjoy singing and playing songs in two-, three- and four-part harmony. While no songs of this type have been included in this manual, almost all music series texts contain such material, and many individually published part songs are available on the commercial market. Teachers are advised to subscribe to publisher's mailing lists and to attend reading sessions of new material often sponsored by major music dealers in order to familiarize themselves with the vast repertoire in this area.

**6.3 Polytonality**: Polytonality involves the simultaneous use of two or more tonal centers. For instance, the combination of two well-known tunes (as in the example below), one in the key of F Major and the other in the key of G Major, is an example of very simple polytonal writing. Many pieces of modern music are written with polytonal technique, a practice which produces results which have very tense chordal structures. When only two different keys are employed, the composition is said to be **bitonal**.

# 7.0 Concepts of Form and Design

## 7.1 Like and Unlike Phrases

7.1.1 Definition: In music, some phrases* are repeated or are, at the least, similar to other phrases. Students should be able to recognize (both aurally and visually) what phrases are **like** phrases (similar) and what phrases are **unlike** phrases (dissimilar).

7.1.2 Concept Statements: **Form or design may be made up of repeated phrases.**
**Form or design may be made up of like and unlike phrases.**

6.1.3 The song "Der Hans" (page 104) consists of three phrases:

After listening and singing the song, children will discover that phrases **one** and **three** are **like** phrases (they are, in fact, identical) while phrases **two** is **unlike** one and three.

## 7.2 Repetition and Contrast

7.2.1 Definition: Music is often organized into phrases that are **alike** and phrases that are **different**, for reasons of interest and variety in musical composition. This type of organization defines the overall **form** or **design** of a piece of music.

The first and third phrases of "Der Hans" are identical (**repetition**) while the second phrase is different from phrases one and three (**contrast**). If we assign letters to each phrase to indicate their relationship to each other in the overall design of the melody, the following pattern emerges:

    **a**   (phrase 1)
    **b**   (phrase 2 **unlike** phrase 1)
    **a**   (phrase 3, **like** phrase 1)

---

*When we speak of **phrases** in this section, we are referring to **musical phrases**, not textual phrases in the context of language. A phrase in music represents a complete musical idea. Musical compositions are created through the linking of musical phrases, both melodically and harmonically.

In place of letters, symbols may be employed to illustrate the form or design of a melody, such as:

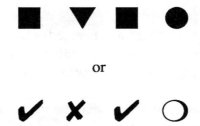

7.22 Sometimes **like** musical sections are similar, but not identical, as we see in the song "Good News."

Phrases one and three are identical, phrase 2 is **similar** to one and three and phrase four is unlike any of the others. The form or design of this tune could be shown as follows:

   **a**  (phrase 1)
   **a₁**  (phrase 2, **similar** to phrase 1)
   **a**  (phrase 3, **identical** to phrase 1)
   **b**  (phrase 4, unlike any other phrase)

These repetitions and contrasts give music a **form** or **design** in much the same way that architects and painters give buildings and paintings a form or design—to make them interesting and appealing.

7.2.3 Concept Statement: **Form or design is created by repeated and contrasting phrases or sections.**

7.3 **The simple forms**: Musical form may also apply to whole **sections** of a composition, each section encompassing several phrases. These designs tend to follow some fairly standard patterns. Look for the following types of patterns:

  **rondo**       ABACAD...
            Some songs with **verses** that vary but with **chorus** sections which remain the same follow this pattern.

**binary forms**   AB
AABB
AAB
ABB

**ternary forms**   ABA
AABA
AABABA

Another important simple formal device to watch for is the use of an **introduction** to begin a work and a **coda** to conclude the piece. (*Coda* is the Italian word for "tail.") Many simple children's songs will present an instrumental introduction, followed by the main song, and then give an instrumental ending to finish the selection.

**7.4 The larger forms**: Not only must the composers be concerned with form and design encompassing only a few measures or phrases of music but they must also be aware of a larger structure which can involve many measures of music. As you delve more and more deeply into music, you will find that composers of large choral and symphonic works are also working to a preconceived plan. While defining these forms is outside the scope of this volume, through listening and reading you will be able to discover the large structure employed in such forms as:

Theme and Variations
Suite
Ballet
Opera
Oratorio
Symphony
Concerto
Tone Poem

## 8.0 Concepts of Timbre

### 8.1 Quality of Sound

8.1.1 Definition: Timbre or tone colour is the quality unique to each voice, instrument, or any other sound source.

8.1.2 Sound can be classified on the basis of descriptive characteristics such as shrill, dull, soothing, jagged, rough.

8.1.3 Sounds can be classified according to the traditional families of instruments:

**Strings**
**Woodwinds**
**Brass**
**Percussion**

8.1.4 Sounds can be classified in a way which acknowledges world instruments and recent technological advances:

**Idiophones** (sound is produced by the vibration of a solid material)
- triangle
- log drum
- washboard
- xylophone

**Membranophones** (sound is produced by the vibration of a stretched skin or membrane)
- conga drum
- tabla drums
- snare drum

**Chordophones** (sound is produced by the vibration of stretched strings)
- mandolin
- banjo
- koto
- piano

**Aerophones** (sound is produced by the vibration of columns of air)
- conch shells
- harmonica
- panpipes
- tuba

**Electrophones** (sound is produced by oscillations of electrical current)
- sound synthesizer
- electric bass guitar (really a chordophone, but the sound may be modified electronically)

8.1.5 One way of classifying vocal sounds is on the basis of range:

**Soprano** (high female voice and children's voices)
**Alto** (low female voice)
**Cambiata** (changing male voice)
**Tenor** (high male voice)
**Bass** (low male voice)

8.1.6 Concept Statement: **Timbre is the unique quality of sound produced by different sources.**

## 8.2 Sound Production

8.2.1 Sounds are produced by blowing, plucking, strumming, striking, scraping, and shaking.

8.2.2 Concept Statement: **The sounds made by instruments are produced in a variety of ways.**

    8.2.2.1 Classroom instruments on which sounds are produced by blowing:
- recorders
- bottles

    8.2.2.2 Classroom instruments on which sounds are produced by plucking or strumming:
- autoharp
- ukulele
- guitar
- kalimba (thumb piano)

    8.2.2.3 Classroom instruments on which sounds are produced by striking:

Non-pitched
- castanets
- claves (*clah-vays*)
- cymbals
- drums
- triangle
- temple blocks (semi-pitched)
- wood block
- finger cymbals
- cowbell
- agogo (2 pitches)
- timpani (tuneable)

Pitched
- piano
- glockenspiel
- tone bells
- xylophone
- metallophone

    8.2.2.4 Classroom instruments on which sounds are produced by scraping:
- guiro (*wee-row*)
- sand blocks
- ratchet
- cabasa

    8.2.2.5 Classroom instruments on which sounds are produced by shaking:
- maracas
- sleigh bells
- tambourine (may also be struck)

## 8.3 Ensembles

8.3.1 A single musical performer is a **soloist.** When two parts are played together a **duet** results. **Trios**, **quartets**, and **quintets** are frequently heard combinations of vocal and instrumental performers of all kinds, from bluegrass to classical. Larger Western groups include the symphony orchestra (strings, woodwinds, brass and percussion), concert band (woodwinds, brass and percussion) and choirs with many different voice groupings. In addition, many new kinds of ensembles are becoming familiar to us as old music and music from other cultures is being heard more frequently.

8.3.2 *A cappella* now refers to unaccompanied vocal music. Originally it described the musical practice of choral singing in churches where instruments were not permitted, thus *a cappella* meant "in chapel style."

8.3.3 Concept Statement: **Music can be played or sung by different kinds of ensembles.**

# Appendix A

## Literacy Concepts in Songs and Listening Selections Cross-Referenced

**Concepts** — **Text Pages**

### RHYTHM

- Steady Beat/Pulse .............. 58. 62, 63, 65, 69, 83, 120
- Accent ................................................................. 107
- Simple Meter
  - duple .................................................... 63, 65, 157
  - triple ............................................ 113, 124, 159, 170
  - quadruple ................................................... 152
- Anacrusis ................................ 79, 115, 118, 128, 129
- Duration
  - sixteenth notes ................................. 80, 97, 133
  - eighth notes ............ 60, 63, 67, 69, 73, 74, 85, 93
  - quarter notes and rests .................. 67, 77, 85, 93
  - half notes ..................................................... 121
  - triplet ............................................ 113, 140, 157
  - fermata ......................................................... 79
  - tie ................................................................ 124
- Even/Uneven ................................................... 141
- Compound Meter ....... 58, 68, 70, 83, 87, 98, 108, 128
- Syncopation .................... 91, 102, 128, 157, 165, 173
- Changing Meter .............................................. 129

### TEMPO

- Faster–Slower ...................................... 127, 145, 186
- Getting Faster–Getting Slower ............................... 73

### DYNAMICS

- Louder–Softer .............................................. 123, 140
- Getting Louder–Getting Softer ..................... 116, 183

### MELODY

- Higher–Lower ............................................. 69, 85, 88
- Melodic Contour ................. 59, 61, 72, 74, 76, 84, 88
- Sequence .............................................. 104, 159, 163
- Cadence .............................. 78, 94, 99, 131, 135, 152
- Tonal Center ........................................... 92, 118, 152
- Major Scale ................................. 72, 76, 84, 118, 146
- Minor Scale ................................. 116, 118, 128, 129
- Major/Minor Mode ................................................ 90
- Pentatonic Scale ........................... 102, 162, 165, 166
- Blues Scale ......................................................... 146

**Concepts** — **Text Pages**

### HARMONY

- Ostinato ................. 60, 66, 73, 83, 89, 102, 103, 126, 127, 139, 154, 163, 177
- Partner Songs ..................................................... 113
- Echo Song ................................................... 145/314
- Rounds ...................... 57, 87, 97, 102, 116, 124, 133, 138, 149, 163, 168, 234
- Major Chords ................. 98, 104, 111, 136, 161, 166
- Minor Chords ...................................... 137/261, 138

### TEXTURE

- Monophonic ........................................................ 116
- Polyphonic .......................................................... 116

### FORM AND DESIGN

- Phrases ........................ 75, 91, 94, 103, 121, 154, 170
- Like/Unlike Phrases ..................................... 106, 149
- Repetition and Contrast ..80, 100, 124, 149, 171, 181
- Form
  - AB .................... 64, 98, 106, 108, 118, 126, 129, 135, 139, 152, 157, 181
  - ABA .............................. 127, 137/261, 166, 173
  - 12-bar blues .................................................. 147

### TIMBRE

- Vocal ............................................. 82, 123, 179, 185
- Instrumental .............. 70, 82, 177, 181, 183, 184, 186

## Melodic Patterns

| Pattern | Text Pages |
|---|---|
| d-r-m | 79, 84 |
| d-m-s | 98, 135, 144 |
| d-l₁-s₁ | 68, 80, 173 |
| d-s | 98 |
| d¹-s-m-d | 87 |
| d-s₁-d | 97, 113 |
| m-d | 94 |
| m-s | 59, 121 |
| m-r-d | 58, 59, 66, 75, 94, 111, 141 |
| m-l | 61, 99, 129 |
| s-d | 60 |
| s-m | 64, 67, 69, 73, 74, 85, 88 |
| s₁-l₁-d | 165 |
| s-m-d | 66 |
| s-m-l | 63 |
| s-l-s | 65 |
| s-l-s-m | 60, 64, 67 |
| s-f-m-r-d | 61 |
| s₁-d | 62, 78, 104, 111 |
| l-s-l | 82, 89, 102, 116 |
| l-m | 89, 118, 139, 149, 163 |
| l-t-d | 62 |
| l-t-l | 82 |

## Rhythm Patterns

| Pattern | Text Pages |
|---|---|
| ♩ | 121, 154 |
| ♩. | 124, 149 |
| ♪ | 85, 93 |
| ♩. ♪ | 78, 131, 141 |
| ♫ ♩ | 60, 61, 63, 69, 85, 88, 89, 93 |
| ♫ ♫ | 60, 73, 88, 89, 93 |
| ♬ | 133, 163 |
| ♬ | 126 |
| ♬♬ | 80, 97, 163 |
| ♪ ♪ ♪ | 91, 102, 103, 165, 173 |
| ♪. ♪ | 99, 124, 142 |
| ♪ ♪. | 126 |
| 𝄽. | 58, 68, 83, 98, 108 |
| ♫ | 58, 68, 83, 98, 108 |
| 𝄽 ♪ | 58, 68, 83, 98, 108 |

## Other Rhythmic Elements

| | |
|---|---|
| 𝄾 | 67, 77, 93 |
| ⌣ | 124 |
| 𝄐 | 79 |

# Appendix B

## 1-, 2-, 3-Chord and Pentatonic Songs

### One Chord Songs

Are You Sleeping? (page 97)
Canoe Song (pages 102, 277)
Charlie Over the Ocean (page 68)
Little Tommy Tinker
Old MacDonald
Row, Row, Row Your Boat (pages 87, 283)
Shortnin' Bread (pages 267, 288)
Swing Low, Sweet Chariot
The Farmer in the Dell
Three Blind Mice
Whistle, Daughter, Whistle (page 290)
Zum Gali Gali (page 345)

### Two Chord Songs

Alouette (page 293)
Billy Boy
Blow the Man Down
Bluebird (page 64)
Buffalo Gals
Clementine (page 312)
Did You Ever See A Lassie?
Down By the Station
Down in the Valley
Down She Sat (page 298)
Drunken Sailor (page 278)
Du, Du, Liegst mir am Herzen
Ezekiel Saw the Wheel (page 111)
Fish and Chips (page 113)
Five Hundred Miles (I-IV, pages 115, 273, 303, 313)
Ghost of John (minor, page 116)
Go Tell Aunt Rhody (pages 252, 267)
He's Got the Whole World (pages 253, 291)
Hokey, Pokey
Hoosen Johnny (page 126)
Hop Old Squirrel (page 299)
Hot Cross Buns (page 75)
How Much is That Doggie?
Joshua Fit (i-$V^7$, pages 137, 261)
Kookaburra (I & IV, pages 138, 301)
Lightly Row (pages 220, 223)
Listen to the Mocking Bird
Little Red Caboose
Liza Jane
London Bridge
Long, Long Ago

### Two Chord Songs (continued)

Mary had a Little Lamb
Oats, Peas, Beans and Barley (page 229)
Oh Dear, What Can the Matter Be?
Old Texas (pages 145, 314)
Polly Wolly Doodle (page 269)
Pop, Goes the Weasel
Shoo Fly
Shortnin' Bread (pages 267, 288)
Simple Gifts
Six Little Ducks
Skip To My Lou (pages 252, 269)
Sloop John B. (pages 157, 253)
Streets of Laredo (page 295)
The Battle of Jericho
The Farmer in the Dell
The More We are Together
This Old Man (pages 252, 265, 270, 294)
Tom Dooley (pages 165, 297)
Where Has My Little Dog Gone? (page 260)
Yellow Rose of Texas

### Three Chord Songs

All Through the Night
Aloha Oe
Amazing Grace (page 231)
Annie Laurie
Auld Lang Syne (pages 242, 316)
Battle Hymn of the Republic
Blowin' in the Wind
Caissons Song
Camptown Races
Can't You Dance the Polka? (page 309)
Cielito Lindo
Cindy
Comin' Through the Rye
Cradle Song (page 243)
Crawdad Song (page 272)
Deck the Halls
Donkey Riding (pages 106, 275)
Drink to Me Only
Eggs and Marrowbones (page 108)
Five Hundred Miles (pages 115, 303)
Goodnight Ladies
Happy Birthday!

**Three Chord Songs** (continued)

    He's a Jolly Good Fellow  (page 277)
    Home on the Range
    I've Been Working on the Railroad
    If Your Happy and You Know It! (page 78)
    Jingle Bells (pages 227, 276)
    Juanita
    Kum Ba Yah (page 259)
    La Cucaracha
    Lavender's Blue
    Little Brown Jug (page 305)
    Loch Lomond
    Lonesome Valley
    Mama Don't 'Low (page 279)
    Michael, Row the Boat Ashore (page 276)
    Muffin Man
    My Bonnie
    Nobody Knows the Trouble I've Seen
    O Bury Me Not on the Lone Prairie
    Oh, Susanna!
    Old Folks at Home
    Old Oaken Bucket
    Old Smokey (pages 144, 272, 307)
    Quilting Party
    Red River Valley
    Rueben and Rachel
    Santa Lucia
    She'll be Comin' 'Round the Mountain
    Silent Night
    Summer Song (page 280)
    The First Noel
    The Water is Wide
    There's Music in the Air
    This Land is Your Land
    This Train (page 274)
    Twinkle, Twinkle Little Star
    When the Saints (page 169)
    Yankee Doodle
    You are My Sunshine

**Pentatonic Songs**

    A la claire fontaine (page 228)
    Auld Lang Syne (pages 242, 316)
    Barnacle Bill (page 58)
    Bee, Bee, Bumble Bee (page 60)
    Billy Bad (page 61)
    Bluebells (page 63)
    Bounce High (page 65)
    Canoe Song (page 102)

**Pentatonic Songs** (continued)

    Categories (page 67)
    Charlie Over the Ocean (page 68)
    Clap Your Hands (page 69)
    Cotton-Eyed Joe
    Coy Malindo
    Do Not Weep
    Draw a Bucket of Water
    Engine, Engine (page 73)
    Ezekiel (page 111)
    Five Hundred Miles (pages 115, 273, 303, 313)
    Get on Board
    Good-bye, Old Paint
    Great Big House (page 121)
    Hoosen Johnny (page 126)
    Hot Cross Buns (page 75)
    Ich-a-back-a (page 77)
    Iroquois Lullaby
    Jim Along Josie
    Land of the Silver Birch (page 139)
    Little Bitty Baby
    Little David, Play on your Harp
    Little Tommy Tinker
    Little Wheel a-Turnin'
    Liza Jane
    Long-Legged Life (page 79)
    Mary had a Baby
    Merrily, We Roll Along (page 141)
    Michael Row the Boat (page 276)
    Mister Frog Went a-Courtin'
    My Bark Canoe
    Now Come On
    Old Brass Wagon (page 80)
    Old Texas (page 145)
    Old Dan Tucker
    Pizza, Pizza Daddy-O
    Riddle Song (page 150)
    Rocky Mountain (page 152)
    Sally go 'Round the Sun (page 314)
    Scotland's Burning
    Skin and Bones
    Sodio
    Starlight, Star Bright (page 89)
    The Train
    There's a Hole in My Bucket (page 162)
    Tom Dooley (pages 165, 297)
    Weavily Wheat (page 91)
    Who's That Yonder (page 94)
    Yonder She Comes

# Appendix C

## Piano Keyboard

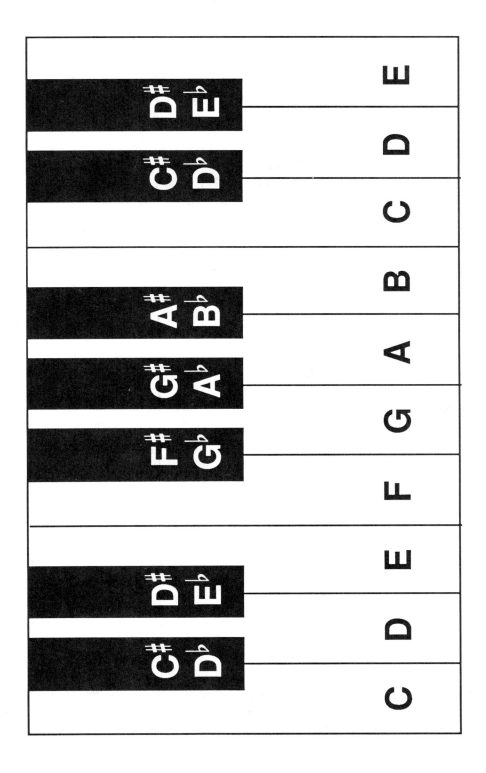

# Autoharp Chord Chart

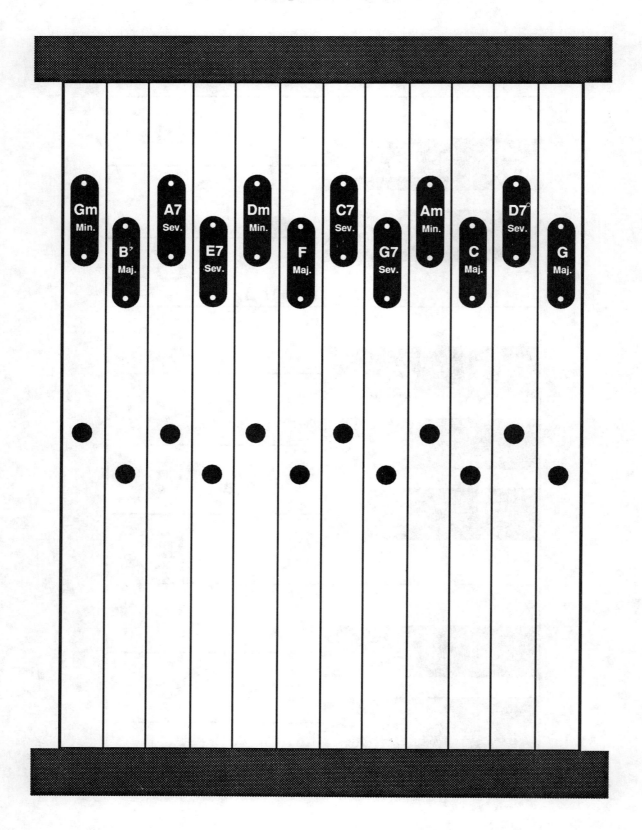

-364-

# Curwen Hand Signs

| Hand Signs | Syllables | |
|---|---|---|
| | Doh (d') | forehead level |
| | Ti (t) | |
| | La (l) | |
| | Sol (s) | neck level |
| | Fa (f) | |
| | Mi (m) | |
| | Re (r) | |
| | Doh (d) | waist level |

# Guitar Chord Chart

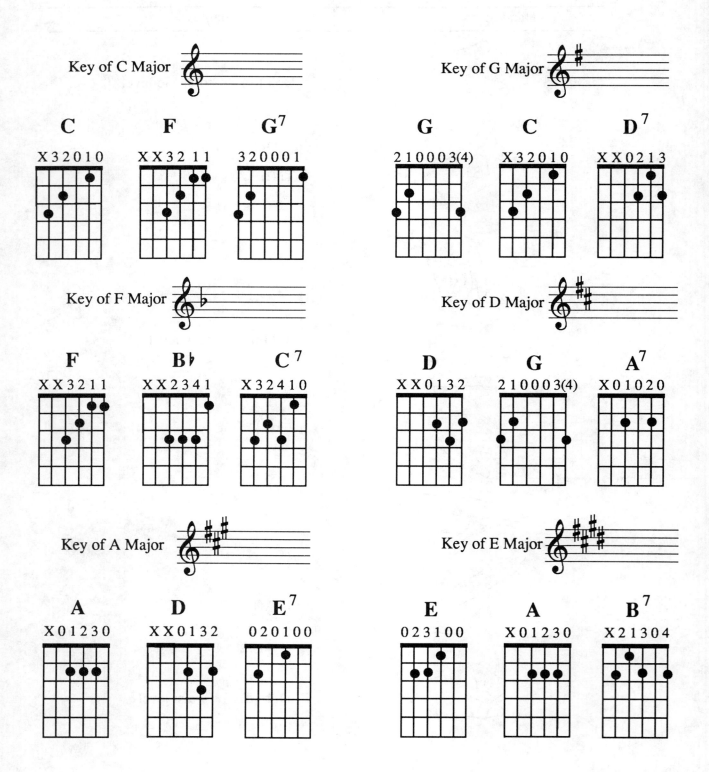

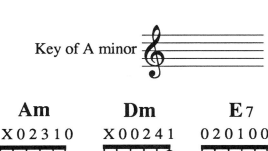
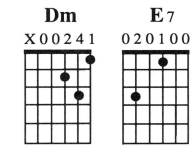
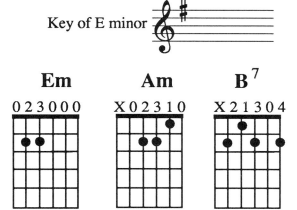

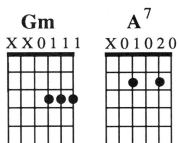
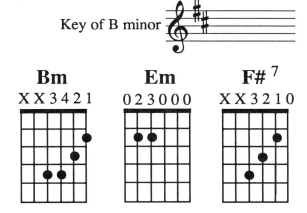

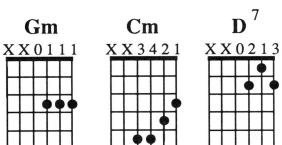
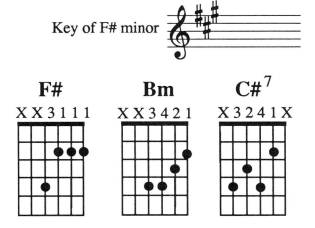

# Ukulele Chord Chart

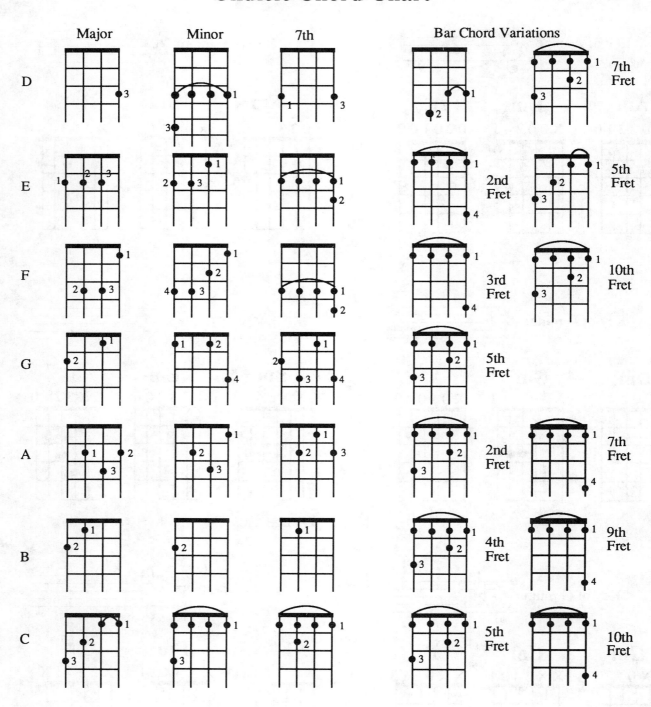

Some Bar Chord Formations which apply in all positions:

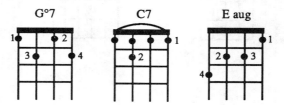

# Appendix D

## Signs and Symbols

### Notes

| | |
|---|---|
| 𝄺 | Double whole note (breve) |
| o | Whole note |
| ♩ | Half note |
| ♩ | Quarter note |
| ♪ | Eighth note |
| ♬ | Sixteenth note |
| | Thirty-second note |
| | Sixty-fourth note |

### Clefs  X shows "middle" C

| | |
|---|---|
| 𝄞 | Treble clef |
| 𝄡 | Alto clef |
| 𝄡 | Tenor clef |
| 𝄢 | Bass clef |

### Bar Lines

| | |
|---|---|
| │ | Single bar line |
| ‖ | Double bar line |
| ‖ | End bar |
| :‖ | Repeat (ending) |
| ‖: | Repeat (beginning) |

### Rests

| | |
|---|---|
| ▬ | Whole rest |
| ▬ | Half rest |
| 𝄽 | Quarter rest |
| 𝄾 | Eighth rest |
| 𝄿 | Sixteenth rest |
| 𝅀 | Thirty-second rest |
| 𝅁 | Sixty-fourth rest |

### Accidentals

| | |
|---|---|
| ♯ | Sharp–raises the pitch by 1/2 tone |
| ♭ | Flat–lowers the pitch by 1/2 tone |
| 𝄪 | Double sharp raises the pitch by 1 tone |
| ♭♭ | Double flat–lowers the pitch by 1 tone |
| ♮ | Natural–cancels a sharp or flat |

### Dynamics

| | |
|---|---|
| *ff* | Fortissimo (very loud) |
| *f* | Forte (loud) |
| *mf* | Mezzo forte (moderately loud) |
| *mp* | Mezzo piano (moderately soft) |
| *p* | Piano (soft) |
| *pp* | Pianissimo (very soft) |
| *fp* | Forte piano (loud, then immediately soft) |
| *sfz* | Sforzando (heavy accent and sustain loud) |

## Dynamics (continued)

  &lt; Crescendo (gradually louder)
or Cresc.

  &gt; Decrescendo (gradually softer)
or dim. Diminuendo (gradually softer)

## Meter (Time) Signatures

Beat note ♪   2/8   3/8   4/8   5/8   7/8

Beat note ♩   2/4   3/4   4/4   C   5/4   7/4

Beat note 𝅗𝅥   2/2   ¢   3/2   4/2

Beat note ♩.   6/8   9/8   12/8

## Articulations

&gt; Long accent

∧ Short accent

— Tenuto (hold note for full value)

𝄐 Fermata (hold at discretion of performer)

## Other Symbols

𝄋 Signa (return to this sign from **D.S. (dal segno)** or **D.S. al coda**

𝄌 Coda (marks the beginning of coda)

8va--, Play an octave higher

8vb--' Play an octave lower

tr Trill (rapid alteration of two pitches)

, Breath mark (phrase mark)

⌐3⌐ Triplet (3 notes in time of 2)

Ped. Pedal (depress damper pedal on piano)

✽ Release pedal

𝄎 Arpeggio (play broken chord)

▦ Guitar Tablature (shows finger position)

∿ Mordent (short trill)

∽ Turn - play like

D.C. (da capo) Return to the beginning

## Key Signatures

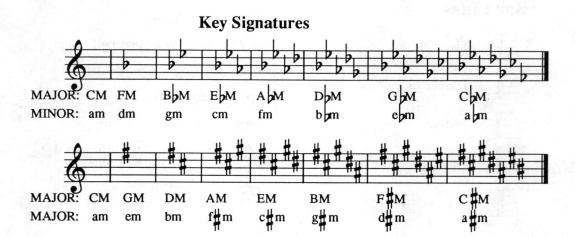

| MAJOR: | CM | FM | B♭M | E♭M | A♭M | D♭M | G♭M | C♭M |
| MINOR: | am | dm | gm | cm | fm | b♭m | e♭m | a♭m |

| MAJOR: | CM | GM | DM | AM | EM | BM | F♯M | C♯M |
| MAJOR: | am | em | bm | f♯m | c♯m | g♯m | d♯m | a♯m |

# Chords in Major Keys

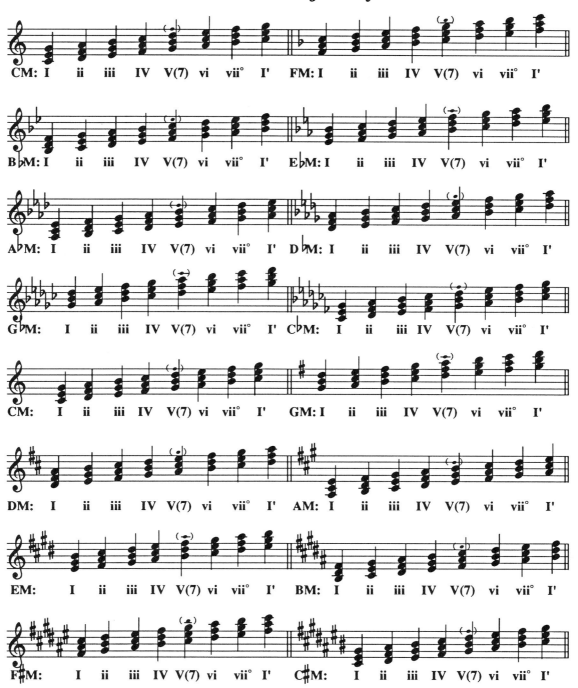

# APPENDIX E

## Glossary

**AB** – symbolic representation of the form of a composition in which there are two contrasting sections (**a b** refers to two contrasting phrases)

**ABA** – symbolic representation of the form of a three-part composition in which the last section is a repetition of the first section

**Accent** ( > ) – emphasis or stress on a note or chord

**Accompaniment** – The music background heard with a melody

**Alto** – lower female voice

**Anacrusis** – An up-beat or incomplete section of a measure which sometimes begins a song

**Articulation** – the manner of producing a tone (see staccato and legato)

**Atonal music** – music purposely constructed so that it has no feeling of tonal center

**Bar line** – a symbol used to mark off measures

**Bass** – lower male voice

**Beat** – the pulse in music (strong/weak; steady/changing); in metrical music, beats are usually grouped in sets of 2, 3, 4, 5

**Cadence** – "punctuation" in music; the ending of a phrase (strong/weak)

**Call and response** (form) – a musical dialogue between a leader and a group which repeats the melody or sings/plays a contrasting refrain

**Canon** (form) – the melody for each voice (part) is the same but the entries occur at planned intervals; differs from a round in that all voices finish together

**Chant** – a kind of liturgical music characterized by free rhythm (Gregorian, Anglican, Byzantine chants); a type of singing using repetitive rhythms and a limited number of pitches

**Chord** – the simultaneous sounding of three or more pitches usually built of consecutive thirds

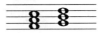

**Chromatic scale** – a scale using all the twelve pitches within the octave

C C♯ D D♯ E F F♯ G G♯ A A♯ B (C)

**Clef** (from French meaning key) – the key to the name of the notes on the staff. The G clef (treble clef) shows where G is located.

The F clef (bass clef) shows where F is located.

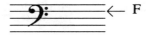

**Coda** – an ending section of a piece

**Compound meter** – a meter (grouping of beats) in which the beat is subdivided in threes

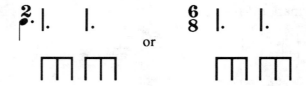

**Conductor** – a musical leader who helps a group of musicians to perform as a unified whole. See page 208 for some conducting patterns.

**Conjunct** – melodic movement by step

**Contour** – the general shape or direction of a melodic line

**Countermelody** – an accompanying melody for the main melody

**D.C. al fine** (*da capo al fine*) – an instruction to go back to the beginning of the piece and perform to the term *Fine*

**Density** – a quality of texture in the music (thick/thin)

**Descant** – a melody added higher than the main melody

**Direction** – melodic movement (upward/downward/repeated)

**Disjunct** – melodic movement by skips or leaps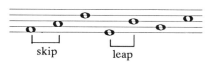

**Dominant** – the fifth degree of the scale

**Down beat** – the first beat of a measure usually conducted with a downward motion

**Duration** – the length of sound or silence in music (long/short)

**Dynamics** – degree of loudness or softness in the music (an expressive quality). See page 331 for musical terms.

**Echo clapping** – the exact repetition of a rhythmic pattern by clapping

**Ensemble** – the whole group of musical performers

**Fermata** (𝄐) – pause, hold; the length of the pause is usually controlled by the performer or conductor

**Flat** (♭) – a symbol placed to the left of a note to lower the pitch a half step

**Form** – the overall construction of a piece; the blueprint (order of events) of a musical composition

**Half step** – the smallest interval between two tones (on the piano); also called a semitone

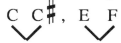

**Harmony** – a result of tones sounding simultaneously

**Homophonic music** – music consisting of a melody with chordal harmony as accompaniment

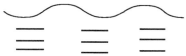

**Improvisation** – creating musical ideas freely within a musical context

**Instrumentation** – the selection of instruments or sound sources for a given piece

**Interlude** – a bridge between parts of a musical composition

**Interval** – the distance between two pitches

**Introduction** – the beginning section of a musical piece (not essential)

**Key** – the name of the pitch which is the tonal center of a piece

**Legato** – smoothly

**Lyrics** – the words of a song

**Major scale** – eight successive pitches with different names bounded by an octave and having the following pattern: ⊔ ⊔∨⊔ ⊔ ⊔∨

⊔ = whole step    ∨ = half step

**Measure** – the events between bar lines (also called bars)   २/४ | ⊓ | ⊓ ⊓
measure

**Melody** – how a series of linear tones is organized into a meaningful whole (includes pitch, rhythm, form)

**Meter** – the pattern of beats produced by musical accents, usually indicated by meter signatures (or time signatures) and written as measures separated by bar lines

२/४ | ⊓ | ⊓ ⊓    for    | ⊓ ⊓ ⊓
                          >   >

**Metronome** – a mechanical device used to sound regular beats at adjustable speeds indicating the exact tempo of the music. It is set to play a given number of beats per minute.

For example, M.M. ♩ = 60 would be one beat per second.

**Minor scale** – eight successive pitches bounded by an octave having the following pattern:

⊔∨⊔ ⊔∨⊔ ⊔

The basic form shown here is the natural minor scale.

**Monophonic music** – music consisting of a single melodic line

**Notation** – written symbols used to represent sound

**Note values** – symbols indicating the duration of sounds. See page 324 for a list.

**Octave** – the interval of the eighth (C to C¹, D to D¹, or doh to doh¹, re to re¹)

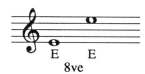

**Ostinato** – a repeated melodic or rhythmic pattern usually throughout the whole song or a large section of the song

**Partner songs** – two or more songs which can be sung together (eg. "Frère Jacques" and "Row, Row, Row Your Boat")

**Patsch (Patschen)** – tap thighs

**Pentatonic scale** – a scale of five pitches without half steps within the octave (eg. d r m s l d¹ is a doh pentatonic scale)

**Phrase** – a unified musical statement; a common phrase length is four bars

**Pitch** – the highness or lowness of a sound (determined by the frequency of the vibrations)

**Polyphonic music** – music consisting of two or more independent melodies

**Pulse** – the regular occurrence of the beat, either real or perceived

**Range** – the spread between the lowest and highest note in a piece (narrow/wide)

**Refrain** – in music, a repeated melody and text heard between verses

**Register** – region of highness or lowness of the sound source (high/middle/low)

**Repeat sign** ( ‖: :‖ ) – perform the section again

**Rest** – a length of silence expressed with musical symbols called rests. See pages 324 and 369 for rest values.

**Rhythm** – how movement in music is organized

**Rhythm pattern** - the grouping of longer and shorter, equal and unequal durations of sound and silence

**Rondo** – a form featuring an alternation of a repeated section with new sections (A B A C A)

**Round** – a work in which the same melody is repeated as each voice enters at regulated time intervals

**Scale** – the successive arrangement within an octave of notes used in a piece

**Score** – the composer's written plan

**Sequence** – a special kind of repetition in which a short musical idea is immediately repeated at a higher or lower pitch level

**Sharp** (♯) – a symbol placed to the left of a note to raise its tone a half step

**Soprano** – higher female voice

**Sound piece** – a score for mixed sound, written usually in graphic notation

**Staccato** – detached, separated

**Staff** – five lines and four spaces used for the notation of pitch

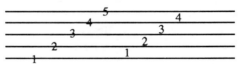

**Step** – melodic movement by the interval of a second

**Style** – characteristic use of music elements resulting in a particular sound

**Syncopation** – a rhythmic device in which the accent occurs in irregular places (not on the beat)

**Tempo** – the speed of the pulse in music (fast/slow/moderate). See pages 329-330 for some tempo terms.

**Tenor** – higher male voice

**Texture** – the density of the sound (thick/thin); the organization of the melody and harmony in a piece (monophonic, polyphonic, homophonic, mixed)

**Theme** – a musical phrase which functions as a main idea in a larger musical work

**Tie** – a notational symbol used to increase the duration of a sound by joining two or more note values

**Timbre** – individual quality of sound made by voices, instruments, and other sound sources. See also tone colour.

**Tonal center** – the focal point of the music, or tonic; some music has no tonal centre (see atonal music)

**Tone** – the sound (includes pitch and quality of sound)

**Tone colour** – see timbre

**Tonic** – the primary note of a key; the tonal focus; the first degree of the scale (I): in the key of C, C is the tonic.

**Triad** – a three note chord (eg. G B D; d m s)

**Unison** – together on the same pitch (but may be an octave apart when men and women sing together)

**Variation** – changes in the original musical idea; a form in which the original melody undergoes several transformations

**Volume** – see dynamics

**Whole step** – two half steps (also called whole tone)   C D

**Whole tone scale** – a successive series of tones within an octave, each a whole step apart

# General References

## Books

Anderson, W.; & Shehan Campbell, P., eds. *Multicultural Perspectives in Music Education.* Reston, VA: Music Educators National Conference, 1989.

Birkenshaw, L. *Music for Fun, Music for Learning*, 3rd ed. Toronto: Holt, Rinehart & Winston, 1982.

Birkenshaw-Fleming, L. *Come on Everybody, Let's Sing.* Toronto: Gordon V. Thompson, 1989.

Choksy, L.; & Brummitt, D. *120 Singing Games and Dances for Elementary Schools.* Englewood Cliffs, NJ: Prentice-Hall, 1987.

de Frece, R. *Canada: Its Music.* Don Mills, ON: Collier MacMillan Canada, 1989. [Tape available]

Fowke, E.; & Mills, A. *Singing our History.* Toronto: Doubleday Canada, 1984.

Nocera, D. *Reaching the Special Learner Through Music.* Morristown, NJ: Silver Burdett Company, 1979. [Recordings available]

Rice, T.; & Shand, P., eds. *Multicultural Music Education: The "Music Means Harmony" Workshop.* Toronto: Faculty of Music, University of Toronto, 1989.

Upitis, R. *This Too is Music.* Portsmouth, NH: Heinemann, 1990.

## Textbook Series  NOTE: Recordings or tapes are available for the following programs.

Birkenshaw, L. *Musictime* (K-3). Agincourt, ON: GLC/Silver Burdett, 1985. [One volume]

Birkenshaw, L.; & Clark, J. *Musictime* (4-6). Agincourt, ON: GLC/Silver Burdett, 1986. [One volume]

Boardman, E.; & Andress, B. *The Music Book* (K-8). New York: Holt, Rinehart & Winston, 1981. [Nine volumes]

Boardman Meske, E.; Andress, B.; Pautz, M.; & Willman, F. *Holt Music* (K-8). New York: Holt, Rinehart & Winston, 1988. [Nine volumes]

Brooks, P., et al. *Musicanada* (3-6). Toronto: Holt, Rinehart & Winston, 1982. [Four volumes]

Colby, D.; Harrison, J.; & Kerr, C. *Canada Is...Music* (3-6). Toronto: Gordon V. Thompson, 1980, 1982. [Two volumes]

Crook, E.; Reimer, B.; & Walker, D. *Silver Burdett Music* (K-8). Morristown, NJ: Silver Burdett Company, 1985. [Nine volumes]

Goodman, J.; Skilling, D.; & Stewart, D. *Canada Is...Music* (7-8). Toronto: Gordon V. Thompson, 1984. [One volume]

Schafer, P.; & Stack, Y. *Musicanada* (1-2). Toronto: Holt, Rinehart & Winston, 1991. [Two volumes]

Staton, B.; & Staton, M. *Music and You* (K-8). New York: MacMillan. [Nine volumes with Canadian supplements]

## Records/Tapes

Hardie, M.; & Mason, E. *Music Builders* (K-6). Agincourt, ON: GLC Publishers, 1983.

Pinel, S.; Mason, E.; & Hardie, M. *Musique s'il vous plaît* (K-3). Agincourt, ON: GLC Publishers, 1989.

# Classified Index

## Action Songs

Blue Bells .................................................. 63
Clap Your Hands ........................................ 69
Eency Weency Spider ................................ 70
Elevator Song ............................................ 72
Hey, Hey Look at Me ................................ 74
I'm a Little Candle .................................... 77
If You're Happy ........................................ 78
Long Legged Life ...................................... 79

## Canadian Songs

Bonavist' Harbour ...................................... 98
Brave Wolfe .............................................. 99
Canoe Song .............................................. 102
Donkey Riding ................................. 106, 275
Hurling down the Pine ............................ 128
Huron Carol ............................................ 129
I'll Give my Love an Apple .................... 131
J'entends le moulin ................................ 133
Jack Was Ev'ry Inch ............................... 135
Land of the Silver Birch ........................ 139
New York Strum ..................................... 281
O Canada ................................................ 142
Orthodontist Blues .................................. 146
Song for the Mira ................................... 159
Summer Song .......................................... 280
Un Canadien errant ................................ 244
Where the Coho Flash Silver ................. 170

## Cumulative Song

Barnyard Song .......................................... 59

## Dance/Movement

Ah, Poor Bird ............................................ 57
Bow Wow .................................................. 66
Come to the Land .................................... 103
Donkey Riding ........................................ 106
The Grand Old Duke .............................. 120
Great Big House ..................................... 121
Old Brass Wagon ..................................... 80
Poor Bird .................................................. 82
Prendés i garde ......................................... 83
Snail, Snail ............................................... 88
Weavily Wheat .......................................... 91
Toembaï .................................................. 163

## Drama

Eggs and Marrowbones .......................... 108

## Echo Song

Old Texas ....................................... 145, 314

## Game Songs

Bluebird .................................................... 64
Categories ................................................ 67
Ich-a-back-a ............................................. 77
Snail, Snail ............................................... 88

## Songs with French Words

Frère Jacques ........................................... 97
J'entends le moulin ................................ 133
O Canada ................................................ 142
Un Canadien errant ................................ 244

## Instrumental Accompaniments

Ah, Poor Bird ............................................ 57
Barnacle Bill ............................................. 58
Come to the Land .................................. 103
Eency Weency Spider .............................. 70
Engine, Engine Number Nine .................. 73
Prendés i garde ......................................... 83
Sakura .................................................... 154
Song for the Mira ................................... 159
Toembaï .................................................. 163

## Narratives

Brave Wolfe .............................................. 99
Eggs and Marrowbones .......................... 108
Jack Was Ev'ry Inch ............................... 135
Old Texas ............................................... 145
There's a Hole in my Bucket ................. 162
Where the Coho Flash Silver ................. 170

## Partner Songs

Fish and Chips ....................................... 113

## Poem

Hallowe'en Night .................................... 123

(Classified Index, cont.)

## Rounds

| Ah, Poor Bird | 57 |
| Are You Sleeping | 97 |
| Canoe Song | 102 |
| Come and Sing Together | 347 |
| Dona Nobis Pacem | 239 |
| Ghost of John | 116 |
| Hebrew Round | 124 |
| J'entends le moulin | 133 |
| Kookaburra | 138 |
| Praetorius Round | 149 |
| Row Your Boat | 87 |
| Tallis' Canon | 234 |
| Toembaï | 163 |
| Tzena | 168 |

## Scale Songs

| Elevator | 72 |
| I'm a Little Candle | 76 |
| Pussywillow | 84 |

## Seasonal Songs

| Auld Lang Syne | 316 |
| Ghost of John | 116 |
| God Rest You Merry, Gentlemen | 118 |
| Good King Wenceslas | 234 |
| Hallowe'en Night | 123 |
| Huron Carol | 129 |
| Jingle Bells | 227 |

## Songs from Other Countries

| Are You Sleeping (France) | 97 |
| Come and Sing Together (Hungary) | 347 |
| Come to the Land (Romania) | 103 |
| Der Hans (Switzerland) | 104 |
| Eggs and Marrowbones (Ireland) | 108 |
| Ezekiel Saw the Wheel (U.S.A.) | 111 |
| God Rest You Merry, Gentlemen (England) | 118 |
| Old Texas (U.S.A.) | 145 |
| Prendés i garde (France) | 83 |
| Riddle Song (U.S.A.) | 150 |
| Sakura (Japan) | 154 |
| There's a Hole in my Bucket (U.S.A.) | 162 |
| Toembaï (Israel) | 163 |
| Tom Dooley (U.S.A.) | 165 |
| Tzena (Israel) | 168 |
| When the Saints (U.S.A.) | 169 |

## Recorder Pieces

| A la claire fontaine | 228 |
| Ah! Si mon moine voulait danser | 233 |
| Ahrirang | 231 |
| Amazing Grace | 231 |
| Auld Lang Syne | 242 |
| Aura Lee | 227 |
| Bransle | 230 |
| Choral Bells (round) | 223 |
| Come, Follow Me (round) | 241 |
| Cradle Song | 243 |
| Dance Tune (duet) | 222 |
| Dona Nobis Pacem (round) | 239 |
| Edi Beo Thu (duet) | 245 |
| En roulant ma boule | 233 |
| Fais dodo | 228 |
| Frère Jacques (round) | 232 |
| Friendly Giant's Theme | 237 |
| Good King Wenceslas | 234 |
| Greensleeves | 243 |
| Gypsy Rover | 230 |
| Hey, Ho (round) | 232 |
| Huron Carol | 236 |
| J'ai du bon tabac | 229 |
| Jingle Bells | 227 |
| Kol Dodi | 238 |
| La Bergamesca (4 part) | 244 |
| Land of the Silver Birch | 235 |
| Lightly Row | 220, 223 |
| Medieval Canons (round) | 237 |
| Oats, Peas, Beans | 229 |
| Poor Wayfaring Stranger | 241 |
| Round (round) | 232 |
| She's Like the Swallow | 242 |
| Song for Recorder | 235 |
| Saint Nick | 221 |
| Sumer is icumen in (round) | 240 |
| Tallis' Canon (round) | 234 |
| Three Farmers | 229 |
| Traditional Round (round) | 238 |
| Troubadour Melody | 236 |
| Turtle Dove | 238 |
| Un Canadien errant | 244 |
| Ungaresca | 231 |
| Viva la Musica (round) | 239 |

# Alphabetical Index of Songs

| | |
|---|---|
| Ah, Poor Bird | 57 |
| Alouette | P293 |
| Are You Sleeping | 97 |
| Auld Lang Syne | P316 |
| Aura Lee | R227 |
| | |
| Barnacle Bill | 58 |
| Barnyard Song | 59 |
| Bee, Bee Bumble Bee | 60 |
| Billy Bad | 61 |
| Bingo | 62 |
| Blue Bells | 63 |
| Bluebird | 64 |
| Bonavist' Harbour | 98 |
| Bounce High | 65 |
| Bow Wow | 66 |
| Brave Wolfe | 99 |
| | |
| Can't You Dance the Polka | P309 |
| Canoe Song | 102, U277 |
| Categories | 67 |
| Charlie Over the Ocean | 68 |
| Clap Your Hands | 69, P285 |
| Clementine | P312 |
| Come and Sing Together | 347 |
| Come to the Land | 103 |
| Crawdad Song | U272 |
| | |
| Der Hans | 104 |
| Dona Nobis Pacem | R239 |
| Donkey Riding | 106, U275 |
| Down She Sat | P298 |
| Draw a Bucket of Water | P314 |
| Drunken Sailor | U278 |
| | |
| Eency Weency Spider | 70 |
| Eggs and Marrowbones | 108 |
| Elevator | 72 |
| Engine, Engine | 73 |
| Ezekiel Saw the Wheel | 111 |
| | |
| Fish and Chips | 113 |
| Five Hundred Miles | 115, U273, P303, P313 |
| For He's a Jolly Good Fellow | U277 |
| | |
| Ghost of John | 116 |
| Go Tell Aunt Rhody | G252, U267 |
| God Rest You Merry, Gentlemen | 118 |
| Good King Wenceslas | R234 |
| Grand Old Duke | 120 |
| Great Big House | 121, P315 |
| | |
| Hallowe'en Night | 123 |
| He's Got the Whole World | G253, P291 |
| Hebrew Round | 124 |
| Hey, Hey Look at Me | 74 |
| Hoosen Johnny | 126 |
| Hop Old Squirrel | P299 |
| Hot Cross Buns | 75 |
| Hungarian Dance | 127 |
| Hurling down the Pine | 128 |
| Huron Carol | 129 |
| | |
| I Love Coffee | P311 |
| I'll Give my Love an Apple | 131 |
| I'm a Little Candle | 76 |
| Ich-a-back-a | 77 |
| If You're Happy | 78 |
| | |
| J'entends le moulin | 133 |
| Jack Was Ev'ry Inch | 135 |
| Jingle Bells | R227, U276 |
| Joshua Fit the Battle | 137, G261 |
| | |
| Kookaburra | 138, P301 |
| Kumbaya | G259 |
| | |
| Land of the Silver Birch | 139 |
| Little Brown Jug | P305 |
| Long Legged Life | 79 |
| Loo-Lah | 140 |
| | |
| Mama Don't 'Low | U2679 |
| Merrily We Roll Along | 141 |
| Michael, Row the Boat Ashore | U276 |
| Mousie, Mousie | P289 |
| | |
| New York Strum | U281 |
| | |
| O Canada | 142 |
| Old Brass Wagon | 80 |
| Old Smokey | 144, U272, P307 |
| Old Texas | 145, P314 |
| Old Woman | P289 |
| Orthodontist Blues | 146 |
| | |
| Polly Wolly Doodle | U269 |
| Poor Bird | 82 |
| Praetorius Round | 149 |
| Prendés i garde | 83 |
| Pussywillow | 84 |
| | |
| Rain, Rain Go Away | 85 |

(Alphabetical Index of Songs, cont.)

Riddle Song .................................................................. 150
Rocky Mountain ........................................................... 152
Row Your Boat .................................................... 87, P283

Sakura ........................................................................... 154
Sally Go 'Round the Sun ............................................ P314
Shortnin' Bread ................................................ U267, P288
Skip to My Lou ................................................. G252, U269
Sloop John B. ..................................................... 157, G253
Snail Snail ...................................................................... 88
Song for the Mira ......................................................... 159
Starlight, Star Bright ...................................................... 89
Streets of Laredo ....................................................... P295
Summer Song ............................................................ U280

Tallis' Canon .............................................................. R234
Telephone Song ............................................................ 90
There's a Hole in my Bucket ....................................... 162
This Old Man ........................... G252, U265, U270, P294
This Train .................................................................. U274
Toembaï ...................................................................... 163
Tom Dooley ....................................................... 165, P297
Turn on the Sun ........................................................... 166
Tzena ........................................................................... 168

Un Canadien errant .................................................... R244

Weavily Wheat ............................................................. 91
What Kind of Cake ....................................................... 92
What the Turkey Said .................................................. 93
When the Saints ......................................................... 169
Where the Coho Flash Silver ..................................... 170
Where, Oh Where Has my Little Dog Gone ............ G260
Whistle Daughter ...................................................... P290
Who Built the Ark ....................................................... 173
Who's That Yonder ...................................................... 94
Whole World in his Hands ...................................... G253

Zum Gali Gali ............................................................. 345

*Legend:* G *numbers indicate guitar section;*
P *numbers indicate piano section;*
U *numbers indicate ukulele section.*